PITTODRIE IDOLS

PITTODRIE IDOLS

The Story of Aberdeen's Cult Heroes

PAUL SMITH

BLACK & WHITE PUBLISHING

First published 2009
by Black & White Publishing Ltd
29 Ocean Drive, Edinburgh EH6 6JL

1 3 5 7 9 10 8 6 4 2   09 10 11 12 13

ISBN: 978 1 84502 268 6

A CIP catalogue record for this book is available from the British Library.

Typeset by Graham Hales Design, Typesetting, Reproduction
www.grahamhales.co.uk

Printed and bound by MPG Books Ltd, Bodmin

CONTENTS

To Coral, Finlay and Mia

ACKNOWLEDGEMENTS

FIRST AND foremost my thanks go to the Red Army, the men and women who over the course of a century have turned a succession of players into heroes. Of course, it is a two-way street and the characters who have graced Pittodrie and adorned the pages which follow have my admiration and gratitude, particularly those who spared their time to reminisce about their special Pittodrie bond. That list includes the worldly-wise transatlantic duo of Graham Leggat and Charlie Cooke, the inspiringly enthusiastic Henning Boel, the affable Willem van der Ark, refreshingly honest Lee Richardson and the endearingly self-effacing pair of Duncan Shearer and Brian Irvine. I am also indebted to the input of my colleagues in the media, with Colin Farquharson joining Frank Gilfeather and Chris Crighton in adding valuable and much appreciated contributions. Ian McNeill and Steve Paterson also lent their time and tremendous experience to give an insight into the inner workings of the game while Hamish Munro shared his memories and Richie Mutch generously agreed to lift the lid on the great Dons cult phenomenon of recent times. Colin MacLeod, a friend and source of eternal encouragement, proved a valuable link in the chain. Graham Hales and Ivan Ponting, as well as John Richardson and all of the team at Black and White, have been a huge assistance with their expertise, attention to detail and advice throughout the production process, while, closer to home, I grow to appreciate more and more with every passing year the encouragement I have always received from my parents. Finally the most heartfelt thanks to my wife Coral and children Finlay and Mia for the love, support, endless inspiration, energy and overwhelming affection which makes each and every day a joy.

FOREWORD BY ALEX SMITH

FOOTBALL CAN be a game of wonderful contradictions and not least when it comes to the relationship between players and the crowd. Why do some strike a chord with supporters whilst others go about their work quietly and without the lavish adulation afforded to the chosen few? It is a question with no right or wrong answer.

Some players achieve cult status through their achievements on the pitch, others more for their approach off the park. Some do it through a blend of both.

I was honoured to serve as manager of Aberdeen Football Club and know at first hand just how much of a lift a player can get from the support of the Pittodrie crowd.

I was also fortunate to work with some wonderful characters during my time with the Dons, several of whom feature in the pages that follow.

Brian Irvine is one who springs immediately to mind, a fine and upstanding man not just in physical terms but also in character. Brian's integrity, honesty and dedication won him many friends amongst the Aberdeen fans and he found himself elevated to the status of an untouchable in the eyes of the Red Army. He was also a player who was far more talented than he was ever given credit for by the wider audience, with a nimbleness that belied his size. Those who followed the club week in and week out knew all too well what he brought to the team.

Willem van der Ark is another from the same era who became a cult hero, perhaps in the first instance because of his unique appearance. But more than that, he had the backing of the Dons fans because he tended to find himself being singled out by the opposition fans as a target from the terraces. The Aberdeen supporters rallied in his defence and from there the mutual appreciation grew and grew.

Willem did not score a barrel load of goals or play in hundreds of games, unlike Joe Harper. Joe is at the other end of the cult spectrum – his adoration was first and foremost based on the incredible number of goals he scored. Mind you, he wouldn't mind me saying that he did not look like your archetypal athlete and his cheeky approach to life and the game did not do him any harm in the popularity stakes.

Going back further in time, I remember vividly watching Graham Leggat and Charlie Cooke go about their business in great style. Leggat rose to prominence with his knack for scoring important goals, Cooke with his amazing ball skills and his appetite for socialising. It is not difficult to see why they became such favourites with the crowd.

Recalling such memorable players, and the men behind those names, raises the question of whether the modern game misses the personalities of old. Setting the rose-tinted glasses to one side, the game we all know and love will always have the ability to produce players to warm the soul.

Zander Diamond, with his never say die spirit and big heart, is the latest to capture the imagination of the Pittodrie crowd but he will not be the last. That is the beauty of the bond between those who play and those who spectate: there's always a new chapter waiting to be written in the story of every club.

The mere mention of some of the great characters from the rich past of Aberdeen Football Club was enough to bring a smile to my face and I hope *Pittodrie Idols* stirs many happy memories for every Dons fan who has laughed, cheered and celebrated along with their favourite sons.

INTRODUCTION

OPEN UP the Collins concise dictionary at C and the tale begins. The third entry under "cult" reads: "devoted attachment to a person, idea or activity." So there it is in black and white, the basic reference point for identifying each cult hero ever to walk the hallowed turf of Britain's football grounds.

That devotion forms the backbone of everything which follows in this tribute to Aberdeen's very own band of *Idols*. To a man, these stars had their own following and their own reason for drawing such a crowd. Some were worshipped by a select band of aficionados, others had mass market appeal – but all shared an unbreakable bond with the Red Army which bridged any potential barriers thrown up by ability, nationality and personality.

Aberdeen Football Club has been fortunate not only to house some of the game's great players but also some of the sport's wonderful characters. More often than not, both collided to give the Pittodrie faithful a collective smile.

Football is not a sport renowned for sticking to confines or adhering to structure, and trying to pin a dictionary definition to its cult heroes is dangerous. Of course, it is useful as a marker, but little more than that. The truth is that the process is not black and white, just as the characters who fill the following 20 chapters are not straightforward or easy to analyse. That is what made them stand out and gave them cult status.

Taking the populist approach to cult heroes, a devoted yet limited following would be a prerequisite for any candidate. But in football, and particularly in the case of Aberdeen FC, the boundaries blur considerably. The Dons, operating in a one-team city, have always had the ability to create a throbbing surge of interest in successful times, yet the club's cult heroes have often flitted comfortably between centre-stage and left-field.

As evidence, look no further than Willie Miller. The most decorated player in Aberdeen's history can rightly lay claim to a place amongst its cult heroes. Yes, the captain fantastic is a legend but nobody could deny a cult element to the adoration surrounding him, particularly among the fully paid-up members of the Miller fan club who were not even born when he strutted his stuff at Pittodrie.

The inclusion of such an established player in a list of cult heroes will rub uncomfortably against the grain for many, but there is a precedent. In 2005 the BBC set out on a concerted campaign to find the ultimate cult heroes for every club in Britain. Aberdeen fans responded and 72 per cent voted in favour of Miller. On the other hand, Gordon Strachan, who was second in that particular ballot with 19 per cent of the vote, does not make the final cut in this volume.

Doug Rougvie, third according to the BBC's calculation after pulling in a nine per cent share, is very much part of this dream team. In fact, Rougvie is arguably the purest of all and ticks every box on a diverse and varied inventory of key attributes. That all three came from the greatest single team the club has ever known, the Gothenburg Greats, is no surprise. Fans love characters but they love them all the more if they are part of a winning side. Unfortunately, that is not always possible.

Not all of *Pittodrie Idols* enjoyed the type of unbridled joy that Miller and Rougvie did. Some, such as modern idol Hicham Zerouali, provided slivers of ecstasy during the more barren years.

The chapters which follow are not all about remembering the players you loved to watch or those still fresh in the minds of Dandies everywhere. Delving deeper into the past, *Pittodrie Idols* also examines the changing relationship between the supporters and their favourites from the early days of the club's existence to the present day. In its infancy there was no distance between the players and those on the terraces; the worship was far from the "us and them" attitude which has crept into the game in recent times and was no poorer for that fact.

While the years have rolled on and the form of the partnership between fan and player has evolved, the common theme throughout is the way in which a succession of Dons players have managed to win the heart and soul of the man on the street by reaching out to him in a way other fine players never did. That was the case in the 1920s just as it is as 2010 looms.

Some stood out physically, whether wider or taller than the average Don, while others had quirks and personality flaws which made them welcome in the bosom of the Pittodrie crowd. Lee Richardson was not a stranger to red mist descending but his commitment to the cause came through loud and clear, winning friends along the way. After all, everyone relates to a loveable rogue – why else would so many film directors and script writers cast them in their productions?

Not that the nice guys never got a look-in. Willem van der Ark, one of the most placid men ever to wander through the front door on Pittodrie Street, is a case in point. The Ark, like Rougvie before him, encapsulated everything great about the unpredictability of football followers. Hans Gillhaus, another of the club's Dutch imports, was far more prolific than affable Willem but he was also far more clinical, perfect almost, and as such a touch more removed from the fans as a result. Van der Ark makes the final cut of *Pittodrie Idols*; Gillhaus for the very reason mentioned above, does not.

Van der Ark also represents another admirable quality among the Dons support. The warmth of the welcome afforded to imported players has, over time, been a charming facet of life in the north-east. Several cult heroes have emerged from the united nations to have represented the team, each bringing their own distinct style and unique appeal.

In a nutshell, whether from home or abroad, that is what every member of *Pittodrie Idols* has brought to the table. Twenty of those men have been included, another 20 were on the reserve list and countless others were valid contenders. There's no definitive list, just as there's no formal definition of a cult hero, but there is a selection of likely lads who had the ability to bring a crowd to its feet. Some have passed away, many have moved to pastures new – but none will ever be forgotten.

'JOCK' 1919–1926

JOHN HUTTON

Magic Moment: With one swipe of a generous thigh, the scarf-wearing Jock Hutton introduced himself to Dons fans with a thunderous debut goal. The strong man and his sideshows had arrived.

Dons Career: Games 282. Goals 17. Caps 10.

THERE IS no better place to start on a whistle-stop tour of *Pittodrie Idols* than with a man who served as the prototype. John Hutton, far better known as Jock, had it all. From his conspicuous appearance to a notorious love of living life to the full and everything in between, the bull from Bellshill was the original loveable rogue.

Hutton plied his trade at Pittodrie in the 1920s but even then, in football's age of innocence, he stood out as a man elevated above the norm. Physicality was a big part of Hutton's dalliance with the early stages of football stardom. The game, particularly in its professional guise, was still a new concept and players had to work hard to be idolised. They had to convince a new audience of their worth, selling the merits of the game as much as promoting their own worth.

"Greatness lies not in being strong, but in the right use of strength."

Henry Ward Beecher, American social reformer

For Hutton that potentially treacherous process was simple. For one thing, he was instantly recognisable thanks to his robust frame. The full-back stood at 5ft 8in tall but the key was in his width, not his height, and the thorny issue of Hutton's weight remains a matter of mystery to this day. Official records have the Dons heavyweight tipping the scale at a hefty 13st 7lb – yet observers noted at the time that the figure was a diplomatic exercise and an additional two stone and more could quite comfortably be added. The Lanarkshire-born player was built like a brick outhouse, a heavily reinforced outhouse at that. It made him easily distinguishable from the Aberdeen crowd and that simple weapon is vital in any cult hero's armoury.

Hutton used his stature to wonderful effect in the black and gold of the Dons, playing before the club switched to the more familiar red kit. He quickly gained a reputation as Scottish football's most formidable defender, a fearsome sight and a no-nonsense figure who never shirked a challenge. That die-hard attitude was another link in the chain between player and fans. There is no better way to get the home faithful onside than showing a willingness to dump the visiting forwards in row Z, not so much taking one for the team but more taking one out for the team. Not that Hutton was a hatchet-man. Those who saw him play always made great play of his hard but fair approach to the game. A bygone Doug Rougvie, if you like.

He was noted as somebody who played the game with a smile on his face, backed up by the many photographs of the big bear of a man grinning from ear to ear, but he had a tough core that every great player needs to succeed. Hutton's steely approach to the game ensured his girth was never likely to make him a figure of fun for even the most daring of terracing hecklers – but he had back-up if anyone did choose to question his credentials as an athlete: lightning pace. The stocky stopper could never be described as looking like a whippet but he could shift like one, being renowned not only for his dogged defending but also for his searing speed down the flank. With his weight estimated conservatively at 16st, Aberdeen's bundle of energy in full flow must have been something to behold.

Coupled with pace was, not surprisingly, strength. The circus strong-man was still a popular attraction in the 1920s and Hutton brought a touch of the big-top fun to work with him. Famously his favourite training party trick was picking up a team-mate with his teeth, just one of the acts in a repertoire full of demonstrations of his incredible power. Life with Hutton around was anything but dull or predictable.

Rolled into the perfect cult-hero package was undoubted ability. Hutton became a Scotland stalwart on the back of his starring performances for Aberdeen and the Pittodrie fans grew to appreciate his contribution to the side. He didn't just provide the muscle; the man could play the game, too. He began his career as an inside-forward, a position reliant on guile as much as guts and power, and when he shifted to the back line those talents transferred with him.

On the field he was well endowed with crucial cult attributes and the trend continued away from his Pittodrie stage, too. Football fans can appreciate the finer things in life and applaud the perfect player. While they clap the polished gem, the raucous cheers and chants are more often than not reserved for the rough diamond. Hutton was most certainly a man in the latter camp and the character flaws he exhibited went a long way to explaining the affinity the supporters felt for their earthy hero. He wasn't perfect, but then neither were they.

Hutton, who went on to star for Blackburn Rovers in the English top flight, was best summed up by those who watched him at his peak. Writing in the *Blackburn Telegraph*, one journalist observed: "He never used his giant strength unfairly, though in his first match he gave Louis Page a perfectly fair shoulder charge which sent the Burnley winger through the air like a guided missile. The referee called it a penalty – but it wasn't. Jock was the most jovial chap who ever wore a football jersey. He roamed through a game as happily as a schoolboy as, in some respects, he did through life. You sometimes felt he would never really grow up. Money used to burn a hole in his pocket, yet he could smile even at times when he couldn't lay his hands on a shilling."

Hutton, it would seem, was ahead of his time in so many respects. Modern football's cult heroes have so often displayed classic tendencies of self-destruction. From George Best to Paul Gascoigne and so many more besides, supporters have grown to forgive the foibles of those at the centre of their attention; it has become part of the territory. Long before the swinging '60s or hedonistic '90s there were loveable rogues in the game, they were just fewer and farther between. Hutton was in that mould and he was happy with his lot.

Post-football, he moved to Northern Ireland, where it was said he continued to live his life in the only way he knew how: wholeheartedly and without a hint of restraint. Exactly what became of Hutton is not certain. He was last spotted on official duty as he took advantage of a sumptuous banquet in Blackburn, having been tempted back across the water in 1960. Rovers had tracked their former star down to his Ulster base and invited him back to England as a guest for their FA Cup final appearance, as he had been an integral part of the Ewood side which won the competition in 1928.

His role in that triumph, coupled with the qualities which made him such a stand-out at Pittodrie, made Hutton a Rovers idol, too. Once could be down to luck or a twist of fate, but to achieve that status at two different clubs makes Hutton stand apart as the genuine article.

At Aberdeen, he could be described as the club's first true cult hero. His imperfections and unique characteristics were befitting of that status. He was not, however, the first object of affection for the Dons fans in their fledgling years of following the club.

Donald Colman, another legendary figure with his own eccentricities, was an idol in a more traditional sense. Colman was one of the first high-profile ambassadors for the club following its foundation in 1903, making his debut four years after the birth of the Dons following the amalgamation of city sides Aberdeen, Orion and Victoria United.

The former Motherwell player famously invented the football dugout, a creation born from his fascination with watching the footwork of the players he took charge of following his move into coaching. Colman became a keen student of dance and boxing as he strived to improve the ground skills of his team and it was that type of dedication to the cause which made him a favourite with the Aberdeen fans.

As a player he was installed as captain of Aberdeen within two years of his arrival and was an ever-present for the club for two consecutive seasons from the summer of 1908. In 1911 Colman won the first of four caps and went on to serve the club with distinction as a coach and the dapper figure cemented his reputation as a man of intelligence and personality.

Colman, a far more straight-laced character than Hutton, was hugely admired and respected but the levels of adulation heaped upon the Dons players grew as the club itself began to flourish. By the time Hutton was on the scene, the characters surrounding the club were beginning to enjoy higher profiles, with every move being keenly watched and the stars beginning to find their place on the Pittodrie pedestals.

Perhaps the biggest rival for Hutton's cult-hero crown during his Pittodrie career was Alex Jackson, who arrived from South Africa in 1924. Jackson made just 40 appearances for the club, lasting all of one season in the north-east, but he quickly burned a place in the memories of those who watched him in action.

Jackson wore the number-seven shirt and filled it in typical fashion, a true winger full of trickery and skill. He became a Scotland player while on the Dons' payroll, still only 19 at the time, and was on his road to Pittodrie immortality. Then the bond was snapped; Jackson was snatched away before he could truly become an established cult hero. Instead he was a one-season wonder, transferred to Huddersfield in a record-breaking £5,000 deal in 1925.

In 1928 Jackson became a Scotland hero when he and his team-mates were christened the Wembley Wizards after trouncing England 5-1 in London, with the former Don netting three goals. He went on to feature for Chelsea and French side Nice before returning early. Jackson died at the age of 41 after a road accident during military service in Egypt. While fondly remembered by the Aberdeen fans, Jackson owed his place in history more to what could have been rather than what his admirers cherished and held dearly. In this he was unlike his team-mate Hutton, who'd had time to win their lasting adulation.

Alex Cheyne was another player of the same era who had Dons fans on the edge of their seats, with the Glasgow-born forward earning five

Scottish caps during his 138-game and 55-goal spell at Pittodrie. He confirmed his place as a fans' hero with a rapid-fire hat-trick against Hibs on home turf in 1927, with all three coming in the space of just ten minutes as he helped his side to a 4-2 victory.

It took another record transfer fee, this time £6,000 was the figure, to take Cheyne away from Aberdeen to the bright lights of London. After four seasons he was bought by Chelsea and went on to sample French football with Nimes before moving into management, winding up in charge of Arbroath in the 1950s.

Colman, Jackson and Cheyne were adored by all who cheered on Aberdeen, but it was the larger-than-life character of Jock Hutton who dominated the 1920s, thundering through the decade with a smile almost as wide as his frame.

His cheeky personality undoubtedly helped Hutton survive the increasing scrutiny to which players found themselves subject. As far back as the club's first year of senior football, the Pittodrie playing staff were aware that every move was watched, with one 1903 reader of the *Evening Express* writing to the newspaper to complain: "Twice since the season opened I have seen members of the team dawdling about the town, apparently doing nothing. Now lads, a football life does not last very long and Satan finds some mischief, so try and get something to do during the day."

If his reputation is to be believed, Hutton did not struggle to fill his day but Mr Angry from Aberdeen may not have entirely approved of the content. Those early observations from Joe Public hint at the way in which Aberdeen Football Club was beginning to grip the city.

Hutton arrived post-war, making his first appearance in a friendly against Partick in 1919 to mark the club's return to action following the restoration of peace. Bizarrely he wore a scarf that day, but did not need accessories to stand out. His contribution included a headed goal and trademark cannonball shot that almost burst the Jags' net.

When the Scottish League resumed on 16 August 1919, Hutton was at the heart of the team. A crowd of 9,000 turned out for the game against Albion Rovers. Attendances were strong as the thirst for top-flight football grew and a crowd of 15,000 was recorded for a Scottish Cup tie against Gala Fairydean that same season.

The game was returning to professionalism after the war, with manager Jimmy Philip back in a full-time post in that period of optimism, and beginning to assume the type of importance that the modern fan has grown to accept.

Entertainment as a whole was beginning to take shape in the 1920s, with the golden age of cinema dawning. Although the first picture house was launched in the city in 1908, two years after His Majesty's Theatre had opened for business, it took time for the concept to catch on. By the 1920s a succession of lavish purpose-built cinemas sprung up throughout Scotland and Aberdeen was at the heart of the movement, with the likes of the Playhouse opening its doors in 1921. Towards the end of the decade the big chains began to dominate the cinema industry, as the advent of talkies increased the investment required to keep track with developments and the paying public began to become more demanding.

There were parallels in football, the other great source of entertainment for the working classes who were on the move in more ways than one. The 1920s and '30s brought slum clearances in the north-east, with 2,955 sub-standard homes in Aberdeen demolished to make way for new council housing in the city. Shiprow, Castlehill, the Gallowgate and Kirkgate were among the areas undergoing modernisation.

Goalposts were shifting in society, aspirations were being heightened and no longer was simply attending a game enough – the fans wanted more from their stars. In Hutton there was an XXL performer who provided more in every sense.

The popularisation of the beautiful game was in full flow during Hutton's period of service in Aberdeen. BBC Radio Scotland was born in 1923, with the Belmont Street relay station in the Granite City opening a year later to broadcast purely local programming to the surrounding area. Sports news was a core feature of the service, with football fans able to keep pace with the latest developments in a way they had not previously been able to. It was the beginning of the transition from player to household name for the stars of the era as tales of their exploits suddenly became available in every home with a radio in the front room.

The Aberdeen studio, overlooking the main rail line to Inverness, was one of the first to begin broadcasting – not surprising when you consider the BBC's first managing director, John Reith, was a minister's son from nearby Stonehaven. Aberdeen's local station was the first to broadcast a weekly 15-minute sports slot, fronted by international football referee Peter Craigmile, to satisfy the cravings of an increasingly enthralled audience for all things competitive.

Craigmile's party piece was answering football rules questions sent in by listeners, arguably the beginning of the interaction between fans and presenters that has manifested itself in the plethora of football phone-ins dominating the airwaves today. A bygone Jim Traynor, perhaps, but the cost to the 1920s listener was less. The initial outlay for a cumbersome radio aside, the ten shillings (50p) licence fee sounds like a bargain.

Just as entertainment's many genres were developing at a hectic pace, the football club's surroundings in Hutton's era were also changing beyond all recognition. The area around the stadium was very different to the present day, with open fields separating the Pittodrie area from nearby Old Aberdeen. At that time Old Aberdeen was a village in itself, while neighbouring Seaton was home to a pottery as well as brick and tile works, rather than the sprawling housing schemes more familiar to matchgoers today.

In the 1920s that scene began to change, with development of Seaton and the Pittodrie area taking shape and St Machar Drive being constructed in 1924 to connect the links area with the planned new housing areas being developed in the Bedford and Powis areas, catering for the upsurge in motorised transport. Throughout the decade horse-drawn carriages remained a feature of everyday life, particularly for commercial haulage contractors servicing the likes of the fish market and the city's other core industries.

Industries thriving in the city included the shipyards, with John Lewis & Sons one of the new kids on the block. Founded in 1907, the yard did not branch out into ship-building until the 1920s when it became a prolific manufacturer to rival the more established Hall Russell. John Lewis was swallowed up by the Wood Group in 1972 as the focus shifted towards vessels servicing the oil industry.

While boat-builders were key employers in the 1920s, road transport was also a major source of conversation as cars and trucks were becoming a more common sight on the streets of the Granite City. The electric tram was king of the public transport sector as it cut through the growing city, which had a population in excess of 150,000, on a variety of routes. Aberdeen Corporation Transport began introducing buses to complement its trams in the 1920s.

In the wider sports community, Aberdeen had a Scottish champion boxer in Steve McCall. His professional career began in 1927, and he once set a British boxing landmark by lasting the 20-round distance in a middleweight title fight. In rugby, Aberdeen Grammar FPs had settled into new surroundings, having moved to their Rubislaw headquarters in 1914, while the many golf clubs established in the previous century were beginning to mature.

The 1920s also brought the introduction of the first non-wool swimming suit by emerging manufacturer Speedo with the creation of the firm's *Racerback* design, but it is fair to assume the bulky Hutton and Speedo was not a preferred combination of the era.

Instead he made do with a generously sized Dons kit and set about his business in a style never seen before or since. John Hutton was born in Dalziel, near Motherwell, on 29 October 1898. He played for local juvenile side Motherwell Hearts before turning junior with Larkhall Thistle and then Bellshill Athletic. During the war he was posted to Aberdeen to serve with the Gordon Highlanders, turning out for Hall Russell in the north-east junior league before being handed a shot at the senior game by the Dons at the age of 20.

He found himself in the front line of a struggling Aberdeen team when he made his competitive debut at the start of the 1919/20 season. The club mustered just 11 wins from 42 outings in the First Division that term but from a personal point of view it was a success for the young recruit, who featured in 38 of those fixtures as well as all four of the Scottish Cup ties the team played. Hutton, handed the number-ten shirt, hit the net six times but that tally was enough to place him joint second in the scoring chart behind Jacky Connon, who had the more respectable haul of 16 goals. The Dons limped over the finish line in 17th place in the 22-team league, which was topped by Rangers, but big Jock was already making a name for himself thanks to his aforementioned cannonball shot.

Hutton was one of five new faces in the opening weeks of his first season and another five rookies were thrown into the team for the opening match of the 1920/21 campaign. The result was a climb to 11th in the table but significantly it also brought the transformation from forward to defender for Hutton, who dropped back to make the number-two shirt his own.

In all he played for seven full seasons and sampled highs at club and representative level. Those included helping the Pittodrie side to fifth in the First Division in 1922/23, a season in which the record attendance at the Aberdeen ground was shattered as 27,000 crammed in to watch their side take on eventual champions Rangers. The Dons led the League for a spell and also posted a record victory, trouncing north-east rivals Peterhead 13-0 in a Scottish Cup third-round tie.

Other notable occasions for Hutton were the Scottish Cup semi-final appearances in 1922, 1924 and 1926 against Morton, Hibs and Celtic. The pairing with Hibs was the most agonising, with the tie going to a second replay before the Easter Road side finally edged their way through to the final with a 1-0 win. Manager Jimmy Philip resigned soon afterwards and was replaced by Pat Travers.

Hutton was picked to represent the Scottish Football League four times during his Aberdeen career and captained that select side. He won seven of his ten caps while on the Dons' books, making his debut in a 1-0 victory against Northern Ireland at Windsor Park in March 1923. Hutton captained his country once, in a 2-0 win against the Ulstermen a year after his debut.

His glowing reputation extended beyond the confines of the Pittodrie terraces and the well-heeled English clubs had been alerted to his obvious talents. The move to Blackburn Rovers just weeks into the 1926/27 season brought a record windfall of £6,000 into the Dons coffers – but all of the money in the world would not have enabled them to replace Hutton like for like. He was one of a kind, and a cult hero because of it.

He went on to spend more than six years with Rovers, the FA Cup win of 1928 the undoubted highlight of that time. The Lancashire side beat Huddersfield Town 3-1 in the Wembley final to lift the famous trophy. Mementoes of Hutton's involvement remain in circulation and are popular fodder on internet auction websites, with everything from autographs on torn pieces of paper to picture postcards available to the modern Hutton devotee.

He retired from playing in 1933 but the legend of Jock Hutton has lived on, passed from generation to generation on both sides of the border. He did not win a single medal with Aberdeen but that did not prevent the likeable Scotland star from winning over the Red Army, typical of the cult heroes who feature in the pages which follow.

Yes, some of Pittodrie's favourite sons sampled the sweet taste of success but for each of them the connection with the crowd was on a far more personal level than simply a reward for a Cup or League victory. Hutton's personality and stature helped him reach out and touch the flat-capped fanatics who were turning out in their droves to find out what the hype surrounding the fast-growing city club was all about.

They were seldom left disappointed by the rotund full-back with the sledgehammer boot and so the tone was set. Future cult heroes had a lot to live up to, but football has an endearing habit of continuing to throw up the unexpected.

The mould was broken like a piece of discarded Seaton pottery when Hutton departed for English football but the characters kept coming. None replicated what the larger-than-life defender had brought to the table but each had their own attraction to the Dons' support. Hutton had put the cult hero ball firmly in play – it was up to his successors to run with it.

'THE ORIGINAL GOLDEN BOY' 1927–1931

BENNY YORSTON

Magic Moment: On an April afternoon in familiar surroundings at Pittodrie, 12,000 Aberdonians could say "I was there" when yet another double from Benny Boy against Queen's Park set the single-season goal-scoring record that stands to this day. In 42 League and Cup games the tally stood at 46 goals, a job well done.

Dons Career: Games 156. Goals 125. Caps 1.

HE WAS the perfect striker and the only one in more than a century of football under the Aberdeen Football Club banner who ever found the route to the holy grail of every attacker in every corner of every football-playing nation: the 100 per cent record.

Benny Yorston's record haul of 38 league goals in a single season will surely never be beaten. His average of exactly one goal per game in that astonishing campaign will surely never be matched.

Yet there is a blot on the copybook of the man with that unblemished scoring chart, or at least a large question-mark stamped across it. Yorston famously was embroiled in what at the time was labelled the Great Mystery, as one of five players hastily shoved through the Pittodrie exit without explanation by the club. Jimmy Blackwell, Hugh McLaren, Frank Hill and David Galloway were the others shown the door but Yorston was the name which caused the biggest shockwaves among the north-east's sporting public. To dispense with the services of the most deadly striker ever to grace the turf was a radical action and led observers to surmise that there must have been a radical cause behind the decision.

Decades later evidence of a betting scam instigated by the group was uncovered but came too late to be confirmed by manager Pat Travers, who unceremoniously dumped the gang of five from his squad. The more modern analysis backed up suspicions which arose at the time, as the conspiracy theories surrounding the Great Mystery swept around the city and its surrounds, that the players involved had been betting on their side to be drawing certain matches at half-time. That could clearly be engineered without unduly hindering the chances of ultimately winning the game, a plausible and workable match-fixing plot.

Up to that point Yorston had been every inch the cult hero. The big unanswerable question is whether he would have retained that status if the cloth-capped, straight-laced supporters of the 1920s and '30s had ever been furnished with the full facts about the circumstances of Yorston's fall from favour. Had they been given the chance to make up their own mind it would have been the ultimate acid test of Yorston's standing in the hero stakes. Would his status have survived in any shape or form had the mystery not been preserved? You wouldn't bet on it.

Right up to his death in London in 1977, Yorston remained reticent when it came to talking about his part in the Great Mystery. Even then, almost half a century after kicking his last ball for the Dons, he was still being pursued and cajoled in a bid to unlock the best-kept secret Aberdeen FC has ever had. Still he would not crack and lift the lid on what was regarded a scandal even though separating fact from fiction and speculation was nigh on impossible at the time.

"Mystery is a resource, like coal or gold, and its preservation is a fine thing."

Tim Cahill, travel writer

Some argue the mere hint of bringing the club into disrepute should be enough to have stripped the diminutive forward of his place as a hero for all time. Playing devil's advocate, it is plausible to argue that the intrigue surrounding the innocent and never-proven-guilty group is actually enough to cement everlasting cult status. Coupled with Yorston's undisputed ability and unmistakable appearance, there's a particularly strong case for his place among *Pittodrie Idols*.

The starting point has to be at the end of the life of one of the club's most enigmatic performers. It was in 1977 that Jack Webster, the Aberdonian author and journalist, knocked on the door of a flat in a London block to finally come face to face with the man he had been tracking for weeks and months. Webster, who went on to pen Aberdeen's official centenary history, was working on his latest book and intent on exposing the truth about the Great Mystery.

Yorston heard him out, but in turn gave little away. He claimed a wartime bang on the head had left him with no memory of the episode. Webster, an award-winning journalist, could not coax the true story of the events of 1932 from his veteran interviewee. Nor could his predecessors in the press, who in 1931 could only report that manager Travers had told them the decision was as the result of "some domestic trouble".

Webster later revealed a pang of guilt about his encounter with the ailing Yorston, claiming: "Benny had already suffered a couple of heart attacks and was clearly in poor health. He had a fatal heart attack soon after our meeting and it has often crossed my mind that our talk might have had something to do with it. I hope it didn't, of course. I was only doing what any good journalist would, trying to unearth the truth behind a story that had been buried for too long. The betting scam went on for several weeks and we can only guess how much money they made. They were rumbled when Yorston missed a sitter seconds before half-time in a game. He was one of the greatest goal-scorers of his time and everyone knew there was no way he would make a blunder like that. It's a real shame that fine group of players tainted their Aberdeen careers for a few pounds."

The truth of the matter is that Yorston had been in poor health for years. As far back as 1958 he had been rushed to hospital in Kensington, the borough which had become his home, with peritonitis. Surgeons rated his chances of surviving the abdominal surgery which was required at no better than one per cent. Yorston, renowned for his battling qualities on the pitch, defied the odds, not for the first time in his life, and pulled through, but as the years wore on he began to suffer heart problems. He passed away in 1977, aged 72, having suffered a heart attack a year earlier. With Yorston's death, the hopes of a full and frank disclosure about the Great Mystery once and for all were also laid to rest.

While those closest to the saga were reluctant to tell all, Webster did gain an insight from others who had been connected to the Dons at the time. He gathered enough evidence, including analysis of half-time and full-time scores from the period in question, to claim that the alleged betting scam was indeed in operation and had been exposed when those responsible attempted to include former Celtic star Adam McLean in the ring. McLean voiced his concern to another team-mate and eventually word reached the management team of Travers and trainer Donald Colman. After that there was only one outcome as far as the disciplinarian boss was concerned. The action was swift and absolute, although Travers remained desperate to protect the reputation of his beloved club and refused to air the findings of his own investigation publicly.

The fact Yorston will forever be remembered for his part in that group of five is a source of frustration for the surviving members of his clan. As recently as 2007 one of his grandsons, Matthew Yorston, made an emotional pilgrimage to his famous ancestor's place of work and claimed: "The way my grandfather left Aberdeen was a bit strange but I don't know anything more about it. My dad didn't tell me any more although I have read up about it a bit on the internet and have a number of press cuttings relating to his career. But I prefer to remember him for his amazing strike rate. His scoring rate was phenomenal and if he was around in the modern game today he would be worth an awful lot of money. He must have been a very big player in his day."

A big player in terms of profile but not in stature. At 5ft 4in tall and weighing just ten stone he was far removed from cult predecessor Jock Hutton. He was lightweight and pocket-sized but at the same time nimble and difficult to pin down. Those attributes made him an impossible handful for opposition defenders to deal with and made him one of the greatest exponents of goal-scoring for a generation. The canny

Aberdonian did not let his lack of inches curtail his physical threat on the park and he developed a reputation for strength which belied his measurements.

Yorston's will and wit was credited with playing a major part in the development of England legend Wilf Mannion, whom he partnered in attack at Middlesbrough in the years after his Dons departure. Nick Varley, in the *Golden Boy* book profiling Mannion, noted: "Yorston protected his fellow inside-forward, shielding him but also encouraging him and pushing him on; master and pupil." In fact, at 'Boro he is said to have pinned a "To be got" note inside his locker, with a hit-list of opponents who had dared to wrong him or his team-mates.

Yorston was terrier-sized but he had the bite of a far bigger breed. He had honed his protective skills on Scottish turf, partly for reasons of self-preservation and partly in his bid to make as big a nuisance of himself as was humanly possible. Spec, the house name for the *Evening Express* football writer of the 1950s, rated Yorston as the finest Dons player ever to pull on a pair of boots. He observed: "There have been more spectacular and more publicised football stars than Benny Yorston but Aberdeen has never had a more effective centre-forward than this 5ft 4in bundle of quick-witted menace to opposing defences."

Adored by the fans and praised by the media, Yorston was also a players' player. He had the respect of his peers for his fearless pursuit of goals. One Pittodrie director, who had been a player during the inspirational forward's Dons heyday, made a telling remark in the build-up to his funeral when he said: "He was one of Aberdeen's best ever forwards and one of the few Aberdonians ever to really be accepted by the Dons supporters. Benny was an amazing goal-scorer despite being small in stature. He was the Joe Harper of his era."

The claim about prejudice against home-grown talent was not new, but a timely reminder that only the chosen few have ever managed to lay claim to the tag of local lad made good. In modern times, former manager Jimmy Calderwood has lamented the reception Aberdonian forward Darren Mackie has endured periodically during his career, at times jeered when being introduced to the play. According to Calderwood, the local players have to work twice as hard to convince the home crowd of their worth and it has been a historic trait.

While Benny Yorston was feted by those who watched him, he did not have to look outwith his own family to see the other side of the coin. In the 1950s his nephew Harry Yorston demonstrated a similar knack for hitting the back of the net, bagging 141 goals in 277 games before dropping the bombshell that he was turning his back on football. Harry Yorston, who died in 1992, stressed at the time that the Pittodrie crowd's failure to embrace him universally was one of the key factors in his decision to embark on a new life in a lucrative new profession as a fish market porter. He said: "I never had any regrets. I was as happy as Larry when I packed it in. Every time Aberdeen lost, I took it personally – or my family and friends got it in the neck. That had a big bearing on my decision."

Harry Yorston, who became a big-money pools winner in later life, was tagged 'The Golden Boy' by the media during his playing days but sections of the crowd would barrack his every move, perhaps motivated by jealousy as the dashing young Aberdonian set about making his mark in the Dons history books. Given his own honest appraisal of his difficult relationship with the home fans, it would be wrong to paint Harry as an out-and-out cult hero in the mould of his elder family member.

For his uncle Benny there were not the same barriers to be overcome. The most logical explanation is that the envy was cultivated on the Pittodrie terraces as the profile and standing of the Aberdeen players grew. In the 1920s and 1930s, when Benny was weaving his magic, the club was still just a part of life in the city. In the post-war years of Harry it had become much more than that, the stars being elevated to the level of their fellow entertainers from stage and screen. That familiar Scottish trait of building heroes up to be knocked back down was beginning to be exhibited and the local players tended to bear the brunt more than most.

For Benny it was a fortunate period to be a professional, hoovering up the fortunes which were beginning to find their way into the game but avoiding the pitfalls of fame which his elder relative would later suffer.

Even before hitting the big time with Aberdeen in the late 1920s, Benny Yorston was making a comfortable living from the game he loved. Having honed his skills with his Aberdeen Boys Brigade company, the Nigg-born sharpshooter played juvenile football for Sunnybank and in the junior ranks with Richmond, Banks o' Dee and Mugiemoss. He first ventured outside of his native Aberdeen to sign for Montrose in the second half of the 1920s and was awarded a £10 bonus for every goal he scored in certain games. In response, he scored four in one cup-tie alone to bag a £40 bounty – the equivalent to four months' wages for the average labourer on the street at that time.

Yorston was born in 1905, an Aberdonian through and through, and into a household packed with energy and exuberance. He was one of six children, living a simple life amid the granite on the periphery of the city centre. From his home on Great Northern Road, Yorston went on to attend Kittybrewster school and between there and the Boys Brigade his marksmanship skills were developed. He was always a goal-scorer and it helped him stand out from the crowd, making a mockery of his short stature.

Before he had hit his teenage years Yorston had already had the privilege of playing on the hallowed Pittodrie turf, even if only in a schools match, and they were surroundings with which he would soon get even more familiar.

His first professional experience of Aberdeen Football Club was not as a player but as an office assistant, after a chance encounter with the son of manager Jimmy Philip when both men attended Webster's College. As it turned out, the aspiring footballer's secretarial qualification was not the skill which would eventually set him on his path to an exciting life.

It was after he had starred briefly for Montrose in non-League football that the Dons finally took the plunge and offered their office boy a playing role. He repaid that faith more than 100 times over, with a veritable goal rush thanks in no small part to his two-footed ability and deadly accuracy.

Jack Webster, in his centenary history of the club, wrote: "Little wonder Benny Yorston became the idol of his day, setting up a tradition of smallish centre-forwards which would be followed by Paddy Moore, Matt Armstrong, Stan Williams, Paddy Buckley and the man of the 1970s who echoed much of Yorston's idolatory of the 1920s, Joe Harper. Fans adored him, but colleagues on the park felt he turned on the brilliance only when he felt in the mood. None denied his supremacy on the day, as the leader of that dashing forward line: Love, Cheyne, Yorston, McDermid and Smith."

In March 1927 manager Paddy Travers clinched the deal of the century when he persuaded Montrose to part with Yorston in exchange for £30. Even by 1920s standards, it was a paltry return given the forward's future exploits.

Travers was an astute man and he did not rush his new recruit. Rather Yorston was eased into life as a Dons player, not featuring at all in the top team at the tail-end of the 1926/27 season but instead introduced to the first XI during the tour of South Africa two months after he had been signed. That overseas adventure did enough to persuade Travers that the Nigg-born star in the making was ready for permanent promotion.

Still only 21, he made his competitive debut in the second game of the 1927/28 season at Stark's Park against Raith Rovers. The Dons won 3-2 and the rookie was on target with one of those goals. Now his account was open and the deposits just kept coming. In his first eight games, Yorston netted ten times and grabbed four doubles in that red-hot run of form.

He went on to score 17 goals in just 28 games, finishing his first season at the summit of the Pittodrie scoring chart as the Dons finished seventh in Division One. In each of his four full terms, Yorston sat proudly at the head of the list of scorers as he outgunned some esteemed colleagues. Alex Cheyne, Bob McDermid and Andy Love were hardly put in the shade by their pint-sized team-mate but they could not match his phenomenal strike rate.

The 1928/29 season saw the Dons stand still in the League but there was no danger of the new talisman treading water. Yorston had the bit between his teeth and crashed home his first hat-trick in the club's colours in a 4-1 demolition of Hamilton on home turf in December 1928. There were two more trebles that same season and a quartet of goals aganst Falkirk in the Scottish Cup for good measure. In all he made the net bulge 33 times in 35 games. It was good, if not quite perfect. But there was still time.

Season 1929/30 brought that momentous achievement: 42 games in League and Cup, 46 goals in total and a ratio of more than one goal per match. It was the stuff dreams were made of and the Dons fans were left pinching themselves to make sure they had not drifted into a fantasy realm. After years of mid-table mediocrity, and worse, they were suddenly right in the championship mix, unbeaten at home for the entire season and only falling out of contention in the final quarter as eventual title winners Rangers and runners-up Motherwell stretched out seven- and two-point margins.

It was the best performance in Scotland's top flight since the second-place finish of 1911 and Yorston was the man shunting on the upwardly mobile team from the Granite City. They were exciting times all round, with the ground beginning to take shape following the completion of the new main grandstand and the neat stone façade of the Merkland End rising up to give a greater sense of identity and belonging for the fledgling club. The roots were being set down and a local boy was helping make the process on the pitch very smooth indeed.

Yorston was an ever-present in his glorious 1929/30 tour of duty, the only one in a pool of 20 players utilised by Travers as he chased the elusive first League trophy.

The bid got off to a rocky start, with a 3-2 defeat at Falkirk, but the consolation was that Yorston had already found his range. He netted both that day and scored in a further 23 League games. The quick-witted number-nine grabbed eight doubles and three hat-tricks in his 38 League games. His heroics continued in the Scottish Cup, scoring a vital first-round goal in a 3-3 away draw against Raith and then hammering home a hat-trick in the 7-0 replay mauling of the Kirkcaldy side. He scored two in the second round as Aberdeen eased to a 5-1 win against Nithsdale and another pair against Partick in the third round, although that was not enough to prevent a 3-2 defeat against the Jags.

That blip aside, there was a real momentum building behind Aberdeen and Yorston. His finest season, by no coincidence, brought record numbers flocking to Pittodrie to see the man many would argue is the greatest ever to wear the crest on his chest. Against Rangers in September 1929 the largest crowd ever seen at Pittodrie up to that point was noted, with 32,000 filtering in to witness a 1-1 draw. Ironically, the master so many had come to see drew a blank that day but it mattered not: the legend of Yorston was growing with every passing week.

One of the finest performances he ever produced came just months after that record turnout. It was in the New Year fixture against Dundee at Dens Park in 1930 and those who witnessed it were left with everlasting memories of Yorston's majesty.

Within 27 minutes he had opened the scoring but there was a price to pay, with Dundee's left-back clashing with his Dons adversary as he rammed the ball home. Both players crumpled to the ground but it was the Dark Blues' player who came off worst, suffering a double fracture.

Yorston was able to carry on after apparently being treated for a shoulder injury – but what the public and the players on that eventful day did not know at the time was that there was no shoulder injury. It was the Aberdeen man's battle-scarred legs which had once again borne the brunt of a defender's challenge. But he did not want to give the opposition an edge by allowing the trainer to highlight the fact that he had taken a severe knock and quickly came up with a Plan B.

The scheming worked, with a header and a neat finish after a clever piece of play in the forward channel completing his hat-trick and a 3-0 win for his side. The *Evening Express* account of the game stated: "Part of the price Yorston was paying for being leading scorer was that his legs were covered with lacerations and bruises, and he took to the field that day bandaged almost to the tops of his stockings. Trainer Billy Russell, knowing about Benny's condition, made to attend to his legs after the clash at the first goal, but although hurt, Yorston, not wishing to reveal to the opposition the real state of affairs, told the trainer to rub his shoulder, which actually was uninjured."

The disappointment for Travers and his team was their failure to build on that memorable season. In 1930/31 they fell back to sixth place, a whopping 19 points off the title-winning pace set by Rangers. They surrendered an 18-month unbeaten home record in the process, and there was an embarrassing Scottish Cup quarter-final exit after a 4-0 thumping at the hands of Celtic.

For his part, Yorston was still doing the business and he added another 22 League and Cup goals, in 33 appearances, to beat Bob McDermid to the leading scorer's spot by eight. It won him a Scotland cap in 1931 as the nation searched for a replacement for Hughie Gallacher, but Yorston was not viewed by selectors as the man to take on the role and the expected flood of international appearances never materialised. The game against Northern Ireland, which ended 0-0, was his one and only Scotland experience.

He was still untouchable in the goal stakes at club level, but would soon discover that he was not bigger than the club. After 18 games and eight goals in the 1931/32 season, the axe fell. Yorston was gone for good. His point-winning strike in a 1-1 draw at home to Kilmarnock in November 1931 proved to be his last for his home-town team. After that game he was unceremoniously dumped, sold to the first rather than the highest bidder.

It was Sunderland who were quickest off the mark and the Roker Park side must have thought all of their Christmases had come at once when their £2,000 offer for the goal king was accepted. Yorston played 49 games, scoring 25 goals, before moving on to Middlesbrough, where his strike rate was 54 goals in 152 games. The rate was not quite as generous as it had been at Aberdeen but as he matured Yorston's role changed, and he played in a support position rather than as an out-and-out finisher. He hung up the boots with the Midas touch once and for all when war brought an end to his playing career at the age of 34. He scouted for Bury for a spell before concentrating his efforts on his business commitments.

Following his 1931 exile he never did return to his Aberdeen roots. Instead Yorston moved into the property sector, letting flats and rooms in his adopted home city of London. He made regular returns to visit friends and family in the north-east, even turning out at Linksfield Stadium in 1941 for a Scottish Command Select alongside Stanley Matthews, but was never tempted to move back lock, stock and barrel.

South Kensington became his business base. At the time of his death he had moved the short distance to World's End in Chelsea, living a quiet, modest and unremarkable retirement in an anonymous block of flats and survived at the time by his wife and his sons, Vincent and Terrence.

Yorston will forever have not one, but two places in the annals of Aberdeen Football Club. One as a possible culprit in one of the club's great scandals and the other as possibly the finest striker ever to don the shirt. For a generation who were enticed through the Pittodrie turnstiles by his skill and tenacity, the latter was all that mattered.

'GENTLEMAN GEORGE' 1938–1947 and 1948–1955

GEORGE HAMILTON

Magic Moment: With two headers and two sweeps of his goal-laden boots, Gentleman George became the first Dons man to score four against Celtic as he helped his beloved Reds to a 5-1 win at Parkhead on 2 January 1947. The Hoops were humbled.

Dons Career: Games 281. Goals 153. Caps 5

THE CULT of modern football has created a media machine, one built up around the ability of the central characters to generate the type of tabloid fodder which has made the game front-page news every week of the year. The lurid tales of ungentlemanly conduct have become an accepted part of football culture. Oh, for the good old days, when men were men and football players were content to go home at night and read a good book. In 'Gentleman George' Hamilton the Dons had a player who proved that sometimes the good guys can win through and that the occasional polished gem can prove as popular as the rough diamonds who so often pull at the heartstrings. Jock Hutton and Benny Yorston had their flaws and foibles but were forgiven for those. The difference with Hamilton was that there was no down side or skeleton in the closet – what you saw was what you got, and what he got in return was the love and respect of tens of thousands.

Respect: a rare commodity in the modern game but on both sides of the war there was still a wealth of it washing around the Scottish divisions and it was a two-way street. Hamilton believed wholeheartedly in upholding the honour and tradition of the club he represented. He was a pillar of the community in the Granite City, while in return he could go about his daily business without fear of intrusion or interruption.

At the peak of his talent, when his star of fame was at its highest point and illuminating the north-east, the silky skilled forward would spend his afternoons manning the till at his Rosemount shop. The masses who swayed to his on-field rhythm every fortnight at Pittodrie thought nothing of cheering his every move one day and the next buying from him the newspapers which contained the images of Gentleman George and retold his weekend glories. It sounds unthinkable now, but that was the reality for the big names of the 1940s and '50s.

For a generation which had survived the war years, it was no hardship to have to graft for a living. They were simply glad to be alive and to have the good fortune to be able once again to take on the role of entertainers, even if it was effectively a part-time profession for those who had the foresight to look beyond the short span of their sporting prime and carve out a dual role with a view to a long-term pay cheque.

Hamilton made his nest in the Rosemount area of the city and as his football career wound down he planned for the future by building up his newsagent's business at 1 Watson Street. He would train in the morning before travelling across town to take his place behind the counter. In his spare time he was into gentle pursuits. He was a member of badminton clubs at Beechgrove Church and the Hardgate as well as working to reduce his golf handicap. He later swapped the news trade for a role with the whisky firm, Bell's, using his familiar face to great effect as a rep on his home patch for more than two decades. He served as a kirk elder at Beechgrove from the early 1970s. No late-night headline-grabbing antics for this cult hero and no life of excess.

> "We sometimes meet an original gentleman, who, if manners had not existed, would have invented them."
>
> **Ralf Waldo Emerson, philosopher and poet**

Despite his popularity and stardom, there was no chance to retire on the back of his Aberdeen heroics. Hamilton later revealed: "When I think of the rewards players get nowadays I often smile wryly. When I started as a senior with Queen of the South I got £7 per week. As an Aberdeen player I started off with £12, but that was raised to £14. You might find it hard to believe that I was still getting that after 17 years. There were, of course, bonuses of £2 and £1 for a win and a draw and there was always something extra for success in Scottish Cup ties."

Hamilton was one of the Dons who performed on both sides of the hostilities, but the vast majority of his 281 appearances came post-war. He was playing to an audience who shared the relief of the players. As normality crept back into life, football returned to centre-stage and Hamilton was the leading man for Aberdeen.

The war had a huge impact on players and spectators alike. Hamilton, who died in 2001, insisted: "People used to ask me if I was ever bitter about the fact that possibly my peak time as a player coincided with the war years, but I never looked on it that way. I was a very fortunate man to come out of the war the same way I went into it. I came back. A lot of men never came back, or came back lame or wounded or not able to do anything with the rest of their lives."

Perhaps that sense of relief manifested itself in Hamilton's play. Certainly something in his make-up made him a figure the fans related to. Writing in the *Evening Express* in 1952, Joe Cowie observed: "Popularity in football is something of a Will o' the Wisp. It can be shining brightly one moment and gone forever in the next. One player who has retained the affections of the football public since he first came into prominence, however, is George Hamilton."

There were myriad reasons for his appeal. For one thing he could play; secondly he scored goals left, right and centre. Thirdly, there was his impeccable character. Finally, he played a key role in the club's most successful period in more than half a century of existence.

Starting at the start, there can be no questioning his talent. Even during his later days, he was still turning on the style. One 1953 report noted: "Hamilton must be considered as approaching the twilight of his football career, but if he continues to walk through future matches with the ease he did on Saturday his position in top-class soccer is assured. He was the most cultured player on the field. He coupled an uncanny knack of being in the right spot at the right moment with an ability to spray made-to-measure passes to right or left."

Ironically the future Scotland international was deemed too small to play as a youngster, picked last for every playground kick-about. The little lad bit back, though, going on to prove his doubters wrong in grand style with club and country. He had come through the ranks playing for his Boys Brigade team and at Irvine Royal Academy before earning an unexpected junior break with Irvine Meadow, called up to fill in for an injured inside-right. He had trials with Rangers and Hearts as a centre-forward but it was Queen of the South who eventually gave him a passage to the senior game in 1937.

At the Dumfries club he happened to be watched by Aberdeen manager David Halliday's brother in a twist of fate which shaped the rest of his life. The reports back to Pittodrie were obviously good. Halliday rustled up a bid of £3,000 in 1938. It does not sound a lot in today's money, but when you consider it eclipsed the previous Dons record transfer by 100 per cent the picture of just how highly the new recruit was rated becomes clear.

He made a quiet debut, slipped into the Dons team to face Chelsea in the wonderfully titled Empire Exhibition tournament hosted by Rangers at Ibrox. Everton and the home team made up the numbers. The pre-match talk was of the Stamford Bridge side's personalities, not of the young inside-right who had joined from Queen of the South. New boys Wilf Adey, from Carlisle United, and Willie Hume, recruited from Hearts, were the other new faces in the ranks for the May 27 encounter. Following the fanfare of trumpets when his record-breaking signing was announced, it was a gentle introduction to the Dons first team for the Gentleman.

He was just 20 when he arrived at Pittodrie and he made an encouraging start to his career with the club, scoring 18 goals in 42 games in his first season to justify the investment. Which brings us to the second point in Hamilton's four-pronged assault on the senses of the Dons followers: goals. Hamilton's record of 153 strikes in 281 appearances stacks up with the best forwards ever to grace Pittodrie. But it was not just the numbers that impressed, it was the manner in which the goals came that won more plaudits. Whether from close range, long range, with boot or head, the net bulged regularly on Hamilton's watch.

The outbreak of war stalled that progress but he returned to pick up where he left off when competitive football resumed in 1946. During the conflict he saw service in North Africa as one of the troops involved in the El Alamein push, before being moved to Italy and Austria. He continued to keep his football skills simmering by playing in a touring forces side which also featured legendary Englishman Tom Finney. The good company rubbed off on him, serving to heighten his enthusiasm for the sport and his determination to go on adding different facets to his own game.

The Irvine-born player had a big impact in the post-war emergence of the club, with a Southern League Cup and Scottish Cup double secured within the first two seasons after the hostilities had ended. It was a purple patch for the team and the individual. Hamilton's finest hour was his four-goal blast in a League game against Celtic in the New Year fixture of 1947. He had already bagged four that season, putting Falkirk to the sword in the League Cup with all of Aberdeen's strikes in a pulsating 4-3 victory. But there were no wild celebrations, no antagonistic gestures towards the Bairns fans. This was, after all, Gentleman George and that brings the attention round to box number-three on Hamilton's cult hero checklist: character.

He played the game the right way, was booked just once in a career spanning the 1930s, 1940s and 1950s. Incidentally, that solitary caution came for a passing remark of "It wasn't a foul ref" to an official during a cup-tie against Hibs. Not quite the foul-mouthed rant which characterises dissent in the modern game. Hamilton knew his style was of its time. In a 1986 interview he admitted: "It's a different game now and I would have had to change if I played today. But I've always said that if the game was worth playing it was worth playing well."

The fact Hamilton played the game in the spirit in which its inventors had intended did not detract from his role as one of the most deadly strikers of a generation. Those who watched him play marvelled at the way he could still look after himself without overstepping the mark. He was also a principled man, as the Dons found to their cost on more than one occasion.

The first was during Hamilton's playing days. In 1952 he was suspended for a short period by the club for refusing to play in a game against Rangers. The circumstances were cloaked in secrecy at the time, although it was reported on the day of the game that the player had only just arrived back north of the border after 14 days of service with the forces in Aldershot. Almost 35 years later the great man lifted the lid on what actually happened – and not for the first time it was the tight Pittodrie purse-strings which were at the root of the furore.

While his fellow football-playing servicemen rested in luxury in sleeper carriages, the Aberdeen star sat up through the night in the cheap seats. The treatment did not go down well with Hamilton, who beneath his gentle character was known as a man willing to stand up for himself with passion, and he informed his manager he was too tired to play after his uncomfortable trip.

It was the same story of strong principles after Hamilton had hung up his boots and moved into coaching at Pittodrie. At the start of the 1955/56 season the club made an attempt to tie the fans' favourite to the Dons on a more long-term basis by asking him to succeed Davie Shaw in the trainer's role. He declined and within a month was on his way to Hamilton. He spent just three months with the Accies before injury forced his retirement on his 38th birthday.

He did return to become reserve coach at Aberdeen but resigned from that role in 1959, making the decision during a match against a junior select side. Even after hanging up his boots, he remained passionate and bloody-minded about the game and a fierce defender of his principles.

His impulsive walk-out came when manager David Shaw entered the dressing room at half-time to read the riot act to Hamilton's young reserves following a disappointing performance in the opening period of the game. It was in stark contrast to Hamilton's softly-softly approach. He preferred a quiet word in the ear of his protégés and an arm round the shoulder rather than a kick up the backside and a verbal bashing, and it pushed him over the edge. He remained friends with Shaw, but would not change his personality to fit in with football and decided on a clean break from the game.

In a 1975 interview Hamilton said: "No longer are players allowed to do what comes naturally. I'm not against coaching – I had my share of it as far as the basics went – but think it can be overdone. If a youngster joining a senior club displays individual skills he should be allowed to express them naturally, but one can't help feeling that sometimes coaching is overdone in the interests of teamwork. Quite often if you watch boys playing in the street you see one who looks a natural footballer, but that's probably the last you'll see or hear of him. Mind you, I must admit that there are exceptions and that some lads don't blossom until coaches take them in hand. Too much coaching could well be the reason for the absence of personality players in Britain these days."

There was no shortage of personalities in the Dons team which Hamilton graced and he is far from the only one who could be categorised as a cult hero. He was also far from the sole attacking threat. Harry Yorston, as mentioned in the previous chapter, was the Golden Boy. The pair struck up a lethal partnership and Yorston was quick to acknowledge his respected sidekick's role in his success when he said: "You have to couple my name with that of George Hamilton. He was a genius. That was the secret of what scoring success I enjoyed. I just cottoned on to Hammy's genius and playing alongside him it was easy to get goals. George was a legend and never got the credit or caps to salute his talent. He was a 90-minute player – absolutely fabulous in the air, able to score with either foot, capable of laying on goals and fearless.

He could do it all. He was the ultimate player in Scottish football and why he never got more caps I'll never know."

In fact, Yorston's big break came due to Hamilton's dalliance with Hearts. He came in as a youthful deputy for Gentleman George following the latter's switch to Tynecastle and announced his arrival by scoring within five minutes of kick-off in his first appearance, which fell on Christmas day in 1947 at Third Lanark.

The Golden Boy rivalled and then bettered Hamilton in the scoring stakes, with 160 goals in 277 appearances. While Hamilton was cool, calm and collected his eventual strike partner was a more high-energy proposition. The bustling Yorston hustled and harried his way through games, playing on the edge and ready to exploit the slightest hint of hesitation in an opposition defence with his pace and sharp thinking.

Yorston had first sprung to attention as a juvenile international, straight from St Clements A in Aberdeen's east end, in 1946. Within a year, on the back of army service, he had been propelled straight into the Dons team and towards life as a household name. It was of course a short career, with the Golden Boy famously quitting the game in 1957 to follow his father into the dockside role of fish market porter. It was more lucrative than his Dons contract and also offered an escape from the barracking he was prone to receiving. Yorston played on briefly in the Highland League with Buckie Thistle, Fraserburgh, Lossiemouth and Deveronvale, but it was off the field that he made the biggest headlines. His £170,000 pools win in the 1970s put the former forward back in the public eye.

For all the controversy which surrounded the Aberdonian, it was his partnership with George Hamilton for which he was best known. The understanding between the two was instinctive, not born from carefully choreographed training ground moves. In fact, getting a ball to work with was a rarity for the players of the time as they instead spent hours pounding the track around the Pittodrie pitch under the watchful eye of their manager Halliday and trainer Donald Colman. Not that the finer points of the game were ignored in that era – the pre-match ritual for home games was for the squad to gather at the Caledonian Hotel in the city centre for lunch, then gather round the manager for a final discussion about the opposition, having been educated through Halliday's blackboard during the course of the week. The immaculately turned out Dons would then walk together through their city to Pittodrie, greeting fans with a cheery wave as they made their way to work for the day.

The happy sentiments were always reciprocated during a period in which the Dons were in the ascendancy. The Southern League Cup, which was the predecessor to the League Cup, was landed in the 1945/46 campaign after a mammoth ten-match run. A crowd of 135,000 saw the Dons shock Rangers with a 3-2 win courtesy of a last-minute goal from George Taylor. That triumph gave Hamilton his first medal as an Aberdeen player but more importantly it sent out a message to the whole of Scottish football that the team from the north-east were ready to push the Old Firm all the way.

The 1946/47 season was a memorable one in every sense for Hamilton, with the victory in the 1947 Scottish Cup final against Hibs the undoubted highlight for the city and its most famous sporting sons. It was the first time the coveted trophy had been won by the Dons and Hamilton was in the thick of the action. Hampden was full of expectant fans as the two east-coast sides took to the field, and before the supporters had settled on the sweeping terraces the opener had already been scored. A misunderstanding between George Taylor and Aberdeen goalkeeper George Johnstone allowed Hibees' Johnny Cuthbertson to nip in and give the men from Edinburgh a dream start.

Step forward Gentleman George to save the day. The Ayrshire forward popped up with a typically imperious header after 36 minutes to bring the final all square, and Stan Williams edged the Dons ahead six minutes later. Then came the tragedy amid the triumph, with Hamilton missing from the penalty spot in the final quarter of the match to set up a nervy finale for his team-mates. They clung on, though, and Hamilton got the Scottish Cup medal which he cherished for the rest of his life.

On the way to the final Aberdeen had overcome Partick Thistle, Ayr United, Morton, Dundee and Arbroath. Hamilton had played in each of the seven ties, which included a replay against Morton and the final, and contributed five goals – three against Ayr, one in that third-round replay against the men from Cappielow and his most important of all in the Hampden final.

He also won his first cap in that whirlwind period, turning out for Scotland against Northern Ireland. It was another six years until Hamilton won his second cap, and he went on to total five in all, having scored a hat-trick in a 5-0 win against Belgium in that second appearance. As Yorston highlighted, the fact that he did not add to that collection of SFA mementoes was a travesty of the post-war era. Hamilton found out to his cost, as so many did before and after, that playing for Aberdeen kept him out of view of the selectors. His subtle skills and authoritative influence remained by and large solely for the consumption of his Dons fan club.

The success of 1946 and 1947, not to mention the warmth of the welcome he had received in the years following his move from west to east coast, did not prevent Gentleman George from becoming unsettled. In the closing weeks of 1947 he requested a transfer and switched to Hearts in a deal which cost the Tynecastle men £8,000 and Archie Kelly in a player-plus-cash deal. Less than a year later he packed his bags and returned to Pittodrie admitting the error of his ways and the club was willing to pay £10,000 to allow him to redeem himself. It was another hefty chunk of cash wagered on one of the most cherished talents of the time.

The fact that the Dons supporters welcomed the returning hero with open arms is testament to the appeal he held in his first period with the club. He ripped up the rule-book which said you should never go back and settled back into the team as though he had never been away, hardly much older but far wiser for his brief desertion.

For the next seven seasons Hamilton was there along with the red bricks of the Pittodrie main stand as a permanent fixture. After his Hearts experience he returned in 1948/49 and topped the club's scoring chart, an honour which flitted between Hamilton and Harry Yorston for four seasons following his return.

While the cup double of the 1940s represented the pinnacle for Hamilton, his influence did extend to the historic 1955 League championship success. By then in his veteran years, the wily forward was called upon four times by his mentor Halliday during the title-winning campaign and scored in two of those. It was a fitting year in which to end his days as a first-team star, having played a part in three major trophy triumphs.

He seldom ventured back to Pittodrie after severing his ties in the late 1950s, aghast at the defensive trends which crept into the game as tactics rather than talents began to take precedence. Instead he turned his attention to golf and was crowned champion at his club, Deeside, in the summer of 1967. Weeks later he shot a record-equalling round at the riverside course to ensure two places in its history books.

Hamilton later reflected: "Whether the game is better or not, it has certainly changed. Clubs complain about falling attendances but it's up to the clubs to attract the fans by playing skilful and attractive football. Teams played good football in my day. The old 2-3-5 line-up made sure of that. Those were the days of wingers, real wingers. Men like Finney and Matthews were a treat to watch. Even in Scotland there were really good teams, especially forwards. I feel sorry for the youngsters who never saw the famous Hibs forward line of Smith, Johnstone, Reilly, Turnbull and Ormond."

In turn, those who saw Hamilton in all his glory would be perfectly entitled to have more than a hint of sympathy with those who missed the opportunity to watch Gentleman George do what he did best.

'TWO-TON DON' 1948–1952

DON EMERY

Magic Moment: With a crunch and a crack, the Partick Thistle crossbar split in two and collapsed to the ground. Another victim of Emery's feared and revered shooting prowess had been claimed.

Dons Career: Games 125. Goals 26.

THE ABILITY to divide opinion has been part and parcel of the game since the first whistle sounded in the very first game. For the cult hero, the crowd-splitting tendency has often come more readily than in any other group of players and proved beyond all doubt that there really is nothing more fickle than a football audience.

When it came to Don Emery, the Dons fans either loved him or they hated him. According to reports from the 1950s, for every supporter who worshipped the ground his giant boots fell on there was another who felt manager David Halliday may have dropped an almighty clanger when he procured the services of the biggest hitter of them all.

> "Be what nature intended for you for and you will succeed."
>
> **Sydney Smith, writer**

'Two-Ton Don', as he became affectionately known among the Emery aficionados, was an imposing man. Standing well under 6ft tall, the charismatic man from Cardiff was a brute of a physical specimen who, according to legend, weighed in at up to 17 stone at one time or another during his playing career. Emery himself preferred to quote 13 stone at his peak, but there was some sporting licence involved in that particular figure.

There were amazing parallels between Emery and Jock Hutton, two formidable looking figures both equipped with the type of shot which should have come labelled with a health warning. Both, crucially, also had personalities to match their size and had detractors at stages during their Pittodrie careers.

For Hutton it was his lifestyle which, at times, led to furrowed brows while with Emery it was far simpler, in that some sections of the Pittodrie crowd did not know what to make of him, particularly in the formative stages of the relationship between star and star-gazers.

The scepticism was understandable. After all, the new man did not match the fleet-footed athleticism of contemporaries such as Paddy Buckley and Jackie Hather. He was a different breed, more power than pace, more force than subtlety. That meant he would have to work to win his share of adulation, and he did that in spectacular style. The imposing defender quickly established his own devoted following and the cornerstone of that popularity was his sheer, unadulterated, breathtaking muscularity. Whether tackling or shooting, nobody before, Hutton included, and nobody since, could lay claim to the same type of impact as Don Emery.

His bone-jarring challenges were enough to draw gasps from grown men standing 50 yards beyond the touchline, while his thunderbolt shots had goalkeepers running for cover ... quite literally. In one match against East Fife, petrified goalkeeper John Curran is reputed to have turned his back as Emery lined up to take one of his spot-kick specials and sidled to the sanctuary of one of his goalposts in an obvious state of fear and alarm. Emery was able to tuck the penalty into an empty net and left the watching Dons fans in states of bemusement and amusement in equal measure. Whether urban myth or solemn truth, it is typical of the type of Emery-inspired tale that has stood the test of time.

The story of the terrified shot-stopper, it is safe to say, may have been exaggerated over the passage of time but there is no doubting the authenticity of the crossbar-cracking shot. The late, great man himself testified to that particular achievement, laying claim to the fame of breaking the bar with one of his ferocious efforts.

Emery, who died in 1993, was justifiably proud of his shooting prowess and vouched for that particular episode when he recalled: "It was Firhill on a filthy, wet day when I cracked the heavy ball off the Partick Thistle bar from 20 yards. There was a loud cracking noise and the bar sagged in the middle. The groundsman used a roll of Elastoplast to repair the woodwork."

It would be fascinating to compare Emery's thunderbolts to the modern game's masters of the power-play. The Sky Sports Replay 2000 ball-tracking machine has ended all debate about who packs the biggest punch, with the equipment able to accurately measure the speed of every shot captured by the station's cameras. While Emery had his not-insubstantial physique squarely behind his woodwork-threatening efforts, he also had the technique of shooting down to a fine art. It's a cold, hard fact that skill rather than muscle is the key to getting pace on a ball and if we accept that Emery did, in fact, have the hardest shot of his generation, it follows that he had the best dead-ball ability. Thanks to Sky's box of tricks, a chart of the modern game's hardest shots has been formulated and, in the main, the entrants are not renowned for their hulking physiques.

Topping the rankings is Sheffield Wednesday old boy David Hirst, who fired a shot clocked at 114mph for the Owls in a match against Arsenal in 1996. David Beckham features twice in the top ten, firstly in second spot with an effort of 97.9mph for Manchester United against Chelsea in 1997 and then in tenth spot with 80.5mph against Derby the previous year. In third place is a bullet from the boot of Monaco's David Trezeguet in 1998 against the men from Old Trafford, with Sheffield Wednesday hot-shot Richie Humphreys not far behind with a 95.9mph strike against Aston Villa in 1996. Matt Le Tissier was measured at 86.8mph while playing for Southampton against Newcastle in 1997, and Alan Shearer's best was one mile per hour short of that for Newcastle against Leicester in the same year. The legendary Roberto Carlos features at number seven on the list, firing in a shot of 85.2mph while playing for Brazil against France in 1997, while Blackburn's Tugay registered 84.2mph against Southampton in 2001.

In more recent times, the 2007 screamer from Newcastle striker Obafemi Martins against Spurs hit the headlines, but in actual fact at 84mph it only just scrapes into the top ten recorded shots of all time.

We can only assume Emery at his peak would have propelled himself well up that list, perhaps to the summit, but the point is that none of those nine modern greats have relied on power alone. Yes, Roberto Carlos has thighs the size of tree-trunks and Alan Shearer was as difficult to push off the ball as it is to lift an oak from the ground, but more than anything their prowess was thanks to their talent, something Emery had in abundance to go with his natural attributes.

Because of that, Emery had an uncanny habit of finding the back of the net, particularly given his posting in defence. No doubt he burst a few nets in his time, too. More than half his goals for Aberdeen came from the penalty spot, and resistance must have seemed futile for the keepers who watched him bear down on them from 12 yards. His attacking talents stemmed from his early days as a forward and he was pressed into action as an emergency striker during his Dons tenure, helping to bolster his goals tally.

Born in Cardiff, Emery was a schoolboy international by the age of 13 and a year later became a fixture in the Cardiff City reserve side. He never made the breakthrough with his home-town club, but Swindon saw enough raw talent to work with and snapped up the Welshman.

The war interrupted his dream of making it big in football, with the player serving six years in the RAF. During that airforce stint he met the Aberdonian who would become his wife, and the north-east link was a key factor in his change in football fortunes post-war as the new Mrs Emery sought a return to her family roots in Scotland.

Emery made his name during a decade of service with Swindon Town, straddling the war years before being tempted to Aberdeen in 1948 in a swap deal which took Andy Cowie south of the border. He joined a team which had finished tenth in the 16-team Division A in 1947/48, a season in which Hibs ruled the Scottish roost.

His debut was at Cathkin Park against Third Lanark on 14 August that year, when his new side fell to a 1-0 defeat. He started at right-back but towards the end of the campaign was thrust into attacking action. Despite a return of five goals in ten matches up front, manager Halliday was not convinced the distinctive figure of Emery was the answer to his striking prayers and he returned him to a full-back berth for the following term.

Aberdeen had struggled against relegation, finishing in 13th spot and just two places and three points clear of Morton in the drop zone. It was not the stuff dreams were made of for the new recruit but better times were on the horizon. In 1949/50 he made the number-two jersey his own and helped lift the club to mid-table respectability and eighth spot. The following season the improvement continued as the Dons climbed to fifth, although form tailed off and Halliday's side fell back to 11th in 1951/52.

Team success may have been limited, but the triumph of establishing Emery as a right-back was a bright spot of the period. It was an inspired move and allowed the player to make the most of his defensive qualities while still having licence to make forward raids when the opportunity arose.

Joe Cowie, writing in the *Evening Express* in 1952, said: "The most remarkable feature of his football make-up is his explosive shot. When Emery's around, a free-kick anywhere within 30 yards is generally good for a goal. As a full-back he must be one of the most prolific scorers in Britain."

Yet the tackling and intimidating physical appearance of the bulky Dons defender was just as remarkable. One look at Emery looming over them was usually enough to knock an opponent out of their stride. He was hard, he was fair and he did not suffer fools gladly on the football pitch.

Rodwill Clyne, a legendary figure in the Highland League from his playing days, recalled with fondness Emery's introduction to the northern game in his post-Aberdeen days. Clyne, in his memoirs *In a Different*

League wrote: "Top of the scoring chart in 1956/57 was big Don Emery with the cannonball shot. Don had a long spell at Aberdeen and had been a firm favourite of the Dons supporters, and was reckoned to have the hardest shot in football. In that season Mr Emery and I were not on speaking terms, although we became firm friends off the field later on. At the start of the season we had a player called wee Hamish Munro, who was just starting to make the outside-left berth his own. We played at Fraserburgh and in the very first minute Hamish, with his head down, went flying down the wing, ball at his feet. Don Emery, who was playing at right-back, waited for Hamish to come level with the grandstand. Bang. He hit Hamish right off the park on to the grandstand wall from where he bounced back on to the field of play. About a five-foot bounce. I was not having this, having looked after Hamish's interests as soon as he came to the club. Up I go to Big Don who at the time was about 17 stone but only about 5ft 10in. I said: 'If you do that once ...' – I never got a chance to finish it. Don took a deep breath, his chest went out about six inches and he appeared to grow a foot in stature. 'You were saying, Rod,' he stated, looking down at me. 'Never mind,' I said – and ran away."

Hamish Munro remembers the incident well and the Highland League veteran, who is still a regular spectator of games across the north, still shudders at the memory of going head-to-head with one of the giants of the Scottish game. Munro said: "I played directly against Don when he joined Fraserburgh in the late 1950s with his long-time friend and Aberdeen team-mate Pat McKenna. For me they formed the finest full-back partnership in the Highland League. Don was an awesome player – not tall, but built like a bull and tackling like one – which I know to my cost. He showed his ability as a player when he moved to centre-forward and topped the scoring charts. That was some achievement. Paddy Buckley, another great hero to the Aberdeen supporters, joined us at Caley after his Pittodrie days, and it was interesting to hear him talk about Don Emery. Paddy always talked fondly of Don; he held him in the highest regard as both player and as a man."

Mind you, even the great Emery was not infallible. Rodwill Clyne noted in his memoirs: "In the Qualifying Cup in 1957 it was 1-1 when Len Grant, our goalkeeper, was injured. Big Jim MacPherson took over in goal. Disaster struck – a penalty for Broch. Don placed the ball on the spot. You could hear Jim's knees knocking in Aberdeen. Don stepped back and let fly. His big toe stubbed the ground and the ball trickled into Jim's hands. Upfield it was punted and Ally Chisholm scrambled it into the net. We were into the Scottish Cup."

Even heroes can slip up from time to time and the imperfections were part of the appeal when it came to the strength of feeling he provoked among followers of every team for which he played. For those in the pro-Emery camp, the appeal was as instant as it was obvious. Aberdonian Colin MacLeod was one of those among the paying public who were won over by the honest big defender. Having attended his first match at Pittodrie alongside his father in the 1940s, he grew up watching the Welshman wreak havoc in the Scottish game with his physical power and legendary ball-striking.

MacLeod, now retired and living in the Highlands, was a starry-eyed Fyvie schoolboy when he first caught a glimpse of the formidable figure. He said: "The very first time I went to Pittodrie was for a reserve game between Aberdeen and Leith Athletic. The visiting goalkeeper was Jock Wallace's father and he produced a fantastic save that I can still picture to this day. The memory of seeing Don Emery in full flight is just as vivid for me.

"Don had an aura around him, a real presence. When you looked out and saw Don Emery lining up in your defence there was a security, you knew that if there was any nonsense he would sort the other team out. Then there were his penalty kicks – you would put your house on Emery to score every time. You could see the fear in the goalkeeper's eyes even from the back of the stand because nobody wanted to get in the way of one of Don's piledrivers. I recently had the pleasure of the company of some fellow football fans of a similar vintage for a car journey through to a match in Elgin, including the former Inverness

Thistle player George Mackenzie. When the subject turned to Aberdeen players of the past, the one name that was on the tip of everyone's tongue was Don Emery. He is one of the figures from the late 1940s and early 1950s that leaps out – he was one of the original tough guys in football. With Aberdeen and then later in the Highland League he was such a committed and colourful character."

Emery, who was an honorary member of the Aberdeen Spartan Physical Culture Club, cut a distinctive figure about town and his profile was raised further when he was bestowed with the captaincy of the team by Halliday. The doubts were being eroded with every wholehearted challenge and every bullet shot that flew past the flailing arms of an opposition goalkeeper. It was a brave man who got in the path of a netbound Emery effort, as Dons goalkeeper Fred Martin found to his cost. Martin tried to keep out a predictably fierce drive from his team-mate in training and even in retirement still exhibits a buckled finger as a result.

Emery was a character on the field and off it. He had an aversion to the pain of breaking in the new pair of boots that each player was presented with at the start of the season, the footwear which had to last them the entire campaign. Rather than suffering the blisters himself, he would hand them to a member of the Pittodrie groundstaff to wear around the stadium until they were suitably softened.

He was a personality player and had earned cult-hero status but his was not a long-term Pittodrie sojourn. Like so often in the history of Aberdeen Football Club, the famed fiscal policy was responsible for nipping a blooming relationship in the bud. In 1952, and with the once dubious Dons support finally won over, Emery found himself forced out of the club.

He later explained the circumstances behind his quick switch to East Fife and admitted: "My departure from Pittodrie was far from amicable. At the end of the 1951/52 season I picked up a copy of a national newspaper after training, only to read that Pat McKenna and I were on the transfer list. Although far from pleased, there was no point in arguing with Davie Halliday because I knew he had no real power. The decision had been taken at a higher level. In those days, after five years with a club each player was entitled to a benefit. I was just one season away from that and Aberdeen, who were notoriously grippy, decided to let me go. This was common practice at many clubs but most of them gave players a free transfer in lieu of a testimonial match – but the Dons wanted a £4,000 fee for a 32-year-old player."

When he left Pittodrie for East Fife, he could scarcely have imagined it would have led to trophy success. He was part of the Methil side's League Cup-winning side in 1954 and came close to earning a Welsh international call-up during his Indian summer. During his time with the Fifers he remained based in Aberdeen and continued to train at Pittodrie, his popularity with team-mates never waned and there was never any danger of him being forgotten in a hurry. Players come and go in football, save for the precious few who make the type of impact which leaves a mark that even the sands of time cannot cover.

Emery was one of those characters, a football man through and through. His passion extended beyond playing and in 1955 he just missed out in a bid to succeed Bill Shankly as manager at the English Third Division North outfit Workington. The post carried a £1,000 salary and a club house, a considerable lure for a man who had made it clear that he never earned a king's ransom during his service at Pittodrie.

In the early 1950s the exposure of Dons players was growing but the wages remained restricted. Players used public transport to reach Pittodrie Street, a road now littered with the BMWs and Audis of the modern heroes. A player could survive on his football salary but could not retire on the back of it. Ploughing on for as long as possible was the preferred option and for Emery the passions still burned bright into the twilight of his career. Duly he continued to make waves wherever he went.

In 1956, Emery was appointed player-manager by Highland League side Fraserburgh, and with the Broch he proved adept in both areas after overcoming the initial scepticism about his physical ability to play on due to his hefty stature and advancing years. As it happened, neither hampered his ability to win over the detractors.

As a player he was an instant hit, scoring 49 goals from a forward berth to become the League's top scorer, and as a manager he masterminded the coastal club's 1959 Scottish Cup giant-killing act against Dundee. The minnows from Bellslea dumped the top-flight Dark Blues out of the competition with a 1-0 victory and Emery had chiselled a permanent place in the annals of the proud northern side. The win against the Tayside team is still spoken about in the coastal town and Emery's part in Dundee's downfall will never be forgotten.

It was Emery's finest managerial hour which led to the creation of the Scottish Cup as we know it now. Until the Broch humbled the men from Dens Park, the national tournament featured an all-in draw. After one of the country's finest teams was embarrassed by Highland League opposition the game's rulers had a rethink and opted for the now-familiar seeding system, where the big guns enter the fray long after the potentially embarrassing non-League and lower-league outfits have played their first-round games.

Aided by that famous victory, not to mention his formidable playing displays, Emery went on to become a Highland League legend. His service in northern football included a place on the board of directors at Fraserburgh and then a spell as president of Deveronvale in the 1980s.

Outside of the game, the affable Emery carved out a living in the motor industry. He began as a sales rep with the Webster Tyre Company before promotion to the role of area manager in the 1960s. He was a powerful individual, blessed with the gift of the gab and charm to go with it. More than a decade later he was nominated as a council candidate for the Conservative party, detailed to contest a ward which included Pittodrie. He also continued to be a familiar figure in and around the ground, intently puffing on a cigar as he watched his successors in the red shirts do their business on the park which was once his stomping ground. Had history panned out differently, his seat could have been in the Dons directors' box.

Emery loved the club as much as the club's fans loved him and that strength of feeling prompted an attempted takeover, along with former

Aberdeen team-mate Tony Harris, in 1969. Harris, a respected dentist in the city, and his sidekick tried to upset the balance of power during a trophy-drought which stretched back to the League Cup success in 1955.

It was a key moment in the rich tapestry of Pittodrie life. Would the reigning shareholders retain their seat at the top table or would the pretenders to the throne be successful in wresting power from them?

In 1958, councillor and architect T Scott Sutherland failed in a bid to take control of the club when his £40,000 offer was rejected by chairman William Mitchell and his directors. As the club toiled in its effort to repeat the championship success of 1955, unrest became a familiar part of life on Pittodrie Street.

By the time Emery and his consortium made their £80,000 move in 1969, Charles Forbes had stepped up to the top seat in the boardroom, having been a director at the time of the previous attempt to topple the administration.

Emery and local councillor AF Mutch had devised the 1969 plan having struck up a conversation in Aberdeen's Conservative club. From then the coup gathered pace, attracting Emery's former Pittodrie team-mate Harris, by then established with his own city dental practice, as well as insurance broker John Leiper, electrical wholesaler Gordon McIver and fish merchant Henry Robertson.

On the opposition side were former school headteacher Forbes, with 33 years' experience on the board, as well as cinema and theatre owner Richard Donald, waiting for his chance to take on the chairman's role and etch his place in future chapters of the twisting tale of Aberdeen FC.

SFA office-bearer Douglas McD Philip was another of the directors and well known in golf circles while, at 43, Chris Anderson, the finance officer and deputy secretary of Robert Gordon's College, aided his older colleagues with his vibrant and innovative approach to the role. Completing the board was Charles Shimmins, a retired Clydesdale Bank area manager.

Emery and his group's trump card was their relative youth, with an average age of 47 compared to the board's average of 60. They also set out a ten-point plan to improve Aberdeen's fortunes. Emery's detail was to concentrate on playing matters, a director of football-style role long before that chain of command was in vogue. He was convinced the strict wage structure, the one he had been so critical of as a player, had to be broken to retain the best Dons talent and also wanted improvements in youth development. Fast forward to 2008 and cynics would suggest the same issues could still be addressed. The consortium's grand plan also included the creation of a Dons social club as a revenue source, investment in a pitch blanket to avoid postponements and the appointment of a public relations officer to mirror the Old Firm clubs and improve relations between the Dons and their supporters. After four months of public debate, the consortium lost the vote at an extraordinary general meeting, with shareholders overwhelmingly backing the existing board.

Speaking after the disappointment, consortium leader McIver said: "If the result, which we most sincerely accept, in any way helps the Dons to be in the first four in the Scottish League then we all, and I repeat all, will be most satisfied."

The rest, as they say, is history. Dick Donald went on to continue his progress with the club and assume the chairmanship. Together with his right-hand man Chris Anderson, Donald plotted a dramatic rise to prominence which culminated in the glory days under the future Sir Alex Ferguson. The takeover bid was a shot in the arm for the club and its board, which awoke from years of slumber to move into top gear and attack Scottish football with a vigour which shook the game to the core. Perhaps Emery, after all, can claim to have been a boardroom influence – although not in the manner in which he had hoped.

When Emery died in November 1993 he was 73, the Welshman by that point having retired to Inverurie. He never made it to the chairman's seat and he did not savour the rush of glory in Cup or League. Instead, Emery had to content himself with something arguably just as fulfilling in the shape of the adulation of his adoring public. The big man won a big place in the heart of the club.

'THE KING OF IMAGINATION' 1948–1953

TOMMY PEARSON

Magic Moment: In a deserted gym hall in the bowels of the Kirkham airbase in Lancashire, a determined Scot stood alone with only a football for company. Hours later he emerged with a sense of sporting satisfaction, the double-shuffle had been perfected and was ready to be unleashed on an unsuspecting football public. Let the fun commence.

Dons Career: Games 115. Goals 16. Caps 2.

IN 1952 one of the great secrets of British football was unlocked when the soccer sorcerer Tommy Pearson opened his box of tricks and allowed the audience the opportunity to discover what lay behind the greatest, most distinguished trademark move ever employed at Pittodrie: the Pearson double-shuffle.

A generation of supporters spent years trying to fathom it, countless aspiring young players tied themselves in knots trying to replicate it, but with just four words the mystery was solved: a change of speed. That was the secret to success revealed in a newspaper interview, so simple it was beautiful. Of course, it did not make it any easier to copy; the Pearson double-shuffle belonged to one man and one man only.

His boots were a blur as he bamboozled defenders and spectators alike with his lightning quick footwork before accelerating past his man with the smoothness and certainty of a thoroughbred racehorse.

The famed double-shuffle was not a quirk of fate – it was a carefully planned and devised piece of football trickery. A magician does not walk out on stage and perform an illusion without putting in hours of practice first and Pearson was just as dedicated to his ball skills, drawing up the blueprint for his move after watching an opponent trying something similar in the English game while playing for Newcastle United, the club from which he joined Aberdeen.

He revised it, refined it and came up with his unique double-shuffle, then spent hours perfecting its execution before taking it on the road as he played to crowds the length and breadth of Britain. Pearson was not the type to leave the paying public longing for more and was happy to give them their fix of his renowned move again and again, with no limit to the number of times he would leave a defender trailing in his wake in any particular game by pulling off the shuffle time after time.

By the time he arrived at Pittodrie in 1948 he was in the twilight of his playing career, aged 34 and expected to be winding down. To their delight, the Dons supporters discovered there was plenty left in the tank and the veteran play-maker went on to thrill the Pittodrie galleries for almost five years before hanging up his boots.

In the modern day the Dons find themselves locked in a chicken-and-egg-type dilemma. The club needs crowds to generate revenue to invest in the playing squad, but the crowds need quality players on the park before they open their wallets and pay money to watch the team. The hardcore support of around 11,000 will turn out in rain or shine, whether fortunes are good or bad, but it is unlocking the potential of a far wider fan base which is the key to business and, consequently, football success for Aberdeen Football Club in its current guise.

Prudence is the buzz word, filtering down from chairman Stewart Milne through to managing director Duncan Fraser and director of football Willie Miller. They all urge the supporters to throw their weight behind the team and help generate cash to be reinvested in Jimmy Calderwood's squad. All the while, Calderwood has been left to pull rabbits from hats in the transfer market while shopping in the bargain basement and clearance sales.

Seldom in football can lessons from the dim and distant past be carried forward into the 21st century but when it comes to attendances there is a recurring sermon: give them excitement and they will keep coming back for more. Tommy Pearson brought fans to their tip-toes as they strained to watch him at work. He was impossible to second-guess, either for supporters or his marker. He was a crowd-pleaser and a tormentor of the opposition, so much so that thousands flocked to see him even in reserve fixtures.

Pearson is not unique in that respect. The introduction of Charlie Nicholas, another import from the English game with a pedigree as a flair player, created a wave of renewed interest in the city's only club with a surge to 20,000 for his home debut against Dunfermline contrasting starkly against the 11,000 for the matching fixture earlier in the season.

"Imagination allows us to escape the predictable. It enables us to reply to the common wisdom that we cannot soar by saying: 'Just watch'."

Bill Bradley, basketball player and US politician

Pearson was not only a hit on the football pitch in the north-east, he also dominated the golf scene in Aberdeen as he romped to victory in almost every local tournament on the calendar. His success on the greens included victory in the prestigious Links Championship, an event still going strong on the coastal course just a stone's throw from Pittodrie Stadium. Pearson's crowd-pulling was not restricted to his football performances. When he defeated legendary north-east golfer Jack Booth in the golf final in 1949, a gallery of 6,000 flocked to the Kings Links to watch the tie. For the record, Pearson won 4 and 3.

Former *Press and Journal* sports editor Colin Farquharson is a man renowned in Scottish golf writing and he remembers Pearson at his peak on the fairways. He also replays in glorious technicolour clips from his memory bank of Pearson the footballer in full attack mode, having first watched the Dons as a schoolboy in the 1940s and been a sports writer in the city since the 1950s.

Farquharson told me: "Pearson came to Aberdeen in his twilight years as a footballer. He was 34 and he arrived in 1948, which was the year after they won the Scottish Cup and five years before they won the League championship. So he came in an in-between period. Although it was a barren period for the team, he was a class act. He was an outside-left in the days when left-wingers stayed on the left wing. There was nothing like his double-shuffle on the run. It is not easy to do and took him some time to perfect – but when he hit Scottish football for the first time, he bemused a lot of defenders with it. The last time I saw him before he died, he showed me the basics across the carpet in his lounge in slow motion. It was fascinating stuff.

"He scored one of the best goals I ever saw at Pittodrie. *The Weekly Journal*, a sister paper of the *Evening Express* and the *P & J*, thought so, too. They devoted a whole front page to it. It was a terrific angular shot, from the left wing of course, about 30 yards out playing towards the Beach End. Pearson did not score many goals and when he did it was almost always from the penalty spot. He introduced a bit of skill to penalty-taking in the Scottish League. Not for him the net-bursting shots. Instead he casually pushed the penalty kick with the side of his foot just inside one of the posts. It was so precise that the ball almost, but never did, hit the post as it went over the line. It sounds simple and you would have thought that goalkeepers would eventually have worked out how to save it, because the ball went past them at no great speed, but agonisingly out of their reach.

"He went into journalism with the *Scottish Daily Mail*, still living at Cranford Road near the Mannofield cricket ground in Aberdeen, and wrote a book or two. A couple of his short stories, about football naturally enough, were published in the *P & J*. He often said that the biggest mistake he ever made was to come back into football as manager of Aberdeen FC. It was a low point in the Dons' fortunes, but he always claimed he had given the club a weekly sweepstake that continued to bring in money, long after his services were dispensed with.

"Pearson was also a very good golfer. It was an era when a lot of good footballers were also good golfers, presumably because they had a lot of time to devote to the game. At the time Jack Booth, who played out of Murcar and Royal Aberdeen, was the number-one but Pearson gave him a run for his money in the Aberdeen Links championship finals in the pre-television entertainment days when these finals drew literally thousands to the course."

Nowadays the same golf tournament attracts a devoted yet shrunken following, usually numbering up to 300. It is a reflection on the way society has changed and the competition in the entertainment sector has intensified with the boom in broadcasting and internet interest in every sporting sphere. Pearson's generation led a far more sheltered existence than their Aberdeen successors. Even as the game moved into the 1950s, the stars of the round-ball game were not set apart from the man in the street until Saturday came.

Farquharson, who began working as a copy boy with the *Evening Express* in 1953, recalls: "In those days, the Aberdeen footballers – Paddy Buckley, Harry Yorston, Bobby Wishart and company – used to take the corporation bus down to Pittodrie for training sessions in the morning. I was on the same Broomhill bus, although I would get off at Broad Street. In 1955 I was promoted to junior reporter in the sports department. In those days the sports staff served both the *Evening Express* and *P & J*."

Farquharson would continue to climb the ladder, eventually becoming the sports editor of the *Press and Journal*, but his earliest memories of the Dons and the characters who served the club will never leave him. He said: "I had been a boy on the terraces at Pittodrie from about the age of 10 or 11, starting to attend in around 1947. I used to go to the reserve matches on the other Saturdays. The world was a safer place then and my parents obviously thought nothing about one of their sons, in short trousers, getting on the bus and going over to the other side of the city to the football.

"I remember seeing players like goalkeeper George Johnstone, whose trick was to come out to a high ball and catch it with his hands raised above the level of his head, instead of clutching it to his body in what was the conventional way. He would have looked a fool if the ball had gone through his hands, but it never did. Frank Dunlop was centre-half, Pat McKenna at full-back, Stan Williams centre-forward and Archie Baird inside-left to Tommy Pearson. I can still picture Pearson's double-shuffle as if it was yesterday."

Farquharson had the pleasure of watching Pearson perform in all his glory. He also gained a great insight into the man behind the magic in 1986 when he travelled to Pearson's Edinburgh home to speak to him at length about his experiences in life and the game for a series of articles which ran in the *Press and Journal*.

Pearson was an intricate character, renowned throughout his playing days and his one dalliance with management as a forward thinker. That coaching spell came with Aberdeen. He was appointed to the top job in 1959 in succession to Dave Shaw and lasted five years in the hot seat before being replaced by the more hard-nosed Eddie Turnbull. The record books mark the wing king's tenure as manager as a failure, but for those who lived through it there is a great debate about whether he was ahead of his time. His approach to playing was at times radical and some of his ideas for the team when he took charge of it were of a similar ilk.

His background had much to do with his approach to the game. Just as he was an unpredictable entity on the pitch, Pearson was far from the archetypal footballer away from it. He attended a rugby-playing school in his native Edinburgh and in addition to the oval-ball game he also excelled at cricket as a schoolboy, as well as becoming a tennis champion. The studious Pearson, who worked in the bacteriology department of the public health department before turning to full-time football, was also a talented and keen writer and he fell back on those skills when he became a journalist after his retirement from the game.

Although he was starved of football as a schoolboy, there was no way Pearson's natural ability was ever going to be suppressed and as a 16-year-old playing for Murrayfield amateurs he was spotted by Hearts. His father, Tommy senior, had played for the Jambos at the turn of the century and the youngster was eager to be a chip off the old block. Two trials with the Gorgie side failed to provide him with a route into the senior game, but in 1933 a Newcastle scouting mission unearthed an Edinburgh gem and the young Scot was soon packing his bags to begin life on the St James' Park playing staff.

He was just 19 when he inked his Newcastle contract and inside a year had been eased into the first team, making his debut against Arsenal at Highbury. Pearson made the left-wing berth his own and was a star performer, twice invited for international trials with England. The proud Scot politely declined those approaches from the FA, pointing out his ineligibility to the blundering Wembley blazers, but even his sternest protests could not spare him the amazing honour of playing for both countries.

In 1939 he was in the stand in Newcastle to watch Scotland tackle England when it was discovered the host country's left-winger was not fit to play and that no deputy was available – so Pearson was press-ganged into slotting in, donning the three lions against his better judgement. It was not a permanent defection and Pearson went on to win the two coveted Scotland caps he craved during the war years, becoming the only player ever to represent both nations.

Between his 15 years with Newcastle, in which he played 212 League games and scored 46 goals, and his time with Aberdeen, he enjoyed a top-level career spanning an incredible 20 years. Amazingly for a player with such talent and longevity, Pearson won just a single medal in more than a quarter of a century playing the game. That came as a 16-year-old, when he helped Murrayfield to the Scottish Amateur Cup.

The lack of gold and silver for his troubles was not lost on the man himself. The winger, who died in 1999, once said: "If you don't believe that Tommy Pearson was born under an unlucky star in 1913, then let me tell you that Newcastle United were a flourishing First Division club until I signed for them from Murrayfield Amateurs in 1933. They were then relegated in my first season at St James' Park and remained a Second Division team throughout my years there. Immediately I left Newcastle for Aberdeen near the end of the 1947/48 season, United won so many matches that they snatched promotion to become a First

Division side again ... and of course, they went on to win the FA Cup three times in the early 1950s.

"At Pittodrie it was almost the Newcastle story all over again. The Dons had won the Scottish Cup in 1947 and then I arrived and that team never reached the heights again when I was a player. But I'd no sooner hung up my boots than the Dons won the League championship for the first time. And there's only one post-war period when Aberdeen Football Club did not win one trophy – the 1960s. Guess who was manager for half of that decade? Me, of course."

Pearson's self-deprecating humour masked the truth about the wonderful game of football. Success cannot be judged by rewards alone and that is what makes it so fascinating. If medals alone were the measure of a man, there would be no such thing as a cult hero. The sport has never had firm borders and there have always been characters such as Pearson to carefully tread the line of logic. Here was a man who played no part in triumph or glory with either of his two senior teams, yet he won the adulation of tens of thousands of supporters. Not because he won things nobody else had won, but because he could do things nobody else could do.

Author and journalist Jack Webster has spent a lifetime devotedly following the fortunes of his local team and meticulously charted the highs and lows of the first 100 years of the Dons in the official history of Aberdeen Football Club, released to coincide with the 2003 centenary celebrations. Webster wrote: "Pittodrie was gathering up some remarkable personalities, some of whom would last through memorable times in the mid-1950s. Others would be best remembered by those who like to absorb the essence of a distinctive player and store it in the crevices of the mind for future bouts of nostalgia. Two names spring readily to mind because they stirred public imagination in totally different ways: Tommy Pearson and Don Emery.

"If I were asked to nominate the players who had brought me the greatest amount of pleasure during 60 years of watching the Dons, I would turn to Johnny Pattillo, Ernie Waldron, Archie Baird, George

Hamilton, then come through the century to classical ball players such as Charlie Cooke, Jimmy Smith, Zoltan Varga and Gordon Strachan. But if I were to name one player who satisfied the highest aspirations of football grace, intelligence and excitement, that man would have to be Tommy Pearson. An Edinburgh man, he had been with Newcastle before and after the war but we caught the tail-end of his genius at Pittodrie and were grateful for the privilege.

"Pearson was one of the supreme artists of this maddening game, a barrel-chested dream of a player with the balance of perfection in his body and the sheer power of poetry in his movement. With the deftness of a conjurer, he practised a kind of sleight of foot that produced his famous double-shuffle. Others have tried it but never matched him. Knowing it would happen half-a-dozen times in a game, some of us would set out to observe precisely what happened. We kept our eyes riveted, waiting for the moment, but when it arrived and he weaved his magical deception, we were left none the wiser. Then, like a conjurer who assures his audience that the trick is really quite simple and that he will let them into the secret, he was capable of taking on the same man again – or any other who cared to be demoralised – and beating him in precisely the same manner. Oh for the benefit of an action replay!

"Some say Tommy Pearson would not be allowed to play like that today but great ball artists have always prospered in their respective generations, whether it was Bobby Walker, Stanley Matthews, Jimmy Johnstone, George Best or Ryan Giggs. It is worth remembering that Pittodrie could draw crowds of 8,000 for a reserve game in the early 1950s, most of them there to savour the magic of Tommy Pearson and his protégé Hughie Hay. That kind of genius comes rarely in a lifetime and lingers like a perfume when so much else that seemed important is forgotten."

Being mentioned in the same breath as Walker, Matthews, Johnstone, Best and Giggs would undoubtedly have caused the modest Pearson to blush had he been around to join the centenary celebrations.

Yet such comparisons were nothing new, with some going a step further. Sir George Graham, the all-powerful secretary of the Scottish Football Association during Pearson's playing days, once declared that Thomas Usher Pearson was even better than the world famous Matthews. It would be hard to find a Dons fan in the same period who disagreed with that sentiment.

The mesmerising double-shuffle played a part in helping to establish that reputation. The move was honed during the war years, when Pearson guested for Blackburn Rovers and Blackpool while serving as a physical training instructor with the RAF in Lancashire. Reflecting on the years of conflict, Pearson once admitted: "To be honest, it was a lovely war for me, purely in terms of the football skill I gained from it. In fact, I learned an awful lot about football during that period and I would say that I did not hit my peak until much later because of that. The funny thing about football during the war was that professional players' contracts were scrapped immediately war was declared. Yet football, instead of fading into the background as expected, came very much to the forefront because what was more useful than football to take the public's mind off the war?

"I got on great with Blackburn and the crowd fairly got behind me there. In fact, when I left the Rovers the fans were talking about starting a public fund to buy my transfer from Newcastle United at the end of the war! I was developing into a different type of player. I had always been a dribbler with a lot of tricks and I could cross the ball accurately. But now I began to develop my secret weapon – although it didn't stay very secret for long. It was to be tagged by somebody as the double-shuffle. If there was an asset I had it was football imagination and in my opinion that's what makes the difference between the great player and the good player who's quite competent but just hasn't got that vision.

"Bert Johnston of Charlton was the player I learned the so-called double-shuffle from. In fact, he didn't know how to do it properly – he was doing it only in miniature, with just one foot over the ball and then taking it forward with the other. I began to think about it and I worked on developing it. Other players perhaps did the double-shuffle one way or another, but I was the only one who injected a jump into the middle of the move. I used to jump in the air and when I dropped down I was off and running. The wartime crowds used to roar when I did it, as though I had scored a goal or something spectacular. It not only used to help me beat the full-backs – it used to infuriate them as well. They thought – and they were right – I was making a fool of them."

Now we understand the crux of just why Pearson was a favourite with the Dons fans. Not only did he excite them, entertain them and bring gasps from the terraces – he also excelled in humiliating the opposition, and there is no greater thrill for a group of supporters than seeing their man wipe the floor with the rivals.

Whatever the club and wherever on the planet they have played, wingers have always shared a bond with the supporters who twist and turn with every glorious fade and shimmy. The fact that the touchline beat they patrol is just yards from the perimeter wall and within earshot of the terraces and stands plays a part, but more than anything it is about giving the customer what they want: action.

Pearson did not disappoint, just as the fine list of flying Dons wingers had captivated generations. From Jackie Hather in the 1950s to Arthur Graham in the '70s, from Peter Weir in the '80s to Paul Mason in the '90s, every decade has brought its own set of wide-men to keep the punters coming back for more. Styles have differed, from the all-out pace of Hather to the trickery of Weir, but the end result has always been the same as the chief providers set about laying the groundwork for striker after striker.

Mind you, Pearson did not just play provider and toy with the opposition. He had the ability to hurt them, too, with his deadly accurate shooting, an asset which made him front-page news. The 1950 *Weekly Journal* front page, containing two photographs of the Pearson wonder-strike which was the second goal for Aberdeen in what turned into a 3-1 victory against Hearts in the second-round of the Scottish Cup, was the most notable indication of Pearson's fame and the growing public thirst for football and its stars.

Pre-war the chances of a sportsman making the front page of any newspaper were limited, save for some heinous and unspeakable crime committed. Moving into the 1950s the cult of celebrity was being spawned and the players of the era were finding themselves shifted from the back to the front by newspapers up and down the land.

Pearson's goal was worthy of the exposure it gained. An all-ticket crowd of 42,000 was squeezed into Pittodrie for the match and the old stands creaked and groaned as the gaze of the Dons faithful switched from end to end following a pulsating tie. It was 1-1 when Don Emery rolled a free-kick into the path of Pearson 25 yards from goal and he produced what has been described by those who witnessed it as the perfect strike. It was goal-scoring utopia.

Pearson recalled the effort with pride, claiming: "The ball took off like a missile and went raging into the top right-hand corner of the Hearts net. Jimmy Brown, their goalkeeper, used to say that he got a hand to it, but he was blethering. From the moment the ball left my foot it was bound for the corner of the net. Brown never got near it. It was one of those shots you hit and hope for the best. If it goes in you're a hero – if it goes miles off the target, you're a pudden. It had to be one of the best, if not the best, of my career."

In all there were 16 goals for Aberdeen, but many more happy memories for the supporters who watched the winger rip opposition defences to shreds and willed him to turn back and do it again. Pearson died in 1999, just six days before his 85th birthday. Four decades earlier he had given up a salary of £1,500 from the *Daily Mail* to test himself at the coal face as Dons manager, a position which carried the same renumeration.

When he left Pittodrie in 1965 he had no job in journalism to fall back on and instead opted to enrol on a course in geology before establishing a gems and rare stones business in Edinburgh, which he ran for almost two decades. His later reflection that he was perhaps ill-advised to give up the security of journalism to try his hand at management was understandable, but as a football man the temptation got the better of him.

He had first got involved in coaching by working with Aberdeen's aspiring youngsters but by 1959 he had been invited by the board of directors to take full control of playing matters. In 1960/61, his first full season in charge, Aberdeen finished sixth in the League. It marked an improvement of nine places from the previous term. The following three years produced indifferent form and League finishes of twelfth, sixth and ninth before, early in 1965, Eddie Turnbull assumed control.

The question of Pearson's merit as a manager ran and ran. In the 1980s, *Press and Journal* reporter Jim Dolan reflected: "Tommy Pearson was full of ideas from the start, involving a scheme to attract the cream of the youth in the area and to establish a long-term policy that would establish the Dons at the top in years to come. He talked very convincingly about the game and had great ideas – possibly well ahead of his time – and soon had established regular training for young players at Pittodrie as he attempted to bring back the glory days. But the club was still bedevilled by old habits in preparation and training, and the ball was still a rarity at much of the training. At the time, everything was done by the clock, with morning training starting around 10am and ending at 11.40am. Sometimes the manager was caught up in discussions on his theories during training and the time seemed to pass so quickly it was time to stop training – and talking – before anyone realised it."

In October 1963 the knives were beginning to be sharpened. The man who was once the darling of Pittodrie was in danger of becoming *persona non grata*, although it was not surprisingly the media rather than the fans who were hacking at Pearson.

Aberdeen sports writer Norman MacDonald wrote: "If the Dons are to survive as a top-class club the time has arrived when manager Pearson must come forward with a more constructive policy. He can no longer defend the present system of weekly team changes. It has produced only four League points from eight matches. Every soccer club manager is a sitting duck for criticism if his team is having a bad time. If he fails to make team changes he is liable to be shot at and if he sticks to the same players he is equally liable to come under fire. Nobody could accuse manager Pearson of adopting a passive attitude; the reverse is the case. His forward permutations have been as frequent as they have been unsuccessful."

The main criticism was of Pearson's penchant for squad rotation. Ahead of his time, indeed, by around 40 years. Scottish Cup defeat against Second Division side East Fife was the straw which broke the camel's back in 1965. Pearson was not dismissed, maintaining the club's record of never sacking a manager up to that point, but there is no question that he was advised his resignation would be the best for all concerned.

It is as a former Dons manager with which the Pearson name strikes the loudest chord for many, yet it was as a player that he was a virtuoso performer. Even into his retirement, Pearson's mind was going 19 to the dozen as he sought to perfect the art of wing wizardry.

In the interview conducted with Colin Farquharson at the ripe old age of 72, Pearson leapt from his seat mid-sentence to demonstrate the move he was working on at the time he opted to retire from the game. He explained: "I played senior football until I was 41, but believe it or not I was still developing my repertoire. As a matter of fact, when I retired at 41, cut my throat and swear to die, I was still developing a brand new trick – and it would have been a smasher! It was something I had never done before, anywhere. It was to use my right foot and it involved dragging the ball past the full-back on the touchline."

It was at that point in the conversation that Pearson sprang into action, wowing Farquharson with "a demonstration of Fred Astaire-type footwork". Pearson continued: "Most players will just meet the ball and run to the side to try to evade the full-back. Well, I used to spend a lot of time on my own, trying to think up ideas for situations on the field of play. I would put myself in the full-back's position and try to anticipate what he would or would not do. There are fewer wingers in the game these days but I don't think players in general show that kind of imagination to work at their game on their own to develop an individualistic style which is not in the text books – or was not in my day."

And there you have it, the text-book attitude of a true cult hero, the maverick winger with his own brand of flicks, tricks and body-swerves which were steeped in ingenuity and sprouted from the seeds sown by one of football's great innovators. Football's original king of imagination.

'THE WING WIZARD' 1953–1958

GRAHAM LEGGAT

Magic Moment: St Mirren goalkeeper Jim Lornie was left with egg on his face in 1956 as a cheeky chip from little Leggat drifted into the net in a typically audacious piece of play from the local loon in front of his Pittodrie fan club.

Dons Career: Games 151. Goals 92. Caps 18.

FRED MARTIN, Jimmy Mitchell, Dave Caldwell, Jack Allister, Alec Young and Archie Glen. Graham Leggat, Harry Yorston, Paddy Buckley, Bob Wishart and Jackie Hather. With the staccato rhythm of a concert pianist those names trip off the tongues for Aberdonians who grew up in and around the 1950s. Legends one and all, the men who brought the first-ever League title to Pittodrie in 1955.

They were lauded in their day, afforded status befitting a group who had finally levered Glasgow hands from Scotland's most cherished football prize and eased the stifling Old Firm dominance from the national game. For the tens of thousands who watched the northern lights illuminate the old Division A that year, there was at last an opportunity to say without reservation that their men were *the* men.

Asking Aberdeen supporters to choose between the members of the 1955 team would be like telling the proud parents of twins to pick their favourite. The collective spirit fostered by victorious manager David Halliday extended beyond the confines of the pitch and spilled over the wall on to the terraces.

There was the colourful character Fred Martin, a forward-turned-goalkeeper who recovered from the ignominy of shipping seven goals against the talented Uruguayans at the 1954 World Cup finals in Switzerland to help the Dons to title success with an impressive 11 shut-outs from 28 appearances. It was a year of highs and lows for the popular Aberdeen shot-stopper, who was in the national team which lost 7-2 at Wembley against England the week before the Dons wrapped up the title. He didn't play for Scotland again after that 'Auld Enemy' embarrassment.

Then there was the powerful Jimmy Mitchell, who reverted to his schoolboy pursuit of rugby with some aplomb after leaving the Dons, and the ultra reliable Dave Caldwell.

The famed half-back line of Allister, Young and Glen had character, too. From the heart-on-sleeve style of Jack Allister, with his fierce tackling and notorious will to win, to the cool and rock-steady skipper Archie Glen, who went on to score the League-winning goal on 9 April 1955 before graduating in pure science upon his retirement from the game. Alec Young offered the classic tale of triumph over adversity, overcoming a hat-trick of injuries which left his career hanging in the balance to etch his name into Pittodrie folklore.

> "You may have the greatest bunch of individual stars in the world, but if they don't play together, the club won't be worth a dime."
>
> **Babe Ruth, baseball star**

Even the back-up players had cult credentials, not least Joe O'Neill. It was O'Neill, who played 12 times on the road to the title, who had fired himself into the stratosphere of Aberdeen's shining stars when he played a major part in the 6-0 Scottish Cup demolition of Rangers the previous season – despite playing with a fractured skull. He had suffered the injury three weeks earlier and played with a protective cap, having been more than a little economical with the truth when he told manager David Halliday that doctors had given him the all-clear to play in the Scottish Cup semi-final against the Light Blues. O'Neill, who had been rejected by the Gers due to his Catholic faith as a boy, banged home a hat-trick in the record-busting 6-0 win to confound the medics who had not surprisingly attempted to veto his attempts to play in the tie. You have to wonder what O'Neill and others of his ilk would have made of the modern scourge of football, the broken metatarsal. They would have played on, of course. It is, after all, a man's game.

O'Neill had a foot in both camps, having filled in for forward Bob Wishart in the 1955 campaign and Allister at the back. While the defence was packed with character it was not surprisingly the dashing forward line which had the potential to dominate the headlines of the day and stake a decent claim for the affections of the giddy Dandies who were on a title high.

Paddy Buckley was the joker in the pack, dubbed the "Laughing Cavalier", but there was nothing funny about his goal-scoring prowess. With 92 career goals in 152 appearances and 17 in the 1955 League procession alone, to finish leading scorer, he was the most potent of attacking weapons.

The affable Bob Wishart was another vital cog, popular on the terraces and in the boardroom thanks to his easy-going manner, while on the left wing was the sprint king Jackie Hather, christened the "Flying Englishman" by the Dons faithful as he tore up and down the flank, demonstrating his sweet left peg and chipping in with a barrel-load of goals for good measure.

With Harry Yorston, the goal machine, through the middle it was a formidable group which was rounded off in considerable style by right-winger Graham Leggat – Pittodrie's very own blue-eyed boy. The baby-faced local lad was just a slip of a kid at 19 when he made his first appearance for the club in 1953, but he was a character the supporters in his home town would see far more of in the years ahead.

Leggat cut a distinctive figure, with his film-star looks and enticing personality. In fact, as his playing career continued in England in the 1960s, he even hit upon a profitable sideline as a very much in-demand male model. More than a decade earlier he had become more of an unwilling photographic subject as he swiftly became the Pittodrie pin-up, his every move tracked by adoring fans and by the press pack swept along in the furore surrounding the precocious new talent.

Leggat's mother even used to invite waiting photographers into the family's home in Aberdeen to shelter them from the elements. The paparazzi hadn't been invented in the 1950s but Leggat had an early experience of what future stars of the round-ball game would experience when the media interest reached fever pitch post-millennium.

The forward, a product of the Banks o' Dee conveyor belt of talent, was a natural player, but many observers predicted a short career for the up-and-coming star of the north-east. Too frail, they said, too slight. But they were wrong. Leggat went on to play at the top level for more than 15 years and even well into his forties he was turning out for veterans' teams, still displaying the silky skills which earned him fame in the first place and revealing the same versatility which saw him operate in all five attacking positions during his career.

Hugh McIlvanney, writing in *The Observer* at the time of Leggat's move to Birmingham in 1967, noted: "Leggat is an intelligent, touchy Scot, who had a great deal to say for himself long before it was fashionable for professional footballers to be articulate. He does not look his age. There is a physical neatness about him that makes most men feel flabby and shabby in his presence. The hair is cut close to the small, well-shaped head, and his features have a symmetry wholesome enough to win him a scholarship to an American university or a contract on Madison Avenue."

McIlvanney watched him blossom and made note of his exemplary goal-scoring record, pointing out: "This record is due mainly to his highly developed sense of positioning, the natural economy of his game, and his ability to kick the ball rather well, a talent which is not too common even among top-class professionals. At his best he materialises in destructive positions with a suddenness that makes one suspect a trap door, and he strikes the ball with the same crisp authority that keeps his golf handicap within reach of scratch."

James Forbes, the *Evening Express* sports journalist who covered the Leggat era, described the flanker as "one of the most exciting players ever to wear Aberdeen's colours". Forbes, at the time of Leggat's emigration, said: "When with Fulham he had a special clause inserted in his contract whereby he got an extra fiver in his pay packet if chosen to play anywhere except outside-right. That was typical Leggat. He had a mind of his own, and although he and I didn't always see eye to eye there has never been any doubt in my mind that he was a natural. I'll never forget the day at Pittodrie Stadium when he bent down as if to place the ball for a free-kick and calmly lobbed it over the defensive wall and into the net. A winger with a flair for scoring goals, Leggat generally reacted to the big occasion."

The Aberdonian's journey to those big occasions had begun in less auspicious surroundings. Born in the city in 1934, he turned out for Woodside Primary School and Central Secondary School. It was during his academy days that he first savoured success, collecting the Aberdeen Secondary Schools' Shield. Leggat went on to hone his skills with Torry FPs in the juvenile game before progressing to Banks o' Dee and, soon after, signing schoolboy forms with the Dons. Within two years he had been promoted to the Aberdeen first team, making his first appearance in a 1-0 defeat at Stirling Albion in September 1953. He had won a Scotland youth cap while on Torry's books and went on to add an under-23 appearance during his Aberdeen days, en-route to the full international side.

Leggat became a club regular immediately after his introduction to the team as a 19-year-old, confirming his star status with 19 goals in the 1953/54 season from just 31 appearances in the League and Scottish Cup. The teenager bagged his first hat-trick in a 5-3 win against Clyde that term and another four trebles and a clinical five-goal barrage in a 6-2 League win at Airdrie in 1957 followed before his departure five years later. Leggat's record of 92 goals in 151 appearances was all the more remarkable since the bulk of those games were played on the wing and far from the traditional line of fire through the middle of the park.

The League success in 1955 was clearly the crowning glory for the fast maturing player in his days as a Red, but the 1955/56 League Cup win was also something of a personal triumph for the irrepressible young winger with the lethal shooting boots. In the group stages of the competition he scored against Dunfermline and claimed a match-winning double against Clyde, but those contributions were just a warm-up for the role he played in the knock-out phase.

The Dons faced Hearts in the quarter-final and the Jambos had no answer to the pace, power and technical ability of the Pittodrie forward line in the first leg in the north-east. Leggat scored three and Paddy Buckley helped himself to two as a 5-2 cushion was created. Leggat scored again in the second leg, which Aberdeen won 4-2, and the scene was set for a Hampden semi-final against Rangers. The spirited number-seven exited the stage early, hospitalised with a shoulder injury, but not before his fourth-minute goal had given the Dons the edge in a game they went on to win 2-1. The injury problems were behind him by the time he took his usual place in the Dons side for the final, where St Mirren stood between the club and another trophy. The game was poised delicately at 1-1 going into the final ten minutes, at which point Leggat took command, clipping home the winner to complete the mission for the team and leaving his record in the competition standing at nine goals in ten games that season.

Despite the immense contribution to the League and League Cup victories within months of each other in 1955, either side of the summer break, there was a baffling wait for Leggat's first cap. It eventually came in 1956 when he made a scoring debut in a 1-1 draw against England at Hampden. It was the first of 18 caps and eight goals during service which included the 1958 World Cup finals in Sweden. Leggat played against Paraguay and Yugoslavia in the tournament as his education continued.

The overseas experiences with Scotland proved limited though, with the Aberdonian one of a number of players who found themselves in the wilderness after apparently irking Scotland selectors by choosing to pursue their club career outwith their home country. Following his 1958 move to Fulham, Leggat continued his impressive scoring form but found himself banished from the Scotland team after making what proved to be his final Dark Blue appearance in the summer of 1960, when the team drew 3-3 with Hungary.

Leggat had dropped his transfer bombshell in April 1958, when he demanded a move. The star man was bristling with media criticism of his unrest, fearing he was being painted as the villain as he sought to better himself. He had received a £750 benefit payment from the Dons, a common gesture at that time to reward long service. It was his on the back of five years with the club but was a drop in the ocean compared to the potential to earn elsewhere. On top of that he was growing increasingly uncomfortable with the interest, both from the public and press, in his day-to-day life and was determined to escape the Aberdeen goldfish bowl.

Explaining his decision to seek a new pool to swim in, he said: "I want to stress that my request for a transfer has nothing whatsoever to do with the team, or our position in the League, or our recent form. In fact, had it not been for the spirit of the team, my request would have gone in long before this. To be quite frank, I have not been happy at Pittodrie for the last two seasons and I feel that I cannot do justice to the side or our supporters in this frame of mind."

Luton Town were the first to close in, succeeding with a £15,000 bid but failing to persuade the talented young wide-man that his future lay in industrial Bedfordshire. Leggat turned down the Hatters and his patience paid off when Fulham entered the bidding. The Second Division side were willing to top Luton's offer by £1,000 and proved more adept at the personal negotiations, luring the man with the model looks to London's fashionable West End on the cusp of the swinging '60s. In Aberdeen he had been a big fish in a small bowl. He had the talent, he had the looks and he had the driven personality, but he felt confined in the city which set him on the road to stardom. By escaping to the bright lights he caught his second wind and embarked on another fascinating period in his life, with the big city presenting a whole new ocean to explore.

He was an instant hit at Craven Cottage, scoring in each of his first six matches to make the fee look like the insult it was. Aberdeen's board has rarely been short-changed, but when they allowed their prize asset to leave for less than £20,000 it represented a wonderful piece of business by the purchasing club. With Leggat in tow, the London side stormed back into the top flight and he was either winner or runner-up in the club's golden-boot award for six of the seven seasons he spent with the Cottagers, scoring 134 times in 277 appearances. Just months prior to his switch to England he had recovered from a broken leg, but worse was to follow with Fulham. A year after joining he suffered an horrendous injury during a summer tour of Italy, coming close to losing a leg as a result. Once again, he came back to confound those who felt he would never play again.

Back at home, filling the slot vacated by the wiry winger proved to be a tall order for a succession of men who tried and failed to make the right-wing berth their own in the decade which followed his departure. Dick Ewan had a go, as did George Mulhall, Billy Little, Graham McInnes, Jim Cooper, Jim McCall, Hugh Baird and Billy McKenzie. There were chances at number-seven for Ken Brownlee, Bobby Cummings, Des Herron and even the veritable left-winger Jack Hather. Charlie Cooke provided a solution when he could be spared from the more central positions, while Jimmy Robertson, Doug Fraser, Willie Callaghan, Jim Hosie, Willie Allan, Bobby Hume and Ian Lister were all tried on the troublesome beat as well as Don Kerrigan, Doug Coutts, Tommy Morrison, Ernie Winchester, Jimmy Wilson, George Scott, Jimmy Noble and Pat Wilson before the emergence of Jimmy Smith in the late 1960s.

Reading that list of pretenders to Leggat's throne is enough to make you breathless, but it demonstrates the value he would have provided had he stayed for the long haul.

When he became available early in 1966, as his Fulham career drew to a close, the Chinese whispers about an imminent Pittodrie return began to whistle through the city, but manager Eddie Turnbull dismissed the idea out of hand. The hopes of the Dons faithful, briefly and tantalisingly raised by the most faint hope of a reunion with their long-lost son, were brought crashing back to earth.

By that stage he was 32 and had dropped back down to the English Second Division, with his international days behind him, to join Birmingham City. Yet Leggat was adamant that the Midlands side were getting him at his peak, reasoning: "I'm sure I'm a far better player than I was when I was young. What did I have then? I wasn't very special when it came to taking somebody on and I wasn't all that fast. But I've picked up a great deal in the past few years. I've never been a great player but I think I'm a good player." That modesty belied the confidence which will be familiar to any of the Dons fans who saw him burst on to the scene.

His Birmingham career never really took off, not helped by a back injury which eventually led to a free transfer to Rotherham under Tommy Docherty in 1968. He teamed up with the Doc again at Aston Villa the following year, in a coaching rather than a playing capacity, before breaking from the game and embarking on life as a salesman with Rank Xerox.

The call from football, however, proved too strong. Leggat, who was inducted to Canada's Soccer Hall of Fame in 2001, left Britain behind in 1971 when he was appointed player-coach of the newly formed North American Soccer League side Toronto Metros. By the following year he had been dismissed, but Canadian life had bitten the exiled Scottish family and he accepted a public-relations role with a brewery. He combined that with a burgeoning broadcasting career, which included covering the Olympics and football World Cup for CBC, although later returned to direct involvement as general manager of the Edmonton Drillers in the NASL.

The true calling was television, though, and in the late 1980s Leggat embarked on what became a long and distinguished period as a presenter with the Sports Network. The new vocation made Graham Leggat a household name all over again, this time on a different continent.

After Leggat had spent near enough half a century in the game in one capacity or another, man and boy, the layman might expect retirement to be a welcome relief. It might be time to let the current batch get on with the business in hand and pave the way for some quiet reflection on a lifetime's service. Yet Leggat does not entirely see it that way, with his craving for the game not diluted by his long service and geography not tempering the enjoyment he gets from a sport which remains a minority affair in his adopted homeland.

Of course, he will never be removed from the game completely, intrinsically linked to football both at home and abroad through his playing and broadcasting achievements. But the departure from frontline duty eight years ago is still taking a bit of getting used to for the energetic 74-year-old, who gives the impression he could yet skip back behind the microphone without a second's hesitation as he still talks about the game with the type of vigour which led him into a highly successful television career in the first place.

Leggat told me: "I retired after Euro 2000 and have not really enjoyed being out of football for the first time since 1951. On the other hand I still get to watch plenty of action without having to worry about passing opinion or analysing it."

Being off the screen also shields Leggat from the familiar Scottish rivalries which followed him all the way to North America following his emigration. He grew used to being bombarded by calls and letters from followers of either Celtic or Rangers, depending on which club he was perceived to be biased against on any given week during his assessment of the Scottish scene. On the other side of the world there was no escape from his Scottish roots, even if he had wanted one.

He was never embraced by the Scottish selectors, or the Tartan Army, in the way he was by the Aberdeen supporters. His cap haul was meagre when compared to his talent. While he has always retained an interest in events back home, there was never any pining for a return to the Granite City he left behind in 1958 and even fleeting visits have been sporadic. He said: "I never gave returning to Scotland a thought. I would like to have returned home more often but never found the time to get round to it. My family is settled in Canada and we enjoy it here."

Had Leggat remained in Aberdeen he could have dined out on his part in the 1955 title triumph for the rest of his days, particularly in the glowing aftermath of that most momentous of periods. Indeed, he and Denis Law were the only two footballers inducted in the city of Aberdeen's Sporting Hall of Fame when 21 stars from all walks of life took their places following its creation in 2007.

For the Aberdonian, who grew up learning the game on the city's muddy playing fields, the League success which made him a household name remains a source of immense pride half a century on. A man who has since made his living from analysing the game is shrewd enough to realise that time does not stand still and that the more recent and more concerted triumphs of the 1980s have since eclipsed his own generation's achievements, but being the first Dons side to land the previously elusive League crown is something that will never be taken away from that esteemed pool of players.

He said: "It had to be the most significant event in Aberdeen Football Club's history up to that point. Events since then have perhaps taken over, but we were very proud to have played a part in the club's first League success. We regarded the championship as the prize we needed to win to put Aberdeen on the map."

In its first 50 years of existence Aberdeen Football Club was led by only three managers. It is hard to imagine that type of continuity ever returning, when three managers in 50 months is now a more realistic tally. Jimmy Philip and Pat Travers were the first to take the helm, moulding a club which was taken to the next level by Dave Halliday. He was appointed to the top job when Travers left to take charge of Clyde late in 1937 and became the first manager to win a trophy with the club. Halliday performed major surgery to turn nearly-men into winners and made a series of shrewd signings as well as introducing young players such as Leggat into the fray.

He had already won the Southern League Cup and Scottish Cup before the championship was delivered to a grateful Dons board. Halliday's squad heralded him as a motivator supreme with the ability to get his team selections spot on. The results backed up their faith in the boss. Observers at the time also made note of his ability to spot potential in a player and his knack of man-management.

Leggat agrees and believes Halliday's team was unique, claiming: "There were several factors that were important in the League title success. Firstly there was the spirit – it was a team without egos to spoil the camaraderie. Secondly we had an excellent manager in Dave Halliday and finally we had the pace of Paddy Buckley and Jack Hather, the best half-back line the club has ever seen, the giant hands of Fred Martin in goal ... every player had a part to play and played it well."

By the time Leggat left in 1958 the manager had long since departed for Leicester, the team he joined on the back of the Division A triumph. Many of the title-winning players had also either retired or moved on, with the one constant during the winger's time with his home-town club coming in the shape of the supporters. While other local products had suffered rocky times in front of the demanding Dons fans, Leggat's memories are all positive. He said: "I always found the supporters most generous towards me and very protective, so for my part the relationship with the fans was excellent."

With his goals, attacking flourishes and medal wins, that special bond was assured. Oceans may separate Leggat from his home town but he will never be truly removed from its football story, thanks to the legacy he and his champion colleagues left behind.

'THE BONNIE PRINCE' 1960–1964

CHARLIE COOKE

Magic Moment: Champions-elect Rangers were routed 6-1 at Pittodrie in spring 1961 and the young man named Cooke capped the day with the sixth goal to announce his arrival on the big stage as provider, finisher and entertainer.

Dons Career: Games 165. Goals 32. Caps 16.

A PERSONALITY player and pin-up who was popular, with immaculate footwork, and brought welcome individuality to the game not to mention an array of defence-splitting passes and mazy runs. Not my words, but those of the many observers who were wowed by the baby-faced Charlie Cooke in the swinging '60s as he began an incredible journey in professional football which has taken him all the way from windswept Pittodrie to the balmy boomtown of Cincinnati.

Along the way millions have watched him play, seen him collect European honours and become an international performer. Yet it is the more modest number, the tens of thousands of Dons supporters tucked away in the north-east of his homeland, that struck one of the biggest chords with Cooke. And vice versa.

Players come and players go at Pittodrie. It has been a fact of life since Jimmy Philip named the first Aberdeen team in 1903 and the bleeding of talent has, if anything, intensified in the days since the Bosman ruling.

Most departures are met with staunch indifference from a level-headed group of supporters not prone to over-reacting. The most recent case in point is the loss in 2007 of Russell Anderson, a home-grown mainstay who had been carefully hand-reared and moulded to become an inspirational captain, leading the club through a dark tunnel and into the daylight beyond by taking his men back into Europe. Then he was gone, with no tears from the fans who had worshipped the sods of grass his studs had fallen on. They wished him well, promised to watch his progress from afar and then got on with life and looked for another player to pick up the baton.

"There is nothing to regret, either for those who go or for those who are left behind."

Eleanor Roosevelt, American First Lady

That, in more than 105 years of Dons history, has been the way of things at Pittodrie, except on the rare occasions when a departure hit an agonisingly raw nerve and sent a shockwave of pain arrowing through the very core of the club. In December 1964 there was one of those torturous moments. Charlie Cookie, the pin-up, was gone. The club were not happy, the manager was frustrated and the Red Army were despondent. Sometimes you just don't know what you've got until its gone – but in the case of Cooke the sense of loss was immediate. Supporters were given the freedom of the press to vent their fury and nobody was missed: from Cooke himself for failing to honour his contract, to the board for sanctioning the move and the manager for presiding over it. The more reasoned, who greeted his exit in the same composed manner that Anderson's would be met with more than 40 years later, wished him well in his new career with east-coast rivals Dundee.

To this day the reaction troubles Cooke. He can still vividly recall the sense of injustice he felt as he was pilloried for daring to move on, but equally he recalls the warmth of feeling subsequently afforded him by the Pittodrie supporters on later visits, as a Dundee player, to his first football home. In recent years the Fife-born legend went through the thought-provoking and soul-searching process of putting together his memoirs. The 2006 autobiography *The Bonnie Prince* was the result of months of meandering jaunts down memory lane, during which time Cooke looked up old friends and sought out former mentors to help jog his mind and take him back to a life so far removed from his current existence in the sunsoaked US state of Ohio. In fact, the nickname so affectionately bestowed on him at Pittodrie is the one he chose to adorn the cover of his book as its title.

He told me: "It was good to be able to really sum up my feelings about my time with Aberdeen through the book. In general I think it paints a pretty accurate picture of me, warts and all. There was certainly no attempt to paint any picture other than the truth. The early part of it was what I found most thought-provoking – the later years, particularly my career with Chelsea, had been played out far more in the public domain than the memories from further back. I feel strongly about my time with Aberdeen and the move to Dundee. In many ways those times, and how it turned out I went to Aberdeen rather than Rangers in the first place, are still the most interesting for me."

The early recollections which stirred Cooke into action include the bitter departure from Pittodrie and the joy of reconciliation with his adoring Aberdeen public. Cooke wrote: "I had no feelings of shame or guilt whatsoever. The Dons had signed me for nothing on provisional forms as a junior four years previously. They had got an excellent four years of service, 34 goals and bunches of free publicity at the under-23, Scottish League and full international levels while paying me as little as they could get away with, only increasing my wages when I pressed for it. Now they were cashing in. It was the biggest bonanza they'd ever had, on top of all the other windfalls they squirreled away over the last few seasons. I didn't feel I was cheating the board, the fans or the city one bit and wasn't about to apologise to anyone. In fact, after seeing the way it was all reported I felt just the opposite and even quite belligerent."

The media and my own newspaper in particular, the *Press and Journal,* left a lasting impression with Cooke on the back of the treatment he received. So, too, did chairman Charlie Forbes, with his statement that the board had a policy of considering offers for all dissatisfied players. Forbes went on to qualify that by pointing out that there would be no sense in retaining players who repeatedly asked to leave the club.

That infuriated Cooke, who said: "The remarks, quoted in various newspapers, incensed me, as the implication was that I had been some kind of regular visitor to Tommy Pearson's office, which was total tosh. I had visited once and made my feelings known to the manager up front and crystal clear, and that had been it. The week after I signed with Dundee, I was tempted to write a response to the Aberdeen *Press and Journal* in my own defence but, happily, thought better of it.

"Like all storms in teacups, it was soon forgotten, and I'm happy to say that every time I went back to Pittodrie with Dundee, the fans were great and treated me like they always did – like their Bonnie Prince. While it may have seemed that the four-and-a-half seasons I spent at Pittodrie ended on a low note, I felt quite the opposite about my whole time there. I had met and married my first wife, Edith, and it was a happy, busy football-playing time in the Granite City that I enjoyed a lot."

More than four deacdes have passed and the writers who lambasted Cooke at the time are long departed, but does he still hold the feeling of injustice or has the passage of time healed those particular wounds?

Cooke, comfortably ensconced in his American home, told me: "It's water under the bridge as far as I'm concerned; it all happened an awful long time ago. I appreciate newspapers and journalists have their jobs to do, but at the time, being only a youngster and with only my own opinions to trust, it was a difficult time. I had no real sounding boards and tended to keep my feelings and opinions to myself, so I have to say I was pissed about the way the *P & J* and others dealt with it. I had worked my backside off throughout my time at Aberdeen and given good service, but there did not seem to be a lot of sympathy about when I left. There was even a suggestion I should return the Player of the Year trophy I had just won – that capped it all for me. I've never been back to Pittodrie since leaving Britain but that's not because there are any sour grapes, just that I've never been back in that part of the country. I'd certainly like to take a dander down to the ground if I do land back in Aberdeen because I have some wonderful memories from that period in my life."

His post-Pittodrie career vindicated his decision to seek greener pastures. Even in his short time at the club, and he was still only 22 when he left for Dundee in the controversial £44,000 transfer, frustrations began to creep in. Aberdeen were proud that Cooke, who had rejected a late bid from Rangers to lure him to Ibrox as a 16-year-old and signed for the Dons from Renfrew juniors, was part of a team which had been almost free to assemble. It was a boast typical of a fiercely prudent administration who had actively encouraged manager Tommy Pearson to scour the junior ranks for fresh talent.

Financially the policy reaped rich rewards, with Cooke's sale bolstering the bank balance in 1964. The fee was a record between two Scottish clubs, eclipsing the £27,500 Rangers had paid for St Mirren forward George McLean, and an Aberdeen record, having shattered the £32,500 paid by Stoke for George Kinnell in 1963. Dundee funded the move with the proceeds of the £72,500 sale of Alan Gilzean to Spurs just weeks earlier as money began to flow around the Scottish game. The Dons were keen not to be left behind in the cash stakes and raised substantial revenue from their zero-cost team, selling Dave Smith, a product of local side Aberdeen Lads' Club, to Rangers for £50,000 less than two years later.

Good news for the directors, but that did not transfer to the fans or, indeed, the players who were part of the frugal regime. Cooke came into the side in 1960, just five years after the club's League championship success. Yet in the five seasons in which he played a part, the Dons peaked at sixth in the table, dropping as low as 12th during that period. It was the failure to challenge the Old Firm which was at the root of his unrest, having expected to be competing for trophies when he signed his first pro contract. Ultimately that ambition took him south of the border as the quest for silverware continued.

Upon leaving the Dons he spent just 16 months at Dens Park before 12 seasons over two spells with Chelsea, which proved to be the making of him. At Stamford Bridge he built on the type of bond he had first savoured at Pittodrie, with the extended timescale intensifying the strength of feeling between the Blues brigade and their 'Chelsea Cavalier', as the by-then moustachioed figure of Cooke became known.

Winning the European Cup Winners' Cup in 1971 with the London club was a career highlight, following the FA Cup final success against Leeds United in the previous season. At Chelsea he became a legend of the English game with a profile to match – but the Aberdeen fans who had watched the sprightly forward in his fledgling years did not need banner headlines or colour photographs to illustrate his talents. They had their own memories to cherish.

He signed along with Renfrew team-mate Jim Geddes in 1959 on provisional forms and was ushered from his Port Glasgow home into lodgings on Great Western Road the following year when he became a fully fledged professional with Aberdeen. By the start of the 1960/61 season Cooke had been promoted to the first team. The speed of his fast-tracking surprised even him, despite an underlying belief in his own ability and a determination to make his football dream become reality. In the blink of an eye, Cooke became hot property among suitors on both sides of the border as scouts were sent scurrying north to begin trailing the talented young Scotsman. For the fans on the terrace the allure was just as strong.

A 1962 programme pen picture of the fearless upstart from the west coast painted a glorious picture of his swift rise to prominence, stating: "A youngster who has made a big impact in a short time is the Dons' clever inside-forward Charlie Cooke. The former Renfrew junior won the enthusiasm of the crowd in a floodlight friendly against Luton Town. Since his competitive debut against Clyde reserves in April 1960, Charlie has steadily climbed the ladder of success and established himself as a popular and much-sought-after teenager. No sooner had he stepped foot on the Pittodrie turf than Newcastle United were offering a substantial sum for his signature. Arsenal, too, have been reputed to be interested in him. Both received answers in the negative. His impact has also extended to the SFA selectors. He was chosen as reserve to Alan Gilzean in an under-23 match, the same year he was chosen as one of the 29 for the World Cup series. Cooke's immaculate footwork and defence-splitting passes are a delight to watch. He also shows keen anticipation and his mazy runs leave us in little doubt as to why he is the pin-up boy of Pittodrie. In his short time in senior football he has added a welcome individuality to the game."

That individuality was what made Cooke special. So what was he? A winger, as most supporters of Chelsea would have you believe, or a forward as the earliest Dons supporters to have watched him play would claim? At Pittodrie he was a jack of all trades and master of each of them. He played in the forward line and as a winger, operating on both flanks. His ability on the ball and precise distribution led to Cooke's valuable versatility, not to mention the vision which made him a vital attacking tool wherever he was deployed. The one criticism levelled at the exciting talent was that he dwelled on the ball on occasion, but he is quick to argue that it was his willingness to keep possession and take on opponents that won him so many plaudits in the first place. You can't please all of the people all of the time, especially in football.

To understand what made Cooke special, what earned him the cult status that a thousand players have craved but missed out on, you first have to understand what made him tick. He was born into a working-class family in Greenock, where his father worked in the Clyde shipyards and his mother dreamed of a professional future for a son who bucked the traditional football trait of skipping lessons to concentrate on the game. Cooke combined both, sticking in at school to complete his Highers in English, Maths and Art and at the same time carving out a reputation as a fine aspiring young player with Port Glasgow Rovers. Mind you, he is the first to admit his academic commitment did wane when the tangible prospect of earning a living from the game began to intensify, but with his usual quiet dedication he saw it through to the end.

He was brought into he world in St Monans in Fife, his mother's home patch, during the period after his family's wartime evacuation from the west coast. By the time he began school the Cooke clan were back settled in Greenock and his education was about to begin in more ways than one. His father, Charlie Senior, came from a long line of circus performers and Junior soon had a penchant for juggling – albeit with a ball, rather than hoops. He would spend hours honing his skills and tricks, sweating to become the artist whose trickery and talent thrilled a generation on both sides of the border and across the globe.

He joined the rough-and-tumble world of junior football with Renfrew as a 16-year-old, soaking up knowledge and skills from his more experienced team-mates while setting about winning one-on-one battles all over the park with youthful exuberance. Even then, close control was everything for a self-confessed "ball-hogger".

The young figure cutting a dash in the notoriously tough junior game was soon headline news in the local press, but despite reports of a string of interested clubs across Britain, it was Aberdeen who stole a march. Once again it was legendary scout Bobby Calder who produced another ace from the pack when he persuaded Cooke that his future was in the east. Rangers followed hot on Calder's heals with a counter-offer, but by then the youngster, a Morton fan but with a leaning towards the Ibrox side, had decided his word was his bond and red was the colour.

At the end of the 1959/60 season Cooke pulled on the club jersey for the first time, in a reserve game at Clyde, and produced a performance straight out of the top drawer. At that moment he was catapulted into the first-team picture for the following term. He had retained the intricate close control born on the streets and playing fields of his home-town but married it to a more direct, more ruthless attacking style straight from the cut-and-thrust of the juniors. It proved to be a formidable combination, difficult to defend against and seemingly impossible to replicate. Cooke was regarded as a one-off and as such his progress was far more rapid than most.

Former team-mate Jim Geddes, who accompanied Cooke on his journey from Port Glasgow Rovers to Renfrew and on to Aberdeen, paid homage to his old friend with an insightful contribution to his book. Geddes claims: "It's ironic that Charlie runs a coaching school because, though he'd probably shoot me down for saying this, nobody could have coached Charlie Cooke. He brought the skills he learnt on the streets and in the playground to the top table. I thought one of his geatest assets was his ability to stay clear of injury. Guys like him and Kenny Dalglish rarely missed a game. Charlie was always a great player in my book, and I never saw him play a bad game. He could perform with any players, anytime, anywhere. The original Martini footballer. He was a master of the ball, in a literal sense. His absolute control was mind-blowing, and combined with style, strength, aggression and just the right amount of arrogance, it made him one of the finest players ever to come out of Scotland. He'd be a £20-million player today, for sure."

That mention of arrogance is important in the Cooke story. Far from perceiving him as a stereotypical gallus west-coast player, those who watched Cooke in his prime talk of a more focused and calculated confidence. To play the way he did required deep-seated belief, but it was controlled; there was no sign of an attitude in danger of alienating him from the north-east public.

Recalling his first days as an Aberdeen player, Cooke wrote: "I was focused and excited like it was a cup final every day. I was fit out of my schoolboy skin and ready for just about anything. I assumed all the players would be excellent and mostly much better than me, and I was afraid that I might not be good enough, no question about that. But I had always gone into games thinking that opponents were better than me, and it was an attitude that had served me well and really wasn't new or hard to live with. My background in the religious bigotries and battles of Greenock juvenile football meant I was pretty used to the rough and tumble of older competition, being on the end of stupid tackles and threats, and giving back the welly, if I could, in spades. I wasn't big, but I was strong and quick with a bit of a temper, and I wasn't at all intimidated by older, bigger and stronger players. In fact, in a strange way, I used to think they were all the same size when I had the ball at my feet. It was a great equaliser for me. But I knew my place going in as a schoolboy at Aberdeen. I would shut my mouth and work my butt off and be a royal pain in the arse to play against, no matter who the opponent was. Just about anybody could do that, I figured. If I got the chance to do things with the ball, I'd try to do them – that was what I wanted to be known for. And if I didn't make it, well, I'd take care of that when it happened. I had no plans if the Dons didn't want me."

But they did want him. In fact, within months he became invaluable. The first game of the 1960/61 season was in the League Cup, played on a sectional basis in those days. Ayr United were the visitors for the curtain-raiser and they arrived to find a new name on the Dons teamsheet: C. Cooke, in at number ten. Aberdeen won 4-3 and in the 41 matches which followed in the old First Division, Scottish Cup and League Cup, he missed just three. For a teenager in his first season on the books of a senior club, it was an extraordinary rise to prominence, a testament to his attitude, durability and drive. Inside that first year he had been christened "The Bonnie Prince" by the appreciative home fans. The press preferred to label him "Boy Wizard" or the "Prince of the Dribble". One way or another, he was making a name for himself.

He scored ten goals in his rookie campaign, including one in the memorable 6-1 demolition of champions-elect Rangers, while the Light Blues were going full tilt for the title. He thrived on the Old Firm fixtures, the perfect setting for his bigger-they-are-the-harder-they-fall approach to life.

Cooke made more than 30 appearances in every one of his four full seasons at Pittodrie, providing the type of dependability which is so often the flaw in the make-up of the flair player. Yet Cooke did display some of the off-field traits of the maverick player, freely talking off his drinking and gambling days as a young Don with time and money to spare. He married a local girl in 1961 and settled in the matrimonial home they built on Leggart Avenue in the Granite City, a stone's throw from the River Dee on the southern edge of Aberdeen, although the couple later divorced and he remarried an American.

He makes no bones about his fast living, claiming the vast majority of his playing years are a blur. Coincidently or not, his memories of the years since he turned teetotal in the early 1980s are far clearer and Cooke has candidly admitted that he could have been categorised as an alcoholic at the height of his hedonism – even if he never saw it that way. In keeping with the best of them, there was an edge to Cooke in every aspect of his life and that added to the appeal he carried throughout his playing career.

That career took him from Aberdeen to Dundee to Chelsea to Crystal Palace and then back to Stamford Bridge. From there he made the transatlantic leap, first with the George Best-inspired LA Aztecs in 1976. Next came the Memphis Rogues from 1978 to 1980 and California Surf in 1980, as well as performing in the indoor league operated in the States. Cooke went on to manage in the US before taking up a post with Nike, developing their soccer interests and then joining the Coerver coaching revolution. Coerver has become integral to Cooke's life for more than two decades, with the company's philosophy replicating his own approach to the game in so many ways. Coerver kids are not told what to do, they are shown how to master the ball and then left to their own devices to try and put those talents to use. There is no gameplan, no set plays – just as there was no predictability to Cooke's own meandering style.

He met Englishman Alfred Galustian at a coaching conference and between them they set about turning the philosophy and methodologies of former Feyenoord manager Wiel Coerver into a global brand which now operates in 17 countries across six continents. The mantra is simple, obvious, yet so often overlooked. Cooke explains: "English players in the Premiership today don't lack nutritional or physical conditioning guidance. They are big and strong and usually just as quick as the imported superstars. The differences lie in their abilities with the ball, their skill to be deceptive and work the ball at speed, pass and receive perfectly under pressure, and above all their comfort and confidence in taking on opponents. These are the things Coerver coaching helps to develop."

So there you have it; you too can learn to play just like The Bonnie Prince. Or can you? After all, there really is only one Charlie Cooke.

'THE GREAT DANE' 1969–1974

HENNING BOEL

Magic Moment: First John Hughes and then Jimmy Johnstone found no way past as the 'Great Dane' tamed two of Celtic's most dangerous attackers to help the Dons to Scottish Cup glory in 1970.

Dons Career: Games 150. Goals 4. Caps 17.

THE REIGN of Eddie Turnbull at Pittodrie was characterised by the legendary squad clearance which rejuvenated a club suspended in slumber for far too long. So much is made of the 17 players who fell victim to Turnbull's swingeing cuts, as his brutal yet effective plan took hold, that the individuals brought in to take the places of those so swiftly ejected can be lost in the mists of time. Which is a shame, because there were some barnstorming pieces of business conducted between the gruff and tough manager's arrival in 1965 and his departure six years later. Henning Boel counts among that number, a cult hero often overlooked in modern times but never by those who treasured his short but entertaining relationship with Pittodrie's connoisseurs of all things imported.

"Drive is considered aggression today. I knew it then as purpose."

Bette Davis, actress

For almost as long as the club has existed there has been a proud tradition of cosmopolitan spirit on the silvery coast of the weather-beaten north. South African livewire Stan Williams really set the tone, arriving in 1938 to alert the Pittodrie droves to the big wide world of footballing opportunity. When Williams grabbed the winner in the 1947 Scottish Cup final his legacy was assured, nine years after Pat Travers had shown the foresight to tempt him to leave Africa behind. Travers was also the man who brought mercurial winger Alex Jackson to the club from America in the 1920s, although Jackson was a fully fledged Scot who went on to win the caps to prove it.

So casting the net wide has always been the policy. The difference between the past and present during the 1960s was mainly in volume. Why have one Scandinavian when you could have three or four? Previous managers had been content with the occasional sporadic venture into foreign markets but Tommy Pearson and his successor Turnbull, considered ahead of his time in so many respects, saw the potential in the overseas leagues long before Alex Smith was plundering the Netherlands or Ebbe Skovdahl had Morocco in his sights.

Between them, Pearson and Turnbull boasted a decent success rate in their long-distance raids and Boel was a shining example of that. He was popular yet effective, charismatic yet reliable, hard but fair. Everything a manager could want in a defender was rolled up in a neatly packaged Danish import with the added extra of the occasional sensational goal into the bargain.

A player who offered style as well as substance was a welcome addition for supporters who harboured hopes of ending a dismal period in the club's history. Boel arrived in the 1968/69 season, the "Great Dane" challenged with putting an end to the defensive frailties which had in part been at the root of a trophyless run which stretched all the way back to the 1955 League title. In his quest to find the winning formula, the manager went through a variety of permutations, with the experimentation almost ending in disaster in 1969 when the Dons avoided relegation by just eight points as they slumped to 15th in the 18-team top flight.

The alarming trait of shipping goals during that disappointing term was the root of the problem and Boel was viewed as part of the solution. Prior to his introduction to the side in January 1969 the team had lost 35 goals in just 19 League games. It was clear to those inside and outside the club that changes had to be made and they were three-fold. First

Ernie McGarr was installed in the number-one jersey in place of Bobby Clark after the confidence-sapping run of results, then Boel was sent to camp in the centre of the defence. Thirdly Martin Buchan returned after a period of enforced absence, the result of a car accident, and the reshaped team did enough to stave off the real threat of dropping through the trapdoor. Lessons had been learnt though, and improved fortunes were just around the corner.

Boel had been parachuted into the Aberdeen line-up on a special mission to preserve their First Division status and had accomplished that. He had arrived as the fourth member of the 1960s Scandinavian quartet, which had begun to fall into place under Pearson in 1965 with the visionary hat-trick of Leif Mortensen, Joergen Louis Ravn and Jens Petersen.

While Ravn and Mortensen fell by the wayside within 15 and 13 months respectively, Petersen went on to captain the Dons and justify Pearson's decision to look beyond his own shores by spending five years wearing the red of Aberdeen with pride. The attraction in the first place was the amateur status which still prevailed in the Danish leagues, allowing the traditionally thorny subject of transfer fees to be bypassed by the enthusiastic Dons board, sensing a bargain as they cut straight to the chase with wage negotiations. In the cases of Petersen, Ravn and Mortensen the princely sum of £5,000 each was the going rate. Those three were the trailblazers for Boel, who trod in what had become well-worn footsteps from the undeveloped Danish League to Pittodrie four years later.

Mortensen, who had played abroad with Udinese in Italy previously, arrived with a reputation as a pacy crowd-pleaser with awe-inspiring ball control. Ravn, at a touch over 6ft tall, was billed as the attacking powerhouse, while Petersen, who had 23 caps in his locker before moving to Scotland and was his country's reigning player of the year, was known as a cultured defender. Petersen settled quickly, gaining the skipper's role for the unsuccessful Scottish Cup final of 1967 under Turnbull's stewardship, but Mortensen slipped away quietly after mustering just 18 appearances and Ravn played 33 times before he, too, disappeared from the Scottish scene.

The speed and aggression in the old First Division caught the more measured and reserved Danes by surprise, although Petersen overcame that initial shock through his exemplary reading of the game and his calmness under pressure, operating behind the defence as the use of sweepers began to change the way the game was played. In their own way, each of the three initial finds had the potential to go on and earn cult status. Petersen, with his intelligent use of the ball and poster-boy image, came closest and enjoyed a special bond with the supporters, but it was countryman Boel who really took that particular bull by the horns.

As with so many of the cult heroes and extraordinary characters who have played their part in Pittodrie's rich tapestry, there was an element of luck in Turnbull's discovery. Having begun his career with Ikast in his homeland, Boel also featured for the Boston Beacons, in their only season in the North American Soccer League, and the Washington Whips. By coincidence, the Dons had adopted the Washington Whips moniker during their tour of America in 1967, with a clutch of top-class teams from Britain and beyond each being assigned a local name in an attempt to sell the game to a still-sceptical US public. For the record, the Dons in their guise as the Whips lost to a Wolverhampton Wanderers side playing under the flag of the Los Angeles Wolves in the President's Cup final. Confused? Not half as much as the American spectators must have been.

All of that is incidental to the fact that the flurry of football activity Stateside not only led to a successful summer tour but to the increase in Boel's football education and the type of exposure to watching British eyes which eventually attracted Aberdeen's interest. When the NASL folded in 1968 he returned to Denmark in search of alternative employment and it was Turnbull who came up with the best offer. He was only 23 when he arrived in Aberdeen for a trial period in November 1968, but had good pedigree, with 13 consecutive appearances for Denmark up to the point of turning professional with Boston in 1968. By accepting the lucre of the paid game, Boel had crossed the divide as far as the Danish Football Federation were concerned. By opting to pursue a pay packet he immediately barred himself from representing his country, although he did return briefly to add a further two caps once the anti-pro rule had been abolished in 1971. Current international or not, he was snapped up without hesitation by Turnbull and taken under the wing of Jens Petersen and his family at the start of what would prove to be a hugely successful assignment.

Having arrived in glamorous style, with his American wife by his side, he looked the part before a ball had been kicked. Rugged, with a rough-and-ready aura, Boel had the appearance of a man who meant business and he backed up the bark with considerable bite. The newcomer made his debut as a centre-half against Dundee United on 4 January 1969, and played his part in a morale-boosting 4-1 victory. What the Dons fans who made the trip to Tannadice found was that they had landed a solid and uncompromising stopper, a player who just loved doing his job. He stood tall and weighed in at 12st 6lb, which was hefty in comparison to many opponents during a time in which nimbleness went before power. But diamonds have many different facets and time would enable Scottish football to see all of Boel's glistening qualities.

Henning's stature made him an obvious choice at centre-half when he arrived to quell the defensive storm that was brewing at Pittodrie, but Turnbull, ever the perfectionist, wanted more. He saw enough in the occasional attacking flourishes launched by Boel to feel there was further potential out wide and eventually moved him to right-back, from whence the Great Dane was free to rampage up and down the flank and satisfy his hunger for the occasional goal. He was the first true overlapping full-back the club had ever had and his raids down the right became a hallmark of the team's play, transforming not only the way the game was conducted but also the way it was viewed by spectators and the media alike.

The *Evening Express* proclaimed: "If you think that the full-back position is a dull, unexciting one, just take a close look at Henning Boel on the field some time. Henning makes a mockery of the full-back berth being an unspectacular one. Aberdeen's Great Dane is as popular with the Pittodrie fans as any forward, and rightly so. If you are one of the many who turn their head and flinch whenever Henning is about to come in for the tackle, then you are missing the sight of an artist at work."

Boel had the ability to turn the often ugly art of tackling into a thing of beauty, but he also had the personality to reel in the willing Aberdeen fans searching for a new idol in the aftermath of Charlie Cooke. They were two contrasting players in different positions but each had a maverick spirit. Boel, after all, listed one of his hobbies as pipe-smoking and liked nothing better than spending his spare time at evening classes. This was not Mr Average Footballer by any stretch of the imagination and the fans cottoned on to his uniqueness.

Boel, who now works in the international travel industry, has recently accepted a new challenge as a tour guide working in Scotland with Danish visitors. Speaking to the Dons hero, who still has a hint of a Scottish lilt if you listen intently enough, there was an audible excitement in his voice at the mention of his imminent return to his home from home.

He told me: "I've never had a better time in football than I had at Pittodrie and the supporters were a major part in that. I guess they liked the way I played the game. I was a no-nonsense type of guy and I soon discovered that the Aberdeen fans appreciated that type of approach. I believed that you should play the way that you can. In Denmark that was what was drummed into us – concentrate on the two or three things that you are best at, rather than trying to do the things you are not good at. It took me a little while to realise that, but it got through in the end.

"Scottish football suited me because it was very physical at that time. The running and the hustle and bustle was no problem to me. The way I played never really got me into trouble with the referees because I wasn't the type to moan. I went in hard and if it was a foul it was a foul, I just got on with it without complaining. I think the refs respected that."

Even today Boel is humbled by the legacy of the Red Army's fascination with his talents. The hair has greyed and face has softened with time, but he remains distinctive to those who witnessed the thunderous impact he had on the Scottish game. The man who thrived on head-to-head contests with the Glasgow giants perks up as he recalls the infamous way he set about his task and will never be allowed to forget some of his finest moments.

He said: "Back here in Denmark they know who I am, but it is nothing like the recognition I get in Aberdeen. Coming back to Scotland is like turning back the clock for me. I was in the city on business last year and as soon as I got into the cab to take me into town the driver spotted who I was and wanted to talk about my playing days. It is very flattering. I loved the games against Rangers and Celtic particularly, and the fans responded when you went into a tackle strongly in those games more than any other. They loved it when you slid into a tackle and got the timing just right; you could hear the cheer from the terraces. I was on business in Kazakhstan recently and ran into quite a few Scottish people who remembered the battles I used to have, particularly with John Hughes at Celtic."

Now the roar of the Pittodrie crowd is a thing of the past but Boel can still vividly remember the Dons choir in all its glory chanting his name and lauding his rare goal-scoring contributions. He added: "The chant just happened one day – obviously my name lent itself to it. Even 40 years later, when I was back for a reunion dinner in Aberdeen, the supporters were still singing that song. It still sends a tingle up my spine. I don't think it mattered particularly that I had come from abroad. Whether I was Danish or Scottish, what they saw was a guy who was fighting for their team and battling for every ball.

"I had some great experiences – the Scottish Cup win in 1970 was amazing. I realise now that you should enjoy the big occasions more because they don't come along all that often. In hindsight I also appreciate just how good Eddie Turnbull was. He was far ahead of his time and quite a few of the players have discussed that in recent years. I'm glad to say I remain friends with many of my old Aberdeen colleagues. At the time all you are interested in is training and playing, you don't get to know the players as people. Once you have finished playing you find out that you actually get on well with them as friends and it is interesting how relationships grow and change. You find out what people are actually like. Joe Harper is a perfect example. I like him far more now as a person than I did when we played together. Then he was the big star, but as we all get older we get to know each other better and I really enjoy his company and that of the other great people I met during that part of my life."

The 1969/70 season was Boel's first as a fully fledged member of the Aberdeen squad, having settled quickly to life by that point. It proved to be a seminal period for both him and the club, and one which would provide Boel with what to this day he classes as his greatest sporting achievement: a Scottish Cup winner's medal. In the League the progress was steady but totally unspectacular, with a modest climb to eighth spot. But in the Cup the Turnbull machine clicked into place as the Dons brushed aside the Glasgow pair of Clyde and Clydebank in the first two rounds before single-goal victories against Falkirk and Kilmarnock, courtesy of the famous 'Cup-Tie' McKay goals, set up the 1970 final encounter with League champions Celtic.

In front of 108,434 supporters the title-winners were put to the sword by the unfancied Dons, McKay's double and Joe Harper's goal earning a 3-1 win and, more importantly, immortality for the team which had taken the glittering trophy back to Aberdeen for the first time since 1947. Defenders Boel, Tommy McMillan, Martin Buchan and George Murray, as well as forward Jim Forrest, were the only men to play in each of the five Scottish Cup-ties and the loss of only two goals was another of the prime factors in the success, although only a sideshow to McKay's heroics.

Another feature of that triumphant 1969/70 season was Jens Petersen's gradual removal from the first-team plans, having started out as a mainstay before fading and being told his contract would not be renewed. Petersen was never expected to struggle to find a new club and ended up earning a lucrative deal with Rapid Vienna, leaving Boel as the last man standing from the Mortensen-Ravn-Petersen-Boel signing splurge.

It had taken time but Turnbull's tinkering was almost complete. The wily coach, who had also completed his backroom team with the addition of Jimmy Bonthrone, began the 1970/71 season with a more settled line-up than he had fielded at any time in the five previous seasons. The defence, in particular, looked as though it was hewn from granite. Anchoring the unit was Scotland keeper Bobby Clark, restored to the team following Turnbull's experimentation with fellow international Ernie McGarr and with his confidence back at the levels which had made him a star in the first place. Clark had been Turnbull's first signing for the club, having arrived as a 19-year-old from amateurs Queen's Park in 1965. The boss had been in charge of Queen's and rated Clark as a future international. His judgement was spot on and within two years Clark was his club's player of the year and the proud recipient of a Scotland cap.

At right-back was the dashing figure of Boel, cutting up and down the flank with flair and attitude. He loved to get forward but there was also a steel to the Dane's play. He was fearless in the tackle and he took no prisoners. Indeed, he was suspended for the start of the 1969/70 season, missing the opening of the League Cup campaign, after a post-match ruckus with Motherwell player John Deans at the end of the previous term. Boel, never perceived as dirty, was dealt with sympathetically and escaped with a nominal three-day ban for violent conduct – while Deans, who was no stranger to the disciplinary panel after five appearances in just four years, sat out two weeks for his part in the confrontation. Boel's enforced absence only delayed his ability to take the place earmarked for him in Turnbull's master plan, and after that minor hiccup he stepped into the new-look back four.

With Boel at right-back, the left-sided berth was filled by the emerging Jim Hermiston, not yet 23 when he reported back for duty in the summer of '69, but already making a name for himself. Hermiston, recruited from junior side Bonnyrigg by Turnbull in 1965 as a raw teenager, would go on to become captain of the Dons before sensationally quitting the game to become a policeman in 1975. Hermiston then emigrated to Australia, where he remains to this day.

In the centre of the defence was Martin Buchan, another Turnbull protégé. Buchan, having lifted the Scottish Cup as the 21-year-old captain just months earlier, was the one attracting most attention. He had been in the team for almost four years, maturing in front of his home-town audience, and at the end of the 1970/71 season his talents were recognised when he was crowned as the Scottish Football Writers' Association Player of the Year, becoming the first Aberdonian to win the award.

His partner at the heart of the Turnbull back four was Tommy McMillan. The Paisley-born stopper was the most experienced of the group, a sturdy centre-half who had played as an inside-forward as a schoolboy and shared Boel's penchant for forward forays when the opportunity presented itself. He was another spotted playing junior football by Turnbull, starring for Neilston. Between them those four defenders, ably supported by Bobby Clark, became one of the finest departments ever assembled at Pittodrie. They went on a British club record-breaking run of 12 games without losing a single goal. That stretched from a 4-0 win against Dundee United on 31 October 1970 to a 3-0 triumph over Kilmarnock on 9 January the following year, ending when Hibs hit a double to win 2-1 the next weekend. As well as United and Killie, the teams which also drew a blank in that amazing period were Clyde, Ayr United, Hearts, Motherwell, Cowdenbeath, Celtic, Falkirk, Airdrie, Dundee and St Johnstone.

In a total of 17 League games at Pittodrie the Dons conceded a stingy seven goals and on the road the damage was limited in much the same way, with just 11 against in 17 matches. Boel missed only one League game in that imperious display of defensive solidarity, Buchan was an ever-present along with Clark, while Hermiston sat out only three games and McMillan played in all but seven. Consistency was central to everything they achieved. Each man had his own qualities and individuality, yet there was a one-for-all mentality which made them the most feared back line in the land.

Certainly Turnbull's side had the best defensive record in the country during 1970/71, but agonisingly that was not enough to usurp Celtic, then in the midst of their nine-in-a-row dominance. The Bhoys won the flag by just two points from Aberdeen, who fell to a 1-0 defeat against Falkirk at Brockville on the final day of the season. The Glasgow side had the edge when it came to scoring goals, with Aberdeen reliant on the undeniable talents of Joe Harper but carrying too little threat from other areas of the park. It had been a wonderful challenge, the closest they had got to League success since 1955, but not close enough for the man they called the Boss, and Turnbull left to rejoin his first love, Hibs, in the summer that followed.

Ironically, events completely outwith the manager's control were a major contributing factor to the League heartache. Midway through the season the Main Stand at Pittodrie was ravaged by fire, with the damage leaving the pitch exposed to the worst of the swirling winds whipping in off the North Sea. That in turn dried out the pitch and it became a liability for a side which had put itself in a strong position with incisive passing play. Aberdeen went to desperate lengths to try and improve the situation, with Turnbull even enlisting Grampian Fire Brigade to flood the surface with water but it was only ever a temporary fix. Whether it would have all worked out differently if the blaze had never happened we will never know, but the history books show Henning Boel left not as a League winner but as a runner-up.

That mattered not a jot to the Dons faithful, who greeted the much-loved big man with the chant of: "It's a goal, goal, goal for Henning Boel". The song always tickled the Dane, given he only ever scored four times for the Dons. The most memorable was his searing 20-yard drive against Dundee United in a 2-0 Scottish Cup fourth-round replay win in 1971.

In conversation with the great man it becomes clear that the fact he remains more famous in the north-east of Scotland than he ever was in his own country, despite his international exploits for Denmark, is a source of great amusement for the hero and his family. Boel to this day insists the thrill of hearing the Red Army chant his name will live with him forever.

It begs the question why he ever chose to break that relationship, but the truth is it was taken out of his hands. Although the defender had asked for a transfer in 1971, it was not until the tail-end of the following year that he finally left the club. A major part in the decision was his desire to return to Denmark to raise his young family but the other decisive influence was football-related.

In 1972 Aberdeen travelled to Germany to play Borussia Moenchengladbach in the UEFA Cup first round, bidding to overturn a 3-2 deficit from the first leg. Boel, as ever, threw himself into the tie with vigour, but as he dived in to block a shot from Josef Heynckes he suffered an injury which ultimately ended his Dons career and his life in top-class football. The ankle ligament damage he sustained kept him sidelined for the bulk of the 1972/73 season and, by his own admission, the defender who had been billed as the best and most entertaining full-back in the Scottish game was never the same again.

He packed his bags in October 1972 to head for Denmark, where Boel had intended rejoining his family's electrical firm. Manchester United had failed in a bid to persuade Aberdeen, who still held the player's registration despite his hasty return to Scandinavia, to loan Boel to them early in 1973. Old Trafford manager Tommy Docherty was a huge admirer but he balked at the Dons' demand for £60,000 for a player who had effectively retired from the game when he walked out of Pittodrie the previous year.

The saga continued when Boel arrived back at Pittodrie in March 1973, six months after turning his back on the club. An emergency board meeting was convened and the directors agreed to allow him to rejoin the squad for training and eventually he pushed his way back into the side. In truth he became little more than a squad man for new manager Jimmy Bonthrone and in March 1974 the club agreed to release him to join the newly formed Boston Minutemen in America. The one proviso was that the Dons could have first refusal if he ever returned to the Scottish game. He later reflected: "When the fans started to chant it was impossible not to respond out on the pitch. They made my time at Aberdeen very special. It was hard leaving Aberdeen because I really loved life at Pittodrie. I carried on for a spell in the USA and got to face up to the likes of the great Pele – but nothing ever matched the thrill I got when I ran out in front of the Dons fans and heard them chanting my name."

Boel was still only 28, but there was an undeniable sense that Aberdeen had benefited from his best years. He went on to play alongside Eusebio for Boston but the club folded, as so many American franchises did. Aberdeen's adopted son remained in the States, going on to play for and manage the New England Tea Men before returning to Denmark to wind down back where it started with Ikast. His career took him from Scandinavia to the US, to Britain and back to America before going full circle to Denmark. That journey makes Boel one of the best-travelled players the club has ever seen, but his heart will always be with Aberdeen.

'THE MAGICAL MAGYAR' 1972–1973

ZOLTAN VARGA

Magic Moment: Less than 270 minutes into his Dons career, the Hungarian entertainer delivered the brilliance his new band of admirers had been promised. With a glance and a deft clip of his cultured foot, Celtic were on the receiving end of Varga's genius as a lob to cherish nestled in the Hoops' net.

Dons Career: Games 31. Goals 10. Caps 14 (Hungary).

DEEP IN the bowels of the *Aberdeen Journal's* headquarters on the western edge of the city lays a shrine to every aspect of north-east life. The company's library, occupying two floors, is filled from floor to ceiling with meticulously logged cuttings on every individual, club and organisation ever to have had an impact on everyday life in the heartland of the firm's newspapers before the modern electronic archive kicked in.

The football aisle presents a wall of unadulterated nostalgia, shelves weighed down with an alphabet feast of names from the near and distant past, from the instantly recognisable to the more niche characters to have turned out for every club from junior level through to the Scotland international team.

Much can be garnered about each individual before their particular file has even been opened. A bulging envelope means one of two things: long service or an ability to make headlines with the regularity of a metronome. Standing out from the pack of slim pickings among those filed under V is a distinctly well-filled wallet containing the paper trail which charts the short but fascinating tale of Zoltan Varga. The worn edges tell another story, one of repeated interest and a timeless obsession with the Hungarian superstar who lit up a cold corner of Scotland for an all-too-brief time.

Within that file is a collection of well-thumbed clippings which could be mistaken in part for fiction, were they not there in the black-and-white-and-sepia tones of yesteryear's newspapers. The Varga story, just like that of Benny Yorston all those decades earlier, had all the makings of a soap opera. From allegations of corruption to the high-rolling lifestyle of a celebrity, nothing about the city's most famous football import was understated.

While Aberdeen had rolled out the welcome mat for overseas players before, they had never had one with quite the same baggage or one who represented the same level of risk. It could have been an unmitigated disaster, but instead the flirtation with foreign flair proved an overwhelming success, at least while it lasted. Zoltan Varga, or 'Salt 'n' Vinegar' as he was christened soon after landing in Aberdeen, lived up to the expectations heaped upon a ready-made Dons cult hero. He brought intrigue, he brought glamour and above all else he brought excitement. Varga fitted the cult checklist perfectly.

"A man travels the world over in search of what he needs and returns home to find it."

George Moore, Irish writer

The tongues first began wagging in the Granite City in August 1972. At the beginning of that month Hertha Berlin had visited Pittodrie to play a friendly match and it would seem conversation in the boardroom soon turned to the 14 members of the German club's squad who did not feature. They were the group who had been banned from plying their trade for two years by the German Football Federation, a punishment meted out the previous year after a probe into bribery allegations. The players had been left in limbo and the club was in the unenviable position of having an entire staff sitting twiddling their thumbs during that lengthy period of forced inactivity.

There was a loophole, though, with the ban only applicable in the German game. In a flash of inspiration, Hertha and the Dons latched on to that gap in the red tape and struck a deal to allow a 27-year-old Hungarian by the name of Varga to spend a week on trial in Scotland with a view to a permanent move. Few, if any, of the Aberdeen supporters had even heard the name before, but the mere possibility of attracting the mysterious international put the Dons back on top of the news agenda.

The fact that the new man required stitches in a face wound after a clash of heads at his first training session helped keep the story in the headlines, but it was his pedigree which created the most interest.

Varga had 14 caps for Hungary and had played in the Olympics twice for his country. In fact, it was the Olympics to which Varga owed his rise to star status. He had defected from what was then a communist state to West Germany while competing in the 1968 summer games in Mexico and never looked back, living his life to the full after gaining that freedom. *World Soccer* magazine lamented his defection from Hungary to Germany, which ended his international career, by claiming: "He is a brilliant player now and could have developed into another Puskas. In the Hungarian forward line, he was a conductor without an orchestra."

Instead of staying on home soil, he became one of the game's great wanderers and the winding paths he followed led him to Aberdeen, even if he was only passing through. When he accepted the offer of a trial with Jimmy Bonthrone's Aberdeen side, Varga spoke little English. It was left to Henning Boel to translate, with the Hungarian's German being passed through the Danish defender's Scottish. It may not have been ideal but the message was able to get through and Varga was quickly integrated into the Dons squad. He immediately spoke of his love of the club, his appreciation of the stadium and the spirit in the squad.

With those public-relations boxes ticked, it was time to get down to the business of proving his worth. The club liked what they saw and after a month of hard negotiations with Hertha Berlin, the target touched back down in the north-east to conclude his part of the deal. The fee was never confirmed, but it was understood a bargain price of £40,000 was shaken on, due to the player's outstanding suspension back in his adopted country. It was less than half his accepted market value, but the thrifty Dons were not complaining after landing a bargain.

Varga had been given a glowing reference by Hennes Weisweiler, the coach of Aberdeen's UEFA Cup opponents Borussia Moenchengladbach just days earlier, and that persuaded Bonthrone that the transfer was worth pursuing. Weisweiler described the Eastern European as one of the foremost players in German football. It was high praise, given that he had played for only two seasons in the Bundesliga, but reflected the play-maker's ability and rapidly growing reputation not just in Berlin but across the continent.

After the contract was signed, Varga was allowed a ten-day period of grace to get his affairs in order in Germany before he returned to throw himself into day-to-day life at Pittodrie. To intensify the sense of anticipation, which had already built to a crescendo in the five weeks between Varga's trial and the conclusion of the deal to bring him to Britain, there was an inevitable red-tape wrangle to keep the Dons fans hanging on just that little bit longer. Or three weeks longer to be precise. By the time clearance from the German Federation came through it was 13 October, what seemed like a lifetime to the expectant Red Army since the 16 August announcement of Varga's original visit to Pittodrie.

The *Press and Journal*'s Norman MacDonald sought to keep collective feet on ground when he wrote: "Capped 14 times for Hungary, Varga is a clever ball player with attacking flair, but allowance will have to be made for the fact that he hasn't played a competitive game for almost a year. It is bound to take two or three games before he gets his eye in again. His football credentials can scarcely be doubted, and while playing in the West German League he was reckoned to be in the £100,000 class."

If the truth be told, the excitement about the job in hand appeared to be one-sided. While the supporters were whipping themselves up to fever pitch as they prepared for the grand unveiling of their new messiah, the Hungarian was doing what he had to do. He would train, he would play – but there was almost a sense of duress about it. As a star of the

German game he was paid handsomely, a basic salary of £12,000 plus bonus top-ups to keep him in the manner to which he had become accustomed. Because of the ban he found himself isolated, that cash cow had vanished and he had been sent out to the highest bidder. By his own admission, Varga had more personally attractive offers from clubs in various corners of the world but none had met Hertha's asking price and he was posted to Scotland on a contract which offered him lower wages than he'd had even during his days in Hungary with Ferencvaros.

Journalist and broadcaster Frank Gilfeather was one of the media pack who fell under Varga's spell in the 1970s. Still covering the Pittodrie patch for *The Times* and *The Herald*, Gilfeather recalls: "It might be argued that Zoltan Varga was ahead of his time. It was an era without the agents and management companies who now look after the world's big-name football stars. The Hungarian was a wheeler-dealer who recognised that his God-given talent was all he had to sell and he was insistent that he would capitalise on it to the maximum. In short, he could look after himself and was not prepared to be brow-beaten by any football club wishing to get him on the cheap. Despite the difficulties he had faced growing up in communist Hungary, he was aware, partly through competing in the 1964 Olympic Games in Tokyo where he won a gold medal as his team emerged as the best of the tournament, that there were great riches in the West for those with the kind of skills he possessed. His problem seemed to be that he was a short-termist who found great difficulty settling down, and when he agreed to join Aberdeen it was largely on his terms. Indeed, the disquiet over his signing, at least as far as chairman Dick Donald was concerned, was highlighted when Donald baulked at the news that Varga collected half the £40,000 transfer fee for agreeing to the move. Perhaps that was a real indication of how the player operated. He was a businessman as much as he was a footballer.

"It was true that he found it difficult to settle, though there was no dispute surrounding the love affair he had with the Aberdeen fans following his superb displays for the team. His precision passing and reading of a game were often breathtaking. Unfortunately, there were too many Pittodrie players not only unaccustomed to such technique but unable to tune in to his wavelength. He once confided in me that he was frequently frustrated by the failure of some of his team-mates to use their brains during games and he could never understand why the Aberdeen squad trained only for a couple of hours each day: 'Why are they not told to return in the afternoon and work on the parts of their game they need to improve?' he said. 'In Hungary and in Germany, no matter how big a name a player might be, he recognises that he still has to work hard to be better. We all have to keep learning and I cannot believe that the Aberdeen players go home after two hours' training and do not return in the afternoon.' And when I asked him which of the Dons team he would take with him should he move to another club, his answer was swift and unequivocal: 'Arthur Graham'. It wasn't so much that he rated the speedy winger as particularly talented. His reason for choosing the man who played in front of him was simple. 'With Arthur I can point to a spot where I want him to be,' Varga insisted, 'and I can place the ball there for him. When I say go he runs, taking my instruction.'

"Varga's work ethic, despite growing discontent at Aberdeen and what seemed like a desperate need to move back to mainland Europe, never diminished. He was seen most afternoons on the Pittodrie pitch, on his own, practising free kicks from various angles and distances and with both feet. It was that kind of attitude that made him an exceptional player whose thought process on the field of play was often light years ahead of colleagues and opponents. He had the ability to change a game – a luxury in today's Scottish football – with one searching, defence-splitting pass, with spectators and players alike realising they were in the presence of a special sportsman."

Having had to reject overtures from clubs in Mexico, Greece and South Africa he found himself in a distinctly chillier outpost. The new man came into a team managed by Jimmy Bonthrone which was more about togetherness than individual stars. The team news for Varga's first game, which came at home to Falkirk on 14 October 1972, illustrated the fact. While the imported play-maker was added to the pool, Bonthrone had fitness doubts over dependable captain Jim Hermiston, Ian Taylor and winger Bertie Miller. The manager's cup was not overflowing with international talent.

As it happened, Taylor did make it and it was just as well. He scored two in a 2-2 draw to steal the show from Varga, whose presence had swelled the crowd considerably as 14,165 filed into Pittodrie for the show. It was a home gate only bettered by those for the visits from the Old Firm and the gala opening day of the season against Hibs,and dwarfed the attendance for the corresponding fixture the previous year, which stood at just under 8,800.

From the offset it was clear that the new man had class. Just as predicted, he hit top gear after getting a couple of games under his belt to blow away the cobwebs that his inactivity had brought. In his third appearance, Varga bagged a double against eventual champions Celtic in front of 34,262 at Pittodrie to prove he was a player for the big occasion, although the Hoops hit three of their own to earn another crucial win in their title quest. But where the points ended up is not what the Red Army remember of that game – they recall in sharp focus the sight of Varga collecting the ball, composing himself and then humiliating visiting goalkeeper Evan Williams with a sublime lob. To this day it is regarded as one of the best goals the stadium has ever witnessed.

He had been handed the number-seven jersey by Bonthrone upon his arrival, switching to number-ten at the tail-end of his first season, but regardless of what was on his back he proved to be a consistent and impressive performer. Many would argue Varga was the finest exponent of technical skills that the club has ever seen and, having joined seven games into the 1972/73 season, he displayed those talents in 31 League and Cup matches that term and netted ten times.

By then aged 28 and conscious that he was no longer a young man in football terms, he promised the best was yet to come when he told reporters: "It has been a hard six months for me and I feel it catching up on me. Having been out of football for a year after my dispute with the

German FA I came to Aberdeen and was in League football almost immediately. It was all right for a time but now, not having done any real preparation before the beginning of the season, I feel very tired. I am looking forward to a holiday and then to getting myself properly fit for the start of the new season. It is then that you will see a better Zoltan Varga."

The observation from the press seats was that the Hungarian had reserved his best performances for Pittodrie. The player was in agreement and suggested the special relationship he had built with the home faithful had a part to play, claiming: "At Pittodrie we play more attacking football and this gives me a greater chance to operate my normal style, setting up chances for the strikers and generally building attacks. But in our games away from home we normally play it tighter and therefore I cannot be as effective. In any case I feel better at Pittodrie as the crowd always seems right behind me."

He scored regularly, though the main thrust of his game was creating rather than finishing. Quickly he became a marked man in more ways than one. Varga found himself being closely shadowed in almost every game he played and his legs bore the scars to prove it as he learned to live with meaty treatment from opposition sides. Yet the slightly built maestro was not deterred, claiming: "It is as tough, if not tougher, in Germany and I am used to hard tackling. While I did take one or two bad knocks, I realise this is part of the game. I have no complaints."

The vow to return fitter, stronger, sharper and ready to help the Dons to silverware proved to be an empty promise. He had been saying all the right things in public, but privately Varga was simmering about the contract he had been pinned to at Pittodrie. He arrived for pre-season training in 1973 complaining of a knee injury and returned to Germany for specialist assessment of the problem. Rumours began to sweep around Scottish football that the trip would also serve the purpose of allowing Varga to negotiate a return to the Bundesliga. That was denied, perhaps diplomatically, by the Dons board.

When the player returned from his overseas visit he came bearing bad news, having been ordered to ensure complete rest for up to six weeks in a bid to cure the niggling knee problem which was dogging him. The midfielder had been pencilled in for a key role in Bonthrone's masterplan but the manager had to quickly redraw the blueprint both in the short and the long term.

At the same time as delivering the medical verdict, Varga also announced that he had no intention of staying with Aberdeen beyond the end of the season. He had joined on a two-year contract. The injury had given Varga time to think, time to think of 101 reasons why he wanted to leave.

He said at the time: "No doctor can tell me if I can play football again or if I cannot. I will know myself when I begin training. I believe I will be able to play again but only time will tell. I will have to be very quick in thinking about my future if I can no longer play football. I would like to return to the continent and find a job as a coach. In any case, that is what I wish to do when my contract with Aberdeen is finished. I am a foreigner here and I am a foreigner in Germany. But my German is better than my English and from there I can possibly work in France, Belgium, Spain or Switzerland. Germany is central."

Varga had been unsettled by the lack of central insurance cover for players in Scotland, another factor he cited in his explanation of his plan to abandon ship. Did he not feel a sense of loyalty to Aberdeen for effectively rescuing him from the scrapheap? Not really. Varga said: "I thank Aberdeen, not because I think they gave me a chance to play football, but because it is a good club with a good atmosphere and I like the players. But I had better offers from Mexico, Greece and South Africa. The Aberdeen club, however, put in a higher bid to Hertha Berlin for my transfer. I do not feel that the club has done me any particular favours. My move to Aberdeen has been to our mutual benefit. The future of my family is what is important to me now and I wish to make sure they have security. I must therefore look to Europe for that."

Oh, and the weather did not help either. Apparently the move to the colder, wetter climes of Britain was one of the reasons for the knee injury which stalled his career in the Scottish top flight, with the problem eventually diagnosed as a muscle and ligament strain which was by no means career threatening. Frank Gilfeather takes up the story: "Latterly, having apparently made up his mind to move on, there were thoughts inside and outwith Pittodrie that the knee injury which kept him out of the team – and often in Germany for treatment – had more to do with his lack of interest in playing for the club than anything else. He had a knowledge of, and a liking for, antique furniture and I remember being in his house in Milltimber one afternoon as he was preparing to drive a Ford Transit vanload of old cabinets and bookcases to Germany. It was my belief that this was part of a business in which he was involved and that, if he couldn't play football, he would nonetheless keep busy and use his free time making money.

"Zoltan Varga was, in many ways, an enigma. His formative years behind the Iron Curtain, where life was tough and goods like washing machines and high-quality television sets – regarded by those in the West as everyday items – could only be dreamed of. Perhaps, having defected to the West and shaken off the repression of being part of the Eastern Bloc, he made up his mind that he had to make up for lost time, in terms of experience, lifestyle and wealth. His short but memorable period as part of Jimmy Bonthrone's Aberdeen team brought from the Dons fans a fondness and a respect, both of which he deserved for his stunning ability as a football practitioner like few others who have worn the red jersey."

It seemed the one positive Varga had taken from his brief association with the Scottish game was the spring in the step he had gained from the cult status bestowed upon him by the club's fans. He said: "I am very happy with the supporters. I was feeling down when I first came here because I was forced out of football and the supporters here gave me fresh enthusiasm."

Varga became a familiar sight on the roads of the city and its suburbs during his recuperation from the troublesome knee injury. As part of the recovery plan he was prescribed plenty of cycling and swimming, so he took to his bike to make the run from his home in Milltimber to Pittodrie each day, being greeted with cheery waves and beeping horns along the route.

He began light work in September 1973, but even after a month was still complaining of pain in the joint when he briefly joined team-mates for full training. At the same time reports in the Netherlands were suggesting Varga was the man Ajax had earmarked for the unenviable task of replacing Dutch master Johan Cruyff following his switch to Barcelona.

Just two days into November the Aberdeen supporters were put out of their misery. Just as expectation had built around the time of his arrival, there was a feeling of inevitability about his departure once it became clear there was interest from some of Europe's big names. When the announcement was made, the main reason given was the player's desire to return to live on the continent. Varga exercised a clause in his contract, which required the fee the club had paid for him to be repaid, and packed his bags to head for what he classed as home. Hertha Berlin footed the bill and took him back.

Dejected manager Jimmy Bonthrone said: "I am very disappointed that this has happened. We have done everything humanly possible to make the player happy and keep him in Aberdeen, knowing as we do how popular he is with the fans and how much he means to the team. In the circumstances, however, there is little else we can do. In view of what has happened this season, with the player unable to turn out for us due to his knee injury, we have reluctantly agreed to his request to be released."

So the wanderer made his way back to Berlin. Then a funny thing happened – within five days of his return to Berlin, Varga had been sold on at a profit to Ajax. The Aberdeen directors could have been forgiven for feeling they should have seen it coming. It was an obvious set-up, with Berlin paying Aberdeen £40,000 and then raking in £70,000 from the Amsterdam side inside a week. It was a cute piece of business for everyone except the Dons.

Initially the Dutch Federation intended to uphold the ban imposed by their counterparts across the border, but they relented within weeks of

Varga's arrival and he made his debut against Sparta Rotterdam in December 1973, unable to hide his delight at the turn of events which had left such a bitter taste in the mouths of everyone connected with Aberdeen.

Varga said: "I am absolutely thrilled at the prospect of playing for one of the best teams in the world. Playing for Ajax will mean that I will be in the international spotlight and it will give me the chance to establish myself as a world-class player. It is a dream come true. I think because I was playing for a club like Aberdeen, the football public on the continent had forgotten about me. Things have now changed and I'm delighted. I must emphasise I liked the players, the manager and my football with Aberdeen. My argument was with the directors of the club. I was unhappy with the financial terms and I thought it was better that I left. As it happened, everything has turned out perfectly for me."

Varga, who won Olympic gold with the Hungarian national team at the 1964 games in Tokyo, did not succeed in filling the boots of Cruyff. Within a year, after being limited to mainly substitute appearances for Ajax, he was off on his travels again and heading to Borussia Dortmund in his spiritual home of Germany. He complained: "You can have so much – conditions, money and a tremendous home – but it doesn't mean a thing if they won't let you play."

He was still a big draw in Germany. More than 2,000 turned out to watch his first training session with Dortmund and the crowd swelled by 30,000 for his first game, which was watched by 45,000 fanatics who were soon chanting his name at every opportunity. Varga had found his home and with it came inner peace. He said: "For the past four years we've spent every Christmas in a different country. That couldn't go on. Now I'm glad its all over."

Back in Aberdeen, the memories lingered on. It was a case of "look at what you could have won" for the Pittodrie support, who had only a one-year cameo to savour while the Dortmund crew were being promised a feature-length version of the Varga story. He was described as a magician by the German club, who marvelled particularly at his ability to conjure up crowds for them.

Bonthrone, who died in 2008, never regretted the gamble he took on the Hungarian. The former Dons boss reflected: "It was a pleasure to have a player with so much skill on the staff. He worked very, very hard at the game and it was a real eye-opener to the rest of the players that a man with so much talent still thought it necessary to practise so much. Watching him working out for hour upon hour with a ball was an object lesson to our youngsters. He acquired his marvellous ball control by sheer hard work and he knew he had to keep at it to retain his skills. The only disappointment about Varga's spell in Aberdeen was that it was not nearly long enough. I knew I had to rebuild the team and I had visions of persuading Zoltan to stay on after his two-year contract was up and being a key figure in the re-organisation. Lads like Willie Miller and Billy Williamson would have become even better players, for some of Varga's brilliance must have rubbed off on them. A player of Varga's class seldom comes the way of a Scottish manager. We were fortunate to have him, even for a short spell."

Despite claiming he would turn his hand to photography rather than stay in the game when his playing days were over, Varga could not resist the lure. He now works in youth development in Budapest, having begun coaching in Germany's lower leagues, around his home in Dortmund, before eventually winding his way back to Ferencvaros in his home city. He had first appeared as a player for the club as a fresh-faced 16-year-old, going on to represent them in European Fairs Cup finals against Juventus in 1965 and Leeds three years later. In 1996 he took charge as manager of the club, albeit briefly, and returned to Britain in that role to face Newcastle United in European competition. Even then the conversation turned to Aberdeen, with Varga recalling: "Aberdeen had very good supporters – they loved me and I loved them."

It was the briefest of sporting flings but the memories linger on, untarnished by the speed of the break-up and the bitterness of the circumstances. For a moment in time the Red Army had a world superstar to call their own and one for which they are eternally grateful.

'CUP-TIE' 1969–1971

DEREK McKAY

Magic Moment: A 'Cup-Tie' double was all it took to halt the green-and-white machine in its tracks and send the Red Army into raptures as the Scottish Cup returned to their grasp.

Dons Career: Games 19. Goals 4.

WHEN DEREK McKay passed away in 2008 it caused a wave of grief among the team-mates who accompanied him every step of the way on his Scottish Cup fairytale in 1970, and plunged a generation of Dons fans into mourning. Before long the tears had turned to fond smiles as the anecdotes flowed and the memories of "Cup-Tie" McKay and his fascinating career began to trip off the tongues of those who knew him best. Immortality may be one of football's great clichés but in certain cases it rings true and this is one of them.

> "Heroing is one of the shortest-lived professions there is."
>
> **Will Rogers, actor**

McKay's death left a void in many lives but his name will always fill a special place in one of the great chapters in the Dons tale. A scriptwriter could not have written the life story of a football nomad who for three glorious months savoured surely the swiftest rise to prominence the Pittodrie club has ever known.

The Scottish Cup heroics which earned the winger his nickname are the stuff of legend, passed down through the decades. Three cup-ties, four goals and a winner's medal. But the devil is in the detail when it comes to getting to the bottom of the real McKay. Who was the man behind the headlines and how do you explain the brevity of his association with the team at which he earned cult status?

The sledgehammer impact with which he hit the club scene in 1970 will be remembered forever, but the circumstances have seldom been fully aired. Aberdeen had negotiated home ties against Clyde, who were beaten 4-0, and Clydebank, who fell 2-1, in the opening rounds of the 1969/70 Scottish Cup. The quarter-final draw threw up an away trip to face Falkirk at Brockville, the epitome of a traditional Scottish ground and a venue which was never comfortable for visiting teams. The Bairns were in contention for the Second Division championship when the clubs met on 21 February, reliant on experienced forwards Andy Roxburgh and Alex Ferguson. Those names would crop up again in years to come.

Falkirk's preparations went without a hitch but the same could not be said for an Aberdeen team beset by illness as a virus swept through the squad and backroom team. Manager Eddie Turnbull and coach Jimmy Bonthrone were among those laid low while a string of first-team players also suffered. The board appealed to the SFA to have the game postponed but the pleas fell on deaf ears and the show had to go on. That rampaging flu bug proved to be the twist of fate which led to the greatest tale of cup heroics in the history of the Dons as young prospect Derek McKay was asked to step into the breach. He had been excelling in the reserves, scoring goals for fun, but had experienced first-team football in only a couple of substitute appearances up to that point.

On a cold winter afternoon and with rain lashing down, McKay ran out with the number-seven shirt on his back. Little did he realise at that point just how iconic that shirt would become. The quarter-final was a tight affair, a real test of endurance in difficult underfoot conditions, and the sides were deadlocked as the players trooped in for some welcome warmth at half-time. It was not until the 72nd minute that the tie burst into life. Jim Forrest was fouled on the left wing, Joe Harper hung an inviting cross towards goal and Jim Hermiston's header was only half-cleared by Falkirk. The ball fell into the path of McKay and his confident half-volley nestled in the back of the net to take the Dons through to the last four of the national cup competition. A crowd of 13,500 had filed into the compact and atmospheric town-centre ground for the tie but soon the legend of Derek McKay would be playing to a far wider audience as the prospect of a Hampden final became very real.

The *Press and Journal* hailed the rookie's performance, with Norman MacDonald reporting: "It was the lad from Macduff who destroyed the Bairns' hopes of cup glory and cash. Playing with refreshing style and confidence he introduced a new dynamic element on the right touch-line and emerged as Aberdeen's best forward at Brockville Park."

McKay's reward for clinching a place in the semi-final was a permanent place in the Dons team for the games in the aftermath of that single-goal victory against Falkirk. Turnbull kept faith with the youngster for encounters against Ayr United, Partick Thistle, St Johnstone and Hibs. The Dons beat Ayr and the Jags before drawing with the Perth Saints but the match before the all-important semi-final did not go to plan as they fell 2-0 against Hibs at Pittodrie.

Despite that setback, the manager kept his nerve and made just one change for the Scottish Cup tie against Kilmarnock five days later. Jens Petersen dropped out and Jim Hermiston returned to the first 11. Both Kilmarnock and the Dons were destined for mid-table finishes that season, with the Rugby Park club pipping Aberdeen to seventh place by a single point when the dust settled on the final day of the campaign.

However, going into the semi-final the Reds had the confidence of a 2-0 victory in the League against Killie earlier in the season and hopes were high amongst the Dandies.

Muirton Park in Perth was picked by the SFA for the tie between two provincial clubs, but the turnout suggested they had miscalculated the interest the 14 March fixture would provoke. A capacity crowd of 25,812 crammed on to the terraces but they were not rewarded with a classic. The stakes were high, nerves were jangling and the teams contrived to cancel each other out in the opening stages.

That all changed in the 26th minute when Turnbull's terriers hit the Ayrshire men on the break, with Jim Hamilton picking out Joe Harper on the left and his through-ball fed Derek McKay for another cool and collected finish. There was still a long way to go to the finish line but the Dons had conceded just a single goal in their three previous ties and never looked likely to crack as Kilmarnock cranked up the pressure on Bobby Clark's goal.

The fans who had trekked south in their thousands faced a nervous 66-minute wait for the final whistle but when it came it sparked joyous celebration as the Red Army began the countdown to their latest cup final experience. Three years earlier Turnbull and his team experienced the pain of a 2-0 Scottish Cup final defeat against Celtic, but the memory of that disappointment did not dampen the enthusiasm for the next challenge, simply serving to heighten the determination to usurp the Parkhead side.

Between that semi-final triumph and the showpiece at Hampden on 11 April there was almost a full month to wait. A full month for the Aberdeen faithful to whip themselves up into a frenzy, a full month for the Pittodrie players to contemplate the might of the task they faced against Jock Stein and his dominant Celtic side. The Hoops already had their latest championship in the bag by the time they lined up in the final and adding the cup to the collection was considered a formality. The bookmakers certainly thought so, at least, rating the Dons as rank outsiders at 6-1. In a final between two top-flight teams, those odds were insulting to a side which had talent in every department, but Turnbull revelled in the role of the underdog.

Martin Buchan, who led the side out that day as captain, tells the wonderful story of the last League encounter between the two clubs before they met at Hampden. The Celts needed a point to win the title and had champagne stacked up outside the dressing rooms at Parkhead in anticipation of the big moment. Turnbull's team talk was short and to the point on that occasion, simply asking his players: "Do you think they are going to celebrate tonight at our expense?" As he expected, the squad answered in style by winning 2-1 with goals from George Murray and Arthur Graham to stall the party. Before running out in the cup final,

Murray asked Turnbull to repeat the same concise team talk deep in the heart of the national stadium. The answer, it turned out, was just as decisive from his men.

In the weeks leading up to the Celtic showdown there was a heavy schedule of League action to shoehorn in. McKay played in four of the six matches but struggled to find his scoring touch in the First Division. That did not unsettle Turnbull, who was all too aware that he had a talisman on his hands. The build-up included wins against Dunfermline, as well as that significant victory at Parkhead, and a draw against St Mirren – but there were also defeats at the hands of Dundee United and Hearts.

In the final League outing before the moment of destiny, it was beaten semi-finalists Kilmarnock who provided the opposition and this time the west-coasters managed to hold their cup conquerors to a 2-2 draw to give the Aberdeen management team food for thought as they prepared their teamsheet for the biggest game of the season.

Turnbull had rung the changes for the Killie game, mindful of taking too much out of his tight squad in what was their second game in the space of just two days, but was certain he had the winning formula in mind for the final. Out went Jim Whyte, Steve Murray, George Buchan and Alex Willoughby. In came Tommy McMillan, Martin Buchan, Jim Forrest and Derek McKay. The stage was set and a gallery of 108,434 assembled in Glasgow for the performance.

Those bedecked in green and white thought they knew the end to the story which was about to unfold but nobody had furnished the outsiders with the script. After 27 minutes the Glaswegian supporters in the boisterous crowd were shocked into silence when Joe Harper held his nerve under extreme pressure to put his side 1-0 up with a penalty. McKay had a role to play, firing in the cross which was handled by Bobby Murdoch to concede the spot-kick. Tensions were running high, with Tommy Gemmell booked for hurling the ball at the referee after the penalty award, and the temperature rose even further three minutes later when Celtic had a goal disallowed for a foul by Bobby Lennox on Bobby Clark.

Aberdeen weathered the storm and held their slender advantage until the 83rd minute. That was when Cup-Tie McKay came to the fore, seizing on the loose ball following a save by Evan Williams from Jim Forrest's run and shot and steadying himself before unleashing a perfect shot from a tight angle to make it 2-0.

Celtic were back in the game six minutes later when Lennox's goal threw them a lifeline. There were only seconds left on the clock but nothing was deemed beyond a Celtic team who had a winning habit and were on the verge of securing a place in the European Cup final, having defeated Leeds in the first leg of the semi-final just days earlier.

Yet the humble Dons proved an able match for their adversaries and in the 90th minute McKay produced the knock-out blow. Harper broke on the right as Celtic pushed for an equaliser; he faked to go one way but instead picked out McKay with a pass in the opposite direction and the hero of the hour lashed home the decisive goal to send the travelling fans into wonderland. Young captain Martin Buchan held aloft the glittering prize to kick-off a party which continued into the early hours after the triumphant team had retreated to their base at the Gleneagles Hotel.

Upon returning to the Granite City the players were greeted by 100,000 delirious supporters, eager to catch a glimpse of the cup which had been absent from their trophy cabinet for 23 years. McKay later recalled: "It was a terrific feeling to score those goals in the final. Returning with the cup along Union Street was unbelievable. I'll never forget that in a million years."

It was an amazing period in his young life, the very best of times. McKay had his grounding in the game on his home territory in the quiet fishing village of Macduff. He was a stand-out in schools football and made his Highland League debut for local side Deveronvale as a 16-year-old, featuring at the tail-end of the 1964/65 season. In that short venture into the northern game he caught the attention of a Dundee scout and, after a month-long trial at Dens, he was handed his big break in December 1965 when he signed on as a professional with the Dark

Blues. He had been an amateur with Vale, but Dundee paid a three-figure sum to the Banffers as a goodwill gesture and a mark of their delight at snaffling such a promising young talent from under the noses of their north-east rivals Aberdeen.

McKay made his Dundee debut in a League Cup group game against the Dons at Pittodrie, replacing the talented Andy Penman on the right wing and filling his boots admirably with a string of neat touches. The Dons gained the upper hand though, running out 4-3 winners.

That promising start led to three seasons dipping in and out of the Dundee first team before being released in the summer of 1969. Eddie Turnbull, with his keen eye for a bargain, stepped in to offer McKay a one-month Pittodrie trial and Cup-Tie did not hesitate in accepting as he embarked on the next stage of his effort to establish himself in the game.

He flew south with the Dons party for friendlies against Sheffield Wednesday and Tranmere, attempting to provide the solution to the club's search for reinforcements on the wing following Ian Taylor's appendix operation. Jim Hamilton and George Buchan were already on the books and vying for the wide berth but Turnbull liked what he saw in McKay, with his fashionable hairstyle and free-flowing style to match his laid-back attitude to life, and signed him on month-to-month deals until finally taking the plunge in October 1969 by making McKay a permanent member of the playing staff.

Up to that point he'd had to be content with regular reserve-team action but he earned immediate promotion on the back of inking his full-time contract, making his first-team debut as a substitute just a day after agreeing the deal. McKay was introduced as a substitute in a 2-1 win at Ayr United, with fellow new recruit Joe Harper also turning out in the club's colours for the first time following his higher-profile switch from Morton at the same time. The two new boys went on to forge a friendship which lasted a lifetime.

McKay made another appearance from the bench against Partick Thistle in a 2-1 win the week after his introduction to the Dons fans, but found himself relegated to the reserves for the next five months. He used that time in the second string to great effect, charging to the head of the reserve scoring charts to finish the season on 15 strikes, one ahead of George Buchan. By the end of the season he had, of course, become a fully fledged member of the first team and a cup-winning star, and was well aware of his rising stock in the club game.

As the 1970/71 season loomed, McKay was one of four contract rebels who held out for better terms from the club. It had been a brave stance from the 20-year-old but not surprising. The *Evening Express* described McKay at the time as "one of the most controversial characters" at the club and added: "His George Best hairstyle and knack of scoring goals in important games have made him a great favourite with the Pittodrie fans." No kidding.

When the season began he was still central to Turnbull's plans, despite the wage dispute, and was a key man in the 3-1 European Cup Winners' Cup first-leg victory against Hungarian cracks Honved at Pittodrie. A hip injury forced him out of the second leg and stalled his progress just when it looked as though McKay was in the team to stay. In fact he never made another appearance for the first team, with his last League match coming in a 0-0 home draw against St Johnstone four days before his one and only European experience in the Honved tie. On April 29 1971, barely a year after his man-of-the-match show at Hampden, it was announced that McKay was not being retained by the club. He was free to walk away, with his Scottish Cup medal tucked safely in his pocket.

Little was made of the circumstances at the time, although McKay later revealed: "The Scottish Cup final marked the end of my Aberdeen career. I didn't play that many games for Aberdeen and looking back that was a real disappointment. Winning that final proved to be the beginning of the end of my Pittodrie career. The final was one of my last games and a year later I was handed a free transfer. I wouldn't sign a new deal and Eddie Turnbull said: 'If you don't sign, you won't play.' I said I wanted a pay rise to sign, but he wouldn't increase my wages. So he sat me in the stand for a whole year even though he continued to pay my wages. Clubs continued to come in for me but he wouldn't let me leave."

It was an incredible fall from grace for the darling of the terraces and yet another example of Turnbull's single-minded nature. There was no room for sentiment and Cup-Tie left the building with the modest record of 16 starts, three substitute appearances and the four vital cup goals against his name.

Not since the one season of wonderment provided by Scotland winger Alex Jackson in 1924/25 had there been a player to rival McKay's short but spectacular impact. Jackson, who was brought to the Dons from American side Bethlehem Star and went on to become an international legend as one of the Wembley Wizards who defeated England 5-1, left in altogether different circumstances, mind you. A megabucks £8,000 offer from Chelsea in 1925 sealed the deal on that occasion.

McKay, on the other hand, was a free agent at a crossroads in his career. Not surisingly the winger who had hogged the headlines throughout Britain just 12 months earlier with his amazing story was the subject of widespread interest when it became clear his Dons days were numbered.

Crystal Palace stole a march on their rivals when they tempted McKay to sample the bright lights of London. But after just 45 minutes of a trial match the Scot was on his way, signing a short-term deal with Forres Mechanics in the Highland League as he weighed up options which included Blackpool south of the border and Montrose closer to home.

Despite dropping out of League football, McKay remained big news on his home patch as Dons fans looked on with a mix of intrigue and regret as one of their heroes plotted his next step. Still in his early 20s, McKay had sampled the type of extreme highs and character-testing lows that most players do not experience in an entire career. From the giddy excitement of his introduction to the senior game with Dundee to the disappointment of his eventual rejection at Dens, from the Hampden celebrations to the shattering blow of his Pittodrie exit. It had been a testing introduction to life in football for McKay and those early experiences shaped his attitude as he embarked on a nomadic period in his life.

After three games and one goal for Forres, McKay made his decision. He had been training with Montrose during his time with the Can Cans but turned his back on Scotland and opted to give the English game a try. Lancashire side Barrow had courted the mercurial winger and manager Don McEvoy had impressed him with his vision for the club after flying McKay south for signing talks. It meant playing at Fourth Division level but the man from Macduff was happy with the terms on the table and made his move as the 1971/72 campaign began. It would be his one and only season with the club, making 22 appearances before moving on in the summer of 1972.

It was then that the wanderlust really kicked in as Banffshire's most famous football son embarked on a globetrotting adventure. Hong Kong, and the Siu Fong club, was his first port of call. He joined three Englishmen on the playing staff but before long had packed his suitcase for his first stint in Australia. By the start of 1974 McKay had added South Africa to his burgeoning CV, recruited first by Durban United and then East London United on the strength of his proven ability to adapt to any surroundings.

On a two-month stop-off back on home soil late that year, at the end of the South African season, he added Keith to his list of Highland League clubs while considering options to play in America and Australia. Maroons secretary Alec Rutherford had no doubt McKay remained a major draw in his native north-east, admitting: "We hope that his presence will prove a crowd-puller and get our turnstiles clicking merrily."

McKay opted to return to the sunshine of Australia when his Keith assignment ended, linking up Down Under with Sunderland of Sydney, Apia near Adelaide and the Ukrainian-run outfit, Kiev. By 1977 he had 14 clubs under his belt in just ten years as a professional. Five of those had been spent on Dundee's books.

McKay, who was celebrating his 29th birthday back home in Macduff and on the verge of joining Ross County for another brief Highland League sortie, admitted at the time: "I don't believe in staying in one place for very long. Although many people will say money isn't everything, you can't do without it. I have made a lot of cash since going abroad and at no time regretted the move. I'm all for club loyalty – but it does not really pay your wages or offer you security for the future. Many players in Scotland remain with their clubs for years but at the end of the day have very little to show for it financially. I'm just making sure that does not happen to me."

It was a refreshingly honest career appraisal from a man who had found out to his cost that loyalty was not a currency readily available in his profession. Having been cast aside by Dundee and then the Dons in relatively quick succession, he set about carving out a living by following the money to some weird and wonderful corners of the world. Settling in the Western Australian city of Perth, McKay established a window-cleaning business to supplement his £80 tax-free weekly football wage, while banking signing-on fees left, right and centre.

Ross County in 1978 proved to be his final Scottish club before he emigrated once and for all to set up home in Australia, eventually settling into life as a hospital porter. Thirty years later news of the death of a legend broke, a heart attack cutting him down before his 60th birthday while holidaying in Thailand. Cup-Tie had never been far from the thoughts of supporters or team-mates alike, but his premature passing brought his contribution back into sharp focus.

Close friend Joe Harper, who had been McKay's sidekick on and off the field, led the tributes when he said: "I'm not ashamed to admit I cried when I was told Derek had died. I've found it hard to cope with knowing I will never have the joy of Derek's company again. My tears this week have been mixed with laughter because of the host of happy memories I have of Derek."

The great and the good of the game followed suit, each with their own favourite piece of McKay nostalgia. Some printable, others best kept locked in the memory bank safe from prying eyes, but all with smiles as standard for one of Aberdeen's most under-used yet most dramatic goal-getters of all time.

'KING OF THE BEACH END' 1969–1972 and 1976–1981

JOE HARPER

Magic Moment: In front of 108,000 fans in 1970, the 'King' kept his cool to shock the Hoops and give Aberdeen the Scottish Cup lead against Celtic to complete his coronation.

Dons Career: Games 308. Goals 205. Caps 4.

EDDIE TURNBULL was a disciplinarian as a manager, somebody who demanded respect and total dedication from his charges. With his army background, he brought a regimented organisation to Pittodrie and a work ethic which brought the Dons kicking and screaming into football's bold new era. Turnbull also signed Joe Harper in a move which, on face value, may just as well have been used to illustrate "contradiction" in the football lexicon. While Turnbull built his reputation on his uncompromising approach, there was very little conventional about Harper other than his indisputable ability to stick the ball in the back of the net.

"There is a certain combination of anarchy and discipline in the way I work."

Robert de Niro, actor

The most prolific of Dons strikers proved to be Aberdeen's very own loveable rogue and man about town, as popular on the city's social scene as he was on the football pitch. His love of the high life was at odds with his manager's strict attitude – yet it proved to be a marriage made in heaven for the odd couple. As long as 'King Joey' continued to bang in the goals, Turnbull was quite willing to forgive and forget the indiscretions which would have proved fatal to the career prospects of any ordinary player.

And there's the crux. Harper was no ordinary player, no ordinary character, and Turnbull was astute enough to let him off the leash if it meant getting the best return on the park. Would a Joe Harper who had been under his manager's thumb have gone on to set scoring records which in all probability will never be beaten? It is unlikely. A content striker, after all, is infinitely more liable to make the net bulge than an unhappy one. It was not a case of free rein, but Turnbull did learn to bite his tongue when it served a purpose and to trust his anarchic forward to do what made him happiest – scoring goals.

During his time with the Dons there was a catalogue of Harper-inspired high jinks, from the traditional stuff of football's bad boys, such as his red card for an off-the-ball scuffle at Ayr in 1972, to the downright bizarre, which included joy-riding in a snowplough. Aided and abetted by willing sidekicks such as Derek McKay and Ernie McGarr, Harper was far from subtle as he galloped through life in the Granite City displaying more vigour in his nocturnal activities than he did on the training field the next morning.

But, just like their wise old manager, the Dons fans could see past the pitfalls and accept Harper for what he was – the master of goal-scoring. He became the subject of the type of worship never seen before at Pittodrie, with every ball which crashed into the back of the net cranking up the volume in the chants for the regal finisher. He had not come cheaply but the signing of Harper reaped dividends beyond the wildest dreams of even the man who ducked and dived to bring him north against the wishes of some within the club.

Eddie Turnbull took up the story in his 2006 biography *Having A Ball*. He recalled: "Joe was a winger-cum-striker and he had impressed me greatly when we played Morton. At the start of season 1969/70, we made a generous offer to Hal Stewart, Morton's legendary chairman and manager. Hal was a law unto himself though, and knocked us back. But I wanted Joe Harper and knew I would get my man eventually. We did well in the League Cup, qualifying from our section only to lose to Celtic over two legs in the quarter-final. Our start to the League could not have been better, as we thumped Clyde 6-0 in the opening match. But we won only one of our next five matches and I went back to the board about Joe Harper.

"He had been down at Huddersfield before returning to Scotland to play for Morton, and I thought he was being wasted on the wing there, as he seemed to me to have all the natural attributes of a striker. We needed someone to score goals, and I thought Joe could be that man. Bobby Calder and I went to see him at Ibrox. It was a very wet day and the pitch was muddy, and Joe was running around with his stockings about his ankles, which Bobby did not like. But I was convinced he was a natural goal-scorer, so I went to see Hal and did the deal for £40,000 – and only then did I tell the board. That was a club-record fee, but it was arguably the best money Aberdeen ever spent.

"Joey was a real character, who was always getting into scrapes. He was funny – he once cracked that he was the only footballer with 20,000 budgies named after him. One night I got a call to tell me that he and Ernie McGarr were in a wee bit of trouble – they had somehow commandeered a snowplough and taken it for a ride. It wasn't the first or last time the phone rang with an Ernie McGarr or Joe Harper story … and I have to say it was big Ernie who was in trouble more than any other player. But there was no malice in Ernie or Joe, and, as with a lot of the players, I was willing to forgive them the odd scrape, as they more than repaid the faith I invested in them.

"I also knew they were young men in a lucky situation; it often seemed to me that there were three women to every man in the city at that time and, of course, playing for the club made them something of a catch. There was no serious bother, however, and I don't think I ever fined Joey Harper or any other player at that time – my bark was enough to frighten them. We also knew that Joe wasn't the best of trainers. The players would be sent out on a run of three laps round nearby Seaton Park. Joe would hide in the bushes on the first lap and come out when the lads were approaching the end of the final lap – and he thought we didn't know. But I didn't care as long as he banged in the goals."

Turnbull also tells the story of how a spot of Harper mayhem disrupted his preparations for the European Cup Winners' Cup tie against Honved of Hungary. The striker turned up at his manager's Aberdeen house on the Sunday prior to the tie with a tale of woe, claiming to have fallen through a glass door at home to explain away the stitches he'd had inserted to deal with some nasty lacerations. Turnbull did not buy the unassisted fall and had his own suspicions that a libation or two may have been involved, but he turned the other cheek ... only after telling his protégé that he would be playing, stitches and all. He did play, he did score and Aberdeen did win.

It was that type of response to manoeuvre out of a potentially sticky situation which kept the west-coast player in Turnbull's good books. It was also the impish nature which helped cement his cult status, as if the goals were not enough. Of course, it was the hardcore fans huddled under the hunchbacked roof of the old Beach End who showered their elected King with the most praise, willing him to venture forward and leave another helpless opposition keeper stranded as the drama unfolded in the penalty box in front of them. The cherished old stand, sitting grey against the backdrop of the North Sea sky, could swallow up thousands of Red Army foot soldiers and produce a deafening roar each time the King of the Beach End put another visiting team to the sword and knelt in front of his subjects to lap up their praise. With its low-slung roof propped up by two impossibly thin pillars, the noise was retained and bounced around to heighten the din.

The acoustics of the Beach End could not be matched when the new all-purpose Richard Donald Stand took its place in 1993 and many would contend that Pittodrie lost something special when the bulldozers moved in. It is questionable whether the atmosphere has ever been the same, although few would argue that the facilities provided have not enhanced the match-day experience. Progress does not come without a price and the tariff on the Aberdeen fans was the loss of something which had been integral to their football lives for generations. Indeed, some still hang on to the past and refuse to call the RDS by any other than the Beach End moniker.

Long before the RDS took its place, the ageing enclosure was the venue of choice for the supporters who did not care for the stuffiness of the Main Stand or exposed slopes of the south terrace in the 1960s and '70s. It was home to a new breed of fan, more vocal and raucous than before, and they had a fitting hero in the boisterous Harper. After the old structure had been knocked down, he reflected: "The Beach End was my stand. The fans in that stand were great. They knew that even if I didn't play well, I'd always be good for a goal. I played for the crowd and my relationship with them is something I will never forget."

Born in Greenock in 1948, Joseph Harper arrived at Pittodrie from Morton less than a month before his 21st birthday celebrations. Even at that tender age he had experienced the merry-go-round of football, having originally joined the Cappielow club as a 15-year-old. He signalled his intent with a debut goal for Ton in a cup game against Partick Thistle and quickly became known as one of Scotland's best goal-getting prospects. In 1967, after finishing as the country's leading scorer with 28 strikes to his credit, he was plucked from Greenock by Huddersfield Town. The sojourn in England was short and by 1968 he was back in the blue of Morton as he regrouped after his flirtation with the game south of the border. It was never more than a minor setback for the irrepressible Harper and, to his club's delight, he attracted another big-money bid the following year when Aberdeen finally got their man for £40,000.

He made the first of his 308 appearances for Aberdeen on 4 October in a 2-1 win at Ayr United. The *Evening Express* noted: "He had a serviceable start for the Dons and looked as if he will fit in." If only the reporter had possessed a crystal ball the praise would have been far more lavish. The serviceable frontman netted for the first time in the next match when Partick Thistle fell to a 2-1 defeat at Pittodrie, winning over the supporters with an impressive all-round display in his first home outing. In the next game, at home to Celtic, he had gone from "serviceable" to "inspirational" according to the reports of the time.

Harper bagged his first hat-trick in January 1970 in a 5-1 demolition of Raith Rovers on home turf. That was despite being used wide by Turnbull as he gently introduced his new recruit to life as a Red. In fact, as the season wore on the expensive recruit found himself dropped to the reserves. With the 1970 Scottish Cup final against Celtic at Hampden looming, the man from Clydeside displayed impeccable timing as he returned to first-team action the week before the Hoops contest and produced a confident performance which assured him of a place in the cup-final team.

He had not scored in the competition since his double in the 4-0 victory over Clyde in the first round but came up trumps in the final, the coolest man in the stadium as he sent the Dons ahead from the spot after just 27 minutes. Thanks to Derek McKay's heroics a 3-1 victory was secured and Harper had his first medal inside his first season at Pittodrie. Then his eyes were opened to the latent potential of his new club when 100,000 supporters turned out to meet the homecoming stars as they paraded down Union Street in a Northern bus. Faces popped out of almost every window along the silvery street while at ground level the masses strained to catch a glimpse of their beaming squad as they lapped up the reception. That is what scoring goals can bring and his haul was a mixed bag, from two-yard tap-ins to deadly accurate penalties and the more spectacular efforts such as his dashing solo run and shot against Hibs in 1976 which has been ranked among the finest goals ever scored at Pittodrie.

Harper had finished third on the club's scoring chart in his first season, with his nine goals not even close to Davie Robb's tally of 19, or runner-up Jim Forrest's total of 18. However, there was about to be a new order put in place as the new boy took control. In 1970/71 he led the scoring charts with 27 goals, the highest total since Ernie Winchester's seven years earlier. The best was yet to come, though, and in the next season Harper became the first Dons player since fellow cult hero Benny Yorton in 1930 to smash through the 40-goal barrier in a single season. His 42-goal haul made him the third highest scorer anywhere in Europe. It had begun with an incredible run of 19 goals in the first 23 games, including three in just four UEFA Cup ties against Celta Vigo and Juventus. He hit four in one match against Ayr as Aberdeen split the Old Firm for the second year in a row, once again finishing second to Celtic.

While that was a disappointment for the team, on a personal level the season had been a runaway success for the number-one striker. His efforts did not go unnoticed and before long Everton weighed in with a £180,000 bid, which proved too tempting to those who held the Pittodrie purse-strings. Harper was an instant hit on Merseyside, forging a partnership with Joe Royle which made the Scottish import the leading scorer at Goodison. Yet again his stop in England was brief, cut short this time by a change in management from Harry Catterick to Billy Bingham, and less than two years later he had rejoined Eddie Turnbull, who had taken charge at Hibs by that point. With the Easter Road club he scored a hat-trick in the 1974/75 League Cup final – but still ended up on the losing side, as Celtic ran out 6-3 winners.

In 1976/77 Harper's career turned full circle as he bowled back into Pittodrie to take his place in Ally MacLeod's Red-and-White Army. True to form, the returning hero looked as though he had never been away and scored in his first game back as Kilmarnock were beaten 2-0 in the League Cup. Harper went on to grab nine goals in that competition, including eight in seven consecutive games, as Aberdeen marched to the final to face Celtic again. This time the result was 2-1 and Harper had helped the Dons to another knockout success and earned himself another opportunity to celebrate with his adoring public.

The great mystery of Harper's career is why he did not add to his four caps. Even when the obvious factor of his ban from the international team after a Copenhagen nightclub incident in 1975 is taken into account, there was still ample opportunity for his country to make use of the Aberdeen talisman. He had made a promising start in Dark Blue, scoring on his debut just 19 minutes after being introduced as a 64th-minute replacement for Jimmy Bone in a 4-1 victory against Denmark in 1972 in Copenhagen. That earned a start in the return game against the Danes but it was not the beginning of a beautiful relationship with the international game.

He scored against Denmark again in his third appearance for his country in 1975, before the nightclub ruckus which led to his life ban, along with similar punishments for Arthur Graham, Billy Bremner, Pat McCluskey and Willie Young. The harsh penalty was later lifted and Ally MacLeod brought his one-time Dons signing back into the fold for the 1978 World Cup finals in Argentina, pushing Harper into action as a substitute for Kenny Dalglish in the disastrous 1-1 draw with Iran. And that was that, the international career of one of Scottish club football's most effective forwards of all time. It simply did not add up.

It could be that Harper's reputation as a lover of the good life went before him, either in the eyes of the managers or the SFA top brass. Certainly his approach did not curry favour universally, with Sir Alex Ferguson among those to frown upon the stocky marksman's lifestyle.

Ferguson used his autobiography *Managing My Life* to vent his feelings on many of the contentious issues in his managerial career. One of the earliest was the decision to dispense with the previously untouchable Harper, a player who had scored 33 goals in Ferguson's first season at the Pittodrie tiller. He mustered 11 appearances in the 1979/80 title-winning campaign, not helped by a knee injury, to ensure he had a full set of domestic badges, but there was no disguising the fact he was not on Ferguson's most-wanted list. Steve Archibald and Mark McGhee were the favoured strike partners, but the manager knew he would not be able to instigate his plan without alienating the supporters who doted on Harper, despite his advancing years.

Ferguson revealed in his controversial book: "The only individual who seemed to present a long-term problem was the little front man, Joe Harper. Joe was a hero with the fans but for me he was a worry. I had misgivings about him as early as pre-season training (in 1978), when I found myself lapping him during an endurance run – three and a half years after I had stopped playing seriously. The suspicion that he was an artful dodger was strengthened one day when he stopped me outside the back door of the dressing rooms to tell me how much the players were enjoying my coaching. 'We never got any coaching when Big Billy McNeill was here,' he informed me. I have no time for such nonsense and Harper's motives for peddling it were exposed the following week when he came to me with a request for a testimonial. I marked him down as somebody to watch."

Those musings provoked a stinging response from Harper, who always suspected Ferguson was jealous of his special relationship with the Dons fans and his success as a player. Using his newspaper column as a platform, the King hit back by claiming: "I admire what Alex Ferguson has achieved as a manager with both Aberdeen and Manchester United. But he didn't win the leagues and cups all by himself. Many of the men he slates in his book – like Jim Leighton, Gordon Strachan and Steve Archibald – helped him get to the top. Having a go at these guys and dredging up old stories from their private lives is no way to repay them. While I respect what he has achieved I don't agree with the way he treats people. He would tear strips off the young lads and throw things about to frighten them, but would never try that with experienced players like myself or Bobby Clark. He stopped many of the young lads enjoying their time at Pittodrie and frowned upon the older players trying to involve them in wind-ups and pranks. I find it strange to see him saying he lapped me during pre-season training. I can't remember him ever taking part. Anyway I was a footballer, not a cross-country runner. I had a job to do and, as my scoring record for the Dons proves, I did it well.

"For Alex Ferguson to say I bad-mouthed Billy McNeill in an attempt to sook up to him is total nonsense. To claim I said his coaching was superior to Big Billy's to get him to give me a testimonial is garbage. I still believe that, at the time, Billy was a better coach than Ferguson. If he had stayed on at Pittodrie I feel he could have been just as successful. I've remained friends with Billy over the years, so for Sir Alex to come out with this sort of thing annoys me. Apart from anything else, my testimonial had already been given the green light before Alex Ferguson ever set foot in the place, so I would have no reason to butter him up. Plus, anyone who knows me will know I speak my mind and never sook up to anyone. Even people who've never met me but read this column every week should see that."

Time would prove that Ferguson's plan for life after Harper was sound, but his unceremonious departure brought a tear to the eye of the club's greatest ever forward. After 308 games and 205 goals the adventure was over. He went on to manage Huntly, Peterhead and Deveronvale in the Highland League and had a spell as commercial manager with Morton in the late 1990s, before carving out a career in after-dinner speaking and the media as a football columnist and broadcaster.

His often controversial views are given credence by the statistics which mark out a phenomenal career. When he retired from the game Harper had been credited with 199 goals but in January 2003 his total was pushed up to 205 when the SFA decreed that his four strikes in the short-lived Dryburgh Cup competition could be added to his tally, along with two he scored in the Anglo-Scottish Cup. For the natural born scorer, it was a timely fillip. Harper said: "It's the best start to a New Year I have ever had. I will go to my grave a happy man now, knowing I will be remembered as the first, and probably only, Aberdeen player to score over 200 goals." Once a striker, always a striker, it would seem.

So how does the King stack up against Pittodrie's other sharpshooters? Well, he is indeed the only one to have made it past the 200-mark. Matt Armstrong made it to 155 in the 1930s, and George Hamilton hit 153 in his 17-year association with the Dons. Jack Hather, with 104 and Drew Jarvie with 130 are also members of the century club, joined by Mark McGhee when he hit the magical 100 just before leaving for Germany in 1984. Willie Mills, another hero of the 1930s, bagged 114, and the Yorstons, Benny and Harry, claimed 125 and 141 respectively. All honourable contributions but every single one was blown out of the water by the pint-sized predator who was hailed as much by his peers as he was by those on the terraces.

Willie Miller, upon being named Aberdeen's player of the century, insisted his vote would have gone to Harper, while Davie Robb once claimed his former sidekick was every bit as good as German World Cup-winner Gerd Muller. High praise, indeed.

When Harper was at his peak the Red Army would not have swapped him for any star of the world game, such was the manner in which he captivated them. Some named their children after him, others contented themselves with the more traditional chants. But all worshipped the ground he walked on. He has not kicked a ball for the Dons in almost 30 years, yet is still assured of a rapturous reception whenever he encounters their fans, revelling in the attention while at the same time insisting one man cannot make a team.

The last word in the incredible story of Joe Harper goes to the man himself, who once said: "It was a blessing being a footballer when I was because I played in what was probably the best era – the '60s and '70s – with some of the most smashing players. We played for the jersey – not the money. I am proud of what I have done but I couldn't have done it without the other players in the team. We were like a band of brothers when we got the '70s team together. I don't think of me as being a hero."

'GOD' 1973–1990

WILLIE MILLER

Magic Moment: With one strong arm outstretched, the glittering European treasure that put the Dons on the map was in the clutches of the 'lord of the manor'.

Dons Career: Games 797. Goals 32. Caps 65.

IN THE early 1990s in a London home a fashion revolution was brewing and Vic Groves, Arsenal star of the 1950s, was the inspiration behind it all. It was when Gunners fan Alan Finch decided to ditch his itchy polyester football kit and seek out a local dressmaker to produce a replica of the shirt made famous by Groves that it all began.

Little did Finch realise his retro quest had created a business monster. Soon he had quit his career in the music industry and founded The Old Fashioned Football Shirt company, or TOFFS as it is better known to football fans across the globe. The empire began in his dining room, with just Finch and his wife as the team behind it, but now is based in a Newcastle factory with a staff of 30 and a multi-million-pound turnover.

The company is servicing a seemingly unquenchable thirst among lovers of the beautiful game for a slice of the past, earning contracts with clubs and international federations across the globe, and has provided its distinctive cotton kit for countless films and television productions. But the real appeal of TOFFS is not on the playing fields and in the games halls of Britain; it is on the high street and in the bars of every major city in the land.

Football fans, it seems, have gorged themselves on an endless diet of man-made modern replica strips but tastes have developed and refined over time. Now the supporter wants something different, something distinctive. In 2011 TOFFS will celebrate its 20th year and in the cyclical world of football fashion a new trend has emerged to rival retro, with an even more subtle approach paying dividends for enterprising companies seeking a slice of the pie.

In 2004 a Glasgow firm by the name of Fitbo Europe appeared on the scene, marketing a 'Legends of Football' series of screen-printed T-shirts. Plain old retro replica had been replaced by a line of products with a clever twist, borrowing from popular culture and adapting to suit the football niche. The Aberdeen range includes a copy of the Abercrombie logo and a take on a Ramones T-shirt adapted to pay tribute to the Gothenburg success.

The firm, which has struck a deal to supply the Debenhams chain and opened its own dedicated store in Glasgow in 2007, also does a roaring trade with its version of what has become a Willie Miller classic: captain fantastic does Che Guevara. Few Dons fans, particularly those of a certain age, could have missed them dotted around the silver city's centre.

No one company has a monopoly on the Willie-Guevara, or Che-Miller if you like, edition of the Guevara revolution shirt, with the Cuban's distinctive profile transposed for that of the Dons legend. But one man can lay claim to igniting the fashion flame which has licked around the Aberdeen football fraternity. Step forward Richie Mutch, the Inverurie-based graphic designer who had the spark of inspiration.

If imitation is the biggest form of flattery then Mutch has reason to feel very flattered indeed. While his original design is still available through Attic, the fashion store with Aberdeen and Inverurie branches which originally had faith in the design, he is well aware of the other versions which have sprung up.

In various guises it has appeared here, there and everywhere in the past decade. The localised fashion phenomenon has made Miller a cult hero to a generation too young to have seen him at his playing peak but that has not stopped the pounds from rolling in.

To those who witnessed Miller break through in the 1970s and mature into the most successful captain the club has ever seen, he is a legend. Plain and simple. Can somebody in that mould be a cult hero too? In some cases, yes, and Miller is one of those rare examples.

The T-shirts are a major part of it but the iconic imagery of the Gothenburg era is another, not least the one-handed trophy display which has come to represent that magical moment: Aberdeen 2, Real Madrid 1. The picture of Miller, arms spread wide with the cup shining bright in the Ullevi floodlights, is the most used photograph in the library of AFC.

> "Design is not just what it looks like and feels like. Design is how it works."
>
> **Steve Jobs, Apple co-founder**

It has come to represent the golden era of the Dons, when the club could humble the giants of the European game. Anyone under the age of 30 will struggle to recall even the smallest detail of the 1983 continental cup run, but only somebody from a different planet could have avoided becoming well versed in all it entailed. Surely none could have missed the Miller cup pose and a significant proportion will have worn the T-shirt despite never seeing the man, labelled "God" by adoring Dons fans, play the game.

Legend, icon and cult hero rolled into one neat, moustachioed package, Miller is the one player more than any other who has managed to bridge the generation gap in Aberdeen. It was John Hewitt who scored the all-important winner against Madrid and the forward will always have a huge place in the city's football folklore, but it is Miller who stands out as the instant reference point for that glorious period of national and European domination.

Designer Mutch, a staunch supporter of the Dons, has seen at first hand the pulling power Miller still possesses. The bulk of the customers who have snapped up his iconic garment are sub-30 yet the Miller-Guevara camouflage T-shirt which sits side by side with some of the world's best-known designer names does a roaring trade.

Mutch said: "It all happened just before Willie returned to the club as director of football. He never asked for any royalties from the shirts – I always joked that the exposure he got was worth more anyway. Willie had become less high-profile after leaving the manager's job and enough time had passed for the dust to have settled and for people to remember him simply as a legendary player. He and Gordon Strachan were two of my favourite players when I was growing up.

"I was working as a designer in Glasgow and one day came across a fabulous picture of Willie playing for Scotland – the idea just hit me. I had a typical student's bedroom but I have to admit the Che Guevara image wasn't on the wall and I didn't have the T-shirt. The image must have struck a chord with me, though, because as soon as I saw that particular picture of Willie it seemed perfect to marry the two together. It wouldn't have worked with any other club because the colour red was so important."

When Attic began stocking the design in the summer of 2002 in their Aberdeen city-centre store they were an instant hit. The initial limited run of 60 flew off the shelves and the design has been a steady seller ever since. The following year the image was used on a giant flag for the Red Ultras supporters group, draped across the Richard Donald Stand.

Mutch said: "I don't have an exact sales tally but it runs into thousands now. The first year was amazing and it has been steady since then. In fact, it started to go crazy the first weekend that the shirts were out. Tam Cowan and Stuart Cosgrove picked up on the design and used it to set up a look-alike theme for their *Off The Ball* show on Radio Scotland. That helped get the T-shirts noticed and the initial run was snapped up. From then on we had to keep re-ordering and re-ordering. TOFFS had already done very well with the retro idea but this was something different. It was perfect timing to tie in with the explosion in logo, statement and ironic T-shirts outside of football. Since then a lot more have appeared on a football theme."

The brains behind the Dons fashion phenomenon has resisted the temptation to try and repeat his classic design – but a few more runs in

Europe could provide the motivation to return to the drawing board. He said: "A lot of people asked us to do other players but that was never going to happen. Willie Miller fitted perfectly; doing something similar with another player would just have watered down the idea. The only time I came close to bending with that was when I needed to fund the trip to a UEFA Cup tie. I looked at the possibility of doing a Zoltan Varga design but there were no images that caught my imagination and I decided against doing something for the sake of it."

For generations of Dons followers, Miller is the all-time great, the man who more than any other epitomises their club. The intriguing fact about him is that he is a Glaswegian who has managed to go through his entire career in football as an Aberdeen man. Not a Celtic man, not a Rangers man – a Don through and through. It sounds innocuous enough but if you look back through the annals of the game you'll find that is a fairly mean achievement, with almost every player from the west coast down through time pinning their childhood colours to the mast. Even Alex McLeish, Miller's great defensive partner, came out of the closet as a Rangers man eventually. For the public at large, the colour red is all that has ever been associated with the most distinguished captain ever to serve at Pittodrie.

Indeed, the first words, first lines and first paragraphs of the first chapter of the Pittodrie director's 2007 biography *The Don* were dedicated to distancing himself from his home city's two most famous sporting institutions.

Miller, who penned his latest book with journalist Rob Robertson, wrote: "Mention Celtic and Rangers anywhere on the planet, and you are likely to gain instant recognition from sports fans. Though it may be hard to believe, as a little boy growing up in a football hotspot I had no real interest in the game or in the fortunes of either Old Firm club. The fact I lived in Bridgeton, a Rangers stronghold situated near Celtic Park, makes it even more difficult for people to accept that, throughout my Glasgow childhood, I was one of the few kids who did not inevitably take an interest in football."

By his own admission, Miller hails from a tough area. He grew up amid raging sectarianism, bitter and brutal gang violence and at a time when Glasgow's housing stock was in desperate need of regeneration. Against that backdrop every youngster had two choices: become embroiled in the culture of the era or turn their back on it.

Miller, showing maturity beyond his years, opted for the latter.

He explained: "I reckon it took some guts not to support a football team when you grew up in Bridgeton, an area that was home territory to some of the most fanatical Rangers supporters anywhere. The community would come alive after victories over Celtic. Flags would be flown from tenement windows, car horns would be sounded and naturally the pubs would be packed to overflowing. The proximity to the Parkhead stadium of such a Rangers stronghold led to some ugly scenes involving Old Firm supporters on match days. I would witness the fights between rival fans from my bedroom window, and these were certainly not spectacles that earned any credit for my home area. In fact, observing such violence close-up was one of the reasons that I did not support either Old Firm team: I just could not understand why the fans were kicking lumps out of each other. It had nothing to do with football and everything to do with bigotry, and I did not wish to be part of that scenario."

By isolating himself from those political troubles, Miller was able to enjoy what he recalls with fondness as a blissful childhood, despite the less than luxurious surroundings of the time. Yet he did not have to think twice when Aberdeen offered an escape route straight from school. The Dons director said: "Much of what was going on in Glasgow at that time, it must be said, I just did not like; the gang fights and the sectarianism bothered me, and I wanted out. Aberdeen suited me and if any doubts lurked in my mind about my destination, they were swept away when I saw a picture in a newspaper of a chap who had attended my school – and he was brandishing an open razor at a police officer during an Orange Walk. More positively, there was something special about Aberdeen and its environs that I could not put my finger on. I had gone on a school trip to Rosehearty, Aberdeenshire, and I loved the place.

Even back then before my football life was mapped out, I felt an affinity to the north-east."

When you consider Miller has been with the club man and boy, it is little surprise that he has become an adopted Aberdonian. He first pulled on the jersey as a 15-year-old in a youth tournament, having been spotted starring in the Glasgow schools league. He began his youth career as a goalkeeper, representing his city select as a shot-stopper, but carved out a niche as a striker during his teenage years. That provoked Aberdeen's interest and after his youth-team cameo for the Dons he was signed as a professional and shipped off from the family home in Glasgow to start a new life in the north-east along with so many other hopefuls from the central belt. His successful loan stint with Peterhead, during which he was a prolific scorer, led to a recall to the Dons squad before his transformation from attacker to defender in the Pittodrie reserves.

He made his first-team debut under Jimmy Bonthrone in 1973 in a 2-1 win at Morton as a 17-year-old and before long was elevated to the captaincy, replacing goalkeeper Bobby Clark. It was Clark who recommended that Miller take over as skipper, being impressed by the young stopper's leadership qualities despite his tender age.

The 1976 League Cup final proved to be a landmark occasion for the player and his club. It was the first time Miller held aloft a trophy in his new role as captain, a scene that would become all too familiar for rival clubs and players throughout the 1970s and 1980s.

Even the celebration became the stuff of folklore. As recently as 2008, one keen reader of Miller's column in the *Evening Express* wrote to the newspaper to seek an explanation for the origin of the long-serving skipper's prize collection routine. The one-arm pose, with a defiant air of satisfaction etched on his face, was, it turns out, more design than accident. Miller guessed it would become a frequent sight and decided early on he needed to find his own distinct style, opting for the one-armed display in part to set him aside from football's crowd and in part to allow him to soak up the occasion and get full view of the jubilant

Red Army on the terraces surrounding him without the obstruction of a trophy in front of his face.

The interest in every piece of Miller trivia remains strong, testament to his lasting mass-market appeal. His status led to a stable career during his Dons hiatus, as he carved out a new place among Scotland's army of football analysts. It is ironic that a man who has made no secret of the fact he loathed the treatment he received by some sections of the press during his managerial dalliance sought solace on the payroll of a string of newspapers, who jostled for the right to count the Pittodrie legend as part of their team.

First The *Herald*, then the *Press and Journal* and subsequently the *Daily Mail* and Aberdeen *Evening Express* have all called upon his expert opinion. The BBC also latched on to Miller's analytical ability and, being cynical about it, his north-east appeal, to give their radio team extra breadth.

The media commitments remain, even now Miller is back on football's fast-moving train with a place on the Aberdeen board, but his preference was always to be someone on the inside making the running rather than one on the outside looking in.

Now he is back at the coal-face, earning a living with the club which made him a star throughout the trophy-laden 1970s and '80s.

At home and abroad, William Ferguson Miller MBE, as he became in the 1980s as a reward for his services to football, charged through his first two decades in the game collecting trophies at every turn. He won the League title three times, the first in 1980, with his one and only club, as well as the Scottish Cup four times and the League Cup three times. Add the European Cup Winners' Cup and the European Super Cup and the extent of the Miller family treasure trove becomes clear.

Miller has been described by Sir Alex Ferguson as "the best penalty-box defender I have ever seen", and the legendary manager has seen a few in his time. He is also not a man to lavish praise recklessly and when he pays tribute to his former Dons captain it is clear he means what he says.

Having arrived at Pittodrie as a promising young striker, it was when Miller was shifted to a defensive role that the Glaswegian hopeful really shone and he went on to become Scotland's leading defender. Yet there were flaws, as the man himself admits as he assesses the quandary which faced both Ferguson and his predecessor, Billy McNeill over whether to retain him as club captain.

Miller said: "Like Billy, Fergie was not sure if he should keep me on as captain. In his eyes I was a bit slow and poor at training." There we have it, the great man had a weakness. There was nothing he could do about his lack of pace over the turf but his lack of love for training was a self-generated glitch in the make-up. That said, it did him little harm and there's an argument for saying that the most talented players need little practice.

Other than that aversion to graft on the training field, there were not the quirks that beset so many other cult figures. Miller, now a connoisseur of fine wines, drank only once on the eve of a game and that was as a teenager while on loan in the Highland League with Peterhead. After that experience, he vowed never again. There were no tabloid scandals, no fall-outs and no on-field disgrace. He went about his business in a determined manner from beginning to end.

A playing career which began in the last game of the 1972/73 season ended after the first match of the 1990/91 campaign, when the gritty defender was forced to concede defeat in his battle against a knee injury. He had been crowned Scotland's Footballer of the Year in 1984 and won 65 caps, but at the age of 35 the legend was forced to retire to focus on his new life as a coach.

At first he served under Alex Smith, but it was only a matter of time before Miller took the helm. That happened following Smith's dismissal in 1992 and initially the results were impressive. Miller steered his side to the runners-up spot in all three domestic competitions in his first season. They finished second in the League again in 1994, but second best was never going to be enough for a man who built his reputation as a winner. So Miller the manager set about demolishing the team he had inherited and starting virtually from scratch. The project was not a success, and in 1995 he left the club, taking a sabbatical from frontline duties which lasted until his reintroduction at Pittodrie as director of football in 2004.

The experience did stand Miller in good stead in later years, hardening him to the fact that in football not every turn provides the type of glittering reward that he had become accustomed to as a player. That realisation has tempered his expectations in later life, vital in his new role at an Aberdeen Football Club which is more humble than during the glory days, and serves as a valuable reference point.

Of his downfall as manager, Miller recalled in *The Don*: "Being ordered to leave your job is a huge blow, whoever you are and whatever you do for a living. I am a confident bloke, but I did have moments of self-doubt after being dismissed. It was the worst moment in my football career. Ever. Managers will tell you that being shown the door is the only certainty when you take the job. That may be true, but nothing prepares you for the emotional turmoil when it happens. Failure ate deeply into my psyche, and though I was much too proud an individual to allow any public demonstrations of my pain, it would be some time before I came to terms with what had happened to me. I was used to winning; it had become a way of life. Now I was the fall guy. I realise in retrospect that I was chasing an impossible dream. I wanted Aberdeen to beat the Old Firm and to be transformd into the dominant team in Scottish football. But if I had been frank with myself, I would have admitted that these days vanished the minute that Alex Ferguson left for Manchester United and Rangers started to spend big under Graeme Souness. I simply cared too much, and managing Aberdeen engulfed me."

You should never go back, so the great football adage goes. In Miller's case he has flown in the face of that advice twice by moving from player to manager and then returning again to accept a place on the board. Has it diluted the affection directed his way by the supporters? Probably, yes.

The management episode did not damage him in the long term, although the shield of invincibility which had cloaked him as a player was removed when he left Pittodrie under a cloud of disappointment on that occasion. The man known as God to sections of the Dons faithful proved to be human after all.

It was the Aberdeen supporters who were so desperate to see Miller installed as manager. He was their great white hope at the time and it would have been harsh for them to have held it against him when that chapter eventually closed and the club took the decision to dispense with his services.

He remained a beloved figure for the supporters, even spearheading the Aberdeen Supporters Trust's movement against the Stewart Milne-led board at the turn of the millennium. Having God on their side gave the trust the type of kudos they required to make an impact. He gave credibility to a fledgling organisation and a sense of purpose. With the former captain and manager involved, anything was possible. A faceless organisation suddenly had the highest-profile face of all to lead the cause and a well-versed public speaker to push the manifesto.

Miller was not just a figurehead, though, a name on the headed notepaper. He had a role in the think-tank that the AFC Trust became. He was outspoken about his unhappiness with the direction the club was taking and he urged more fans and shareholders to join forces to push for change. In part that aim was met in 2002 when trust member Chris Gavin was invited to join the Pittodrie board to act as a voice for the supporters at large, but the Milne regime did not stop there. Despite his criticism of the stewardship of the club up to that point, Miller himself earned a boardroom call-up.

The acid test for many was whether he continued to wage his campaign for change once back in the inner sanctum – the truth is, it is impossible to judge. On the face of it Miller has rocked few boats since his return, perhaps understandably appreciative of his place at the table after so long in exile, but the club has progressed and the work of a director is very rarely seen in public. Those in the seats of power are best placed to judge his work in his latest Dons incarnation, and there has been no dissent from those quarters.

After Miller joined the same board he had criticised so fiercely, his new position as director of football has understandably led to occasional conflict with the support who once felt he could do no wrong. Ultimately he has become accountable for all aspects of the football operation and as such has had to learn to dodge the slings and arrows of outrageous misfortune on his latest watch, which have included humiliating knockout defeats at the hands of amateur side Queen's Park and unfancied First Division battlers Queen of the South in the Scottish Cup semi-final.

Many of those supporters now judging Miller in his executive role never saw him kick a ball in anger. Any Dons fan under the age of 25 is too young to have seen him boss games from his defensive berth and knows only Miller the coach and Miller the administrator. Even in those testing circumstances, the cult of Willie Miller has outlasted its natural life expectancy. God's appeal, it would appear, is most certainly eternal.

The imagery of the Gothenburg glory in 1983 has gone a long way to preserving that cherished status but, of course, the 50-something has also become a fashion icon along the way, courtesy of those Guevara shirts. That is something not cultivated by the man himself, but in a more traditional sense his public persona has been. Always immaculately turned out, Miller has become a media-savvy individual mainly through his work as a newspaper columnist and radio broadcaster. Those two arenas have helped reach out to a new audience and given something for the cult followers to hang their adulation on. Through his media work, Miller has never been far from the public eye.

The publication of *The Don* added some depth to the personality for those too young to have read *A Miller's Tale*, the first book to have charted the life and times of the Pittodrie legend. The new volume entered a fiercely competitive area, with sports books vying for a slice of a market which in recent years has become increasingly tough to crack.

Once upon a time football biographies were restricted to the game's big achievers, but now there is barely a week that passes without a new launch, some from names you will recognise instantly and others which will leave even the most ardent fan scratching their head and delving into the memory bank. With Miller, the latest book would provide an indication of whether his appeal had survived the passage of time – and the answer was loud and clear.

The title was unmovable from the top 1,000 on Amazon's sales ranking for months following its release, and locally was cleared from Aberdeen bookshop shelves with impressive frequency. The Amazon figure may not sound significant, until you quantify it with the fact that most similar products were ranked around the 200,000 mark on the online giant's chart just weeks after first appearing. With *The Don* out in time for Christmas in 2007, it proved to be a festive hit. Just like the T-shirts, just like the images of the famous Gothenburg trophy parade. In essence that demand vindicates Miller's place in this roll-call of *Pittodrie Idols*.

A legend, yes, but so too were figures such as Alex McLeish and Jim Leighton who accompanied him on many of the steps along the way. They are, and always will be, club greats, yet for their one-club colleague there is that extra-special bond between fan and player. He really has been there with the supporters through some incredible journeys, done all that the fans could have asked for and they, in turn, have bought the book and worn the T-shirt.

'THE BALLINGRY BAT' 1975–1984

DOUG ROUGVIE

Magic Moment: On a cold December night, Big Doug ran out at Windsor Park to earn a cherished Scotland cap and join the proud ranks of the Dark Blue Dons.

Dons Career: Games 308. Goals 21. Caps 1.

STEAK AND chips, the Incredible Hulk and Clint Eastwood – just a few of his favourite things, circa 1979. Whether in food, film or choice of stars, a glimpse back through the dusty cuttings of three decades ago reveal a recurring theme in the uncompromising defender's vox pop answers, and an indication of how he would set about the spectacular Dons career which was about to unfold in front of him. In Doug Rougvie we have a man's man, no quarter asked or given in his quest to drive Aberdeen to success at home and abroad. His passion was plain to see and it made him perhaps the club's ultimate cult hero, revered and remembered by an adoring Pittodrie public.

"People with courage and character always seem sinister to the rest."

Herman Hesse, German author

Among the Gothenburg greats there was silk and steel in equal measure. Rougvie, all 6ft 2ins of him, was most certainly in the latter camp, rugged and ready to mix it up in some of football's most hostile and testing environments. Nine times out of ten it was the towering Fifer who came out on top, as striker after striker found out to their cost and pain.

While feared by all who crossed his path on the football park, Rougvie had a split personality in the nicest possible way. To the Dons fans he was just Big Doug, somebody to love, not to loathe, and behind

Jock Hutton was built like and ox and had the heart of a lion

Benny Yorston's time with Aberdeen was packed full of incident and intrigue

Don Emery was big in character as well as physique

Tommy Pearson (right) was football's king of imagination

George Hamilton (left) and Harry Yorston celebrate

Graham Leggat scores against Airdrie at Pittodrie in 1956

Charlie Cooke in action for the Dons

The strapping figure of Henning Boel (centre) runs out in the red shirt he treasured

Zoltan Varga's quiet personality belied his devastating ability

Cup Tie McKay with the Scottish Cup he played such a major part in winning in 1970

Derek McKay and Joe Harper together again in 1995

Joe Harper scores against Celtic in the 1970 Scottish Cup final

The image of Willie Miller which has become a fashion icon after being used as a tee-shirt design

Doug Rougvie and Willie Miller celebrate the 1983 triumph in Gothenburg

Willem van der Ark with manager Alex Smith

Brian Irvine and Theo Snelders celebrate after the Scottish Cup final victory in 1990

Willem van der Ark after netting for the Dons

Duncan Shearer scores the winner in a game against Rangers in 1995

As a coach, Duncan Shearer returned to Pittodrie as assistant to Steve Paterson in 2002

Lee Richardson in full flight against Torino

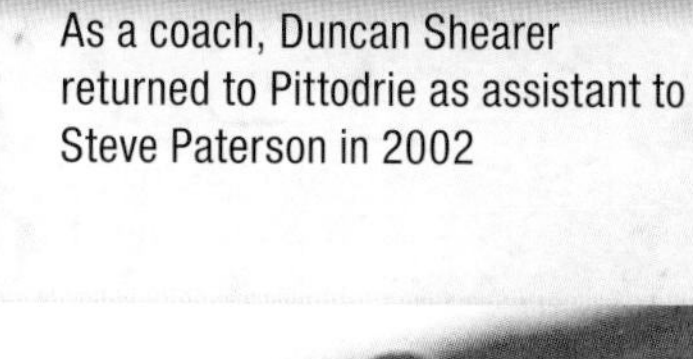

Lee Richardson became an Aberdeen icon with his wholehearted midfield performances

Lee Richardson lets off some steam through his passion for music

Ebbe Skovdahl checks into Pittodrie in 1999

Ebbe Skovdahl in a reflective mood at Pittodrie

The man dubbed 'Uncle Ebbe' by Dons fans salutes the Red Army

Hicham Zerouali's summersault celebrations became his trademark

Left: The shirt made famous by Zerouali hangs alone on the Pittodrie entrance in a tribute from a supporter following Zero's death

A banner paying tribute to Hicham Zerouali draped over the Richard Donald Stand at Pittodrie

Zander Diamond connects with the Dons supporters in typical style

Zander Diamond launches the celebration as Aberdeen go 1-0 up against Rangers allowing his boyhood heroes Celtic to win the league in 2008

the menacing on-field persona lay a gentle giant with a carefree spirit and almost childlike appeal.

It was Rougvie's refreshingly unpretentious approach to life and his profession that led to so many of the capers that have become the stuff of legend. Everyone has their favourite Big Doug story. It could be the one about the teeth and the open-top bus, or perhaps the motorbike at the training ground; maybe the fish suppers or the pre-match warm-up routine. He was a character who left a trail of anecdotes in his wake, some unbelievable yet all appear to be truth rather than urban myth.

The pearly-whites one certainly is; in fact, it was one of the last Dons adventures in Rougvie's career with the Pittodrie club. That particular tale stems from the 1984 open-top bus parade down Union Street following the Scottish Cup final win against Celtic, when the false front tooth Rougvie sported flew from his mouth and landed in the crowd below. Fortunately for him, and his dentist, the stray gnasher was handed straight back by an honest fan and he was free to flash his familiar grin for the rest of the procession. The winner of the mad scramble at street level was a schoolboy who launched it back to the top deck, only for Rougvie to let it slip from his grasp. At the second attempt it was thrown back to his grateful palm and one young Aberdonian had a story tucked away in his locker for the grandchildren in years to come.

It can be said celebrity breeds celebrity and in the case of cult hero Rougvie that certainly became true. Even his dentist became famous on the back of the tooth-overboard incident. He leapt to the player's defence in the press to hit back at the well worn "toothless grin" line that was trotted out in report after report. In fact, claimed the tooth doctor, Rougvie was a shining example of dental health and had just one missing peg due to a football accident – although the Dons star did get a public reprimand from the same dentist for his part in a cream cake advertising campaign. You can keep your multi-million pound Adidas deal; Rougvie's marketing potential was very much local and proud.

The motorbike story is far better known than the tooth one, yet still worth retelling. The familiar line is that Rougvie turned up at Pittodrie one day on a powerful bike – to the horror of manager Ferguson. The legendary hairdryer treatment was meted out as the gaffer, in his less than subtle manner, attempted to persuade his defender of the error of his ways and urge him to ditch the dangerous two-wheel transport in favour of a more traditional mode.

In fact, a month before pre-season training had begun, bringing with it the opportunity for Rougvie to show off his hot metal to his team-mates, and manager, he had given a newspaper interview proclaiming his love of his Kawasaki. Whether the manager had read it and was waiting for him, primed and ready to explode on the first day back at work, we'll probably never know. Not that Rougvie was unused to dealing with Fergie tirades. Long before David Beckham received a royal boot in the head from the king of management, the same fate almost befell the Dandies defender – except the big man had faster reactions than the ex-England skipper and managed to duck out of the way when the kit started flying.

The manager's warning was heeded, at least for a while. Rougvie is still a keen biker to this day, and Ferguson's mandate caused only a temporary halt in his motorcycle dream. Doug splashed out on a Kawasaki 200 in the summer of 1980, his reward to himself for playing a major part in that year's Premier Division title win. He invested in the machine to speed him to the Isle of Man TT races and further indulge his passion for bikes – but bowed to his manager's demand that he ditch his new toy.

It was not until he was sacked as manager of Montrose in 1992 that he dusted his leathers down and got back in the driving seat with a new bike, believing his life in football was at an end and aiming to replace the buzz he got from sport with the adrenaline-rush of biking.

His playing career was revived nine months later with Huntly, but new manager Steve Paterson was happy to let his new addition indulge his two-wheel obsession and the veteran stopper was a familiar sight at training, roaring into the car park on his bike. He would even use it as his match-day transport, chasing the Huntly team bus on the long and winding road to Inverness on one occasion after being held up at work in Aberdeen.

His appetite was almost as legendary as his choice of wheels during the height of Rougvie-mania. He strongly denied the suggestion that he regularly demolished four fish suppers on the return coach journeys from away fixtures. Three, according to the man himself, was a more accurate count.

As for the warm-up, it has become part of Dons legend. In the hostile hot-bed of Old Firm passions, Rougvie would add fuel to the flames at Parkhead and Ibrox by conducting his pre-match routine in front of the baying home fans. Unfazed by the sight of tens of thousands of Glaswegians screaming for his blood, the fearless Aberdeen star would continue to milk his exaggerated stretching session and whip the opposition fans to fever pitch before doing the same to their players minutes later. All with the familiar Rougvie grin never far from the surface.

But the likeable big man was more than just a character or a football equivalent to a court jester. He was also more than a destroyer; he was a player. It takes all kinds to make an Alex Ferguson team tick but above all it takes quality in every department and in Rougvie he had a defender who defended as though his life depended on it. He could also pass a ball when he was given the time and space to do it, something so often forgotten when the popular stopper is remembered.

His abilities were not lost on Chelsea, the team who fought tooth and nail to tempt him away from his beloved Dons in the aftermath of the Gothenburg triumph. It was just 12 months after the European Cup Winners' Cup success that the Stamford Bridge side's Scottish assistant manager Ian McNeill, deputising for manager John Neal, got his man.

McNeill, now retired after distinguished spells as chief scout for Chelsea and Leeds United, spent months watching Rougvie and admiring him from afar. As far as he is concerned, the defender is one of the game's misunderstood men. The renowned talent spotter, himself a former Dons player, told me: "Big Doug really is a gentle giant, a tremendous big fellow. He was always a softly spoken lad, which was at odds with his big frame and appearance. On the pitch he was uncompromising, totally committed, but that did not spill over into everyday life."

Rougvie's wholehearted displays for the Dons had made him hot property among the alert clubs in England, and with McNeill on the staff there was no doubt Chelsea were ahead of the game when it came to sniffing out signing opportunities. As it happens, the glowing praise the charismatic defender won from his adoring supporters helped persuade the Blues to take a closer look.

McNeill said: "When we signed Doug for Chelsea I had been away from Pittodrie for almost 30 years but I still kept in touch with what was happening at the club. I still had family in the city and knew all about the great team Alex Ferguson had put together at that time. Whenever that team was spoken about by Dons fans, Doug's name always cropped up. We soon decided he could do a job for us and it wasn't difficult to persuade him to move to London. I think he was attracted by the challenge of something new. It quickly became clear he would be great for team spirit, a really wonderful character to have at any club."

McNeill had made the same transition from Aberdeen to English football many years earlier, joining Leicester City in the 1950s when he left the Dons. He had seen enough in Rougvie to believe that the big defender could adapt quickly to the game south of the border. The stars of the game in England helped speed up the process.

The Glaswegian super-scout said: "On the pitch Doug soon found out what he would be up against. Playing at left-back, his strength was close man-to-man marking. Not many players relished going up against him in that situation. He wasn't as comfortable when players ran at him from deep and I can still remember one game against Spurs when Glenn Hoddle kept picking out their outside-right to go at Doug. They gave him a torrid time that day but he never gave up. That was the great thing about him."

Despite those stern examinations, and mixed reactions to Rougvie's style south of the border, McNeill was a convert. The player, in fact, was so good he signed him twice. He said: "When I left Chelsea to become manager at Shrewsbury Town I went back to Stamford Bridge to sign Doug for a second time. He's just the type of player every manager would like in their squad, on and off the field. I have always kept in touch with Doug and he's an absolute gem. It's no surprise that supporters always had a soft spot for him wherever he played."

The endorsement for Rougvie from McNeill carries substantial clout. Deep into his 70s, he was still in demand. He served as chief scout for Chelsea during the early days of the Roman Abramovich revolution, having filled the same role for George Graham at Leeds United. With a track record of unearthing talent such as Jimmy Floyd Hasselbaink, and prior to that the likes of Chelsea goal machine Kerry Dixon, the credentials are clear to see.

McNeill, who celebrated his 76th birthday in 2008, retired from his post as Leeds United's chief scout recently to return to his family ties in Aberdeen. Despite being born and brought up in Baillieston, McNeill retains a strong affection for the Dons. He joined the playing staff as a teenager and was a reserve player at the time of the historic first championship win in 1955. He saw at first hand the way the Pittodrie crowd warm to certain players and admits the fact that Rougvie, as a no-nonsense defender, won a place in their hearts is a remarkable achievement. McNeill continued: "During my time with Aberdeen the forwards were all big favourites with the crowd. Harry Yorston, Jimmy Delaney, George Hamilton, Archie Baird, Jackie Hather and Tommy Pearson all excited the fans. In fact, the only reason I left was because it was so difficult to get a place in the team because there were so many great players ahead of me."

Leicester City, under former Dons manager Dave Halliday, provided the way out and McNeill went on to play for Brighton before cutting his coaching teeth with Ross County and taking over as manager at Wigan on two occasions in the 1960s and '70s. The stints with Chelsea and Shrewsbury followed, leading to Rougvie's break in the English game. McNeill, whose son Ian junior is part of the current Dons scouting team, has seen players come and go during a long and distinguished career in the game but the mere mention of Big Doug is enough to bring a smile to his face and a lift in his voice. Clearly, here was a player who left a big impression wherever he roamed the turf.

Unfortunately for McNeill, Neal and successor John Hollins, Rougvie never really settled at Chelsea – but more on that later. Some players fit some clubs but not others and for Rougvie the perfect match was Aberdeen. He knew it and the supporters knew it. In fact, even while living in London he could regularly be found at the Metropolitan and South England branch of the Aberdeen Supporters Club and travelled with the exiles to Dons games when his playing commitments permitted.

The big defender's playing association with the Dons lasted 12 years in total and his commitment to the cause was the key constant throughout that distinguished period. Even in the 1970s the Aberdeen scouting network was wide and in one trawl of the east coast it came up with a prime catch among the boys club teams of the Kingdom of Fife, God's own country according to those who hail from that part of the world. Apart from divine claims, Fife is also home to some of Scotland's most rugged yet wonderful coastlines – and was the birthplace of one of Aberdeen's most rugged yet wonderful defenders. Rougvie, born in Ballingry, was a 16-year-old turning out for Dunfermline United in the juvenile leagues when he was snapped up during Jimmy Bonthrone's tenure as Aberdeen manager.

He helped to win a Scottish juvenile cup with his Dunfermline boys club as a teenager and a welcome twist of fate brought him to Pittodrie, with a tip-off from Leeds United alerting the Dons. The Yorkshire side had opted against signing one-time target Rougvie but the old-boys network led to his name being flagged up to the Dons and the rest, as they say, is history. After a loan spell with Keith in northern football, where he earned a Highland League Cup winner's medal, Rougvie was deemed ready to be unleashed on the Scottish Football League's unsuspecting forwards.

He may not have been a household name yet, but soon every attacker and every set of fans in the country would know all about the rough and tough stopper playing out of the red corner. He made his debut in a League Cup defeat against Celtic on 9 August 1975 but did not become a regular until the arrival of Alex Ferguson as manager three years later.

Ferguson, in his own playing days, was renowned as a battler and was never a character who had endeared himself to the opposition or their followers. As a manager he has maintained those characteristics and maybe, just maybe, he saw something of himself in Rougvie.

The stopper was comfortable in the esteemed company he kept during the glory days in the Granite City. On top of that he had an infectious enthusiasm for the game, a spirit which saw him play on into his twilight years on the public parks of Aberdeen in the amateur leagues. No crowds, no money, but still the same old commitment and attitude – it's hard to imagine any of the Real Madrid stars he helped to conquer in 1983 turning out in the Spanish equivalent, more is the pity.

He had opportunities to leave the Dons during his 12-year tour of duty, with Falkirk and Middlesbrough among the suitors in the late 1970s and early '80s, but first Ally MacLeod and then Alex Ferguson rebuffed all approaches. He could have kicked and stamped his feet to force the hand of the management and force a move, but Rougvie was comfortable in the red shirt he filled with such distinction. There was no need to look elsewhere for success, with a steady stream of honours falling into his path at Pittodrie. First was the Premier Division title in 1980 and then came a hat-trick of Scottish Cup triumphs in consecutive finals from 1982. Add the 1983 continental double, with the European Cup Winners' Cup joined by the European Super Cup in that memorable period, as well as the league title in 1984, and the happy picture becomes clear.

Unfortunately for Rougvie and the supporters, that glory did not bring riches. While the famous faces of 1983 helped create history they did not return from Gothenburg to streets paved with gold and had to battle to try and win the rewards their status as kings of Europe could be expected to merit. The Dons, in keeping with the city's reputation for thriftiness, were a well-oiled machine on and off the park. In the season that Real Madrid were well and truly humbled, the club reported a profit of £200,000. It stayed in the black by sticking to a rigid wage structure, and only a chosen few broke through the £30,000 per year salary ceiling. According to official records the lucky number earning that magic figure was, in fact, just two, and it is safe to assume the manager was one of those. The rest had to make do with what they were offered and when Rougvie came to renew his contract in the summer of 1984 he found the deal on the table simply did not reflect his achievements on the park.

He had been capped by Scotland in the final month of 1983, called upon by Jock Stein for a trip to face Northern Ireland in Belfast. The news was greeted by praise from his club manager, with Ferguson claiming: "We're all absolutely delighted for the big lad. I know that he won't let himself, the club or his country down. He has an appetite for football and an attitude to the game which many other players could well copy."

It proved to be Rougvie's one and only cap but there was no way the Aberdeen board and management team could have known that as they prepared the package they hoped would persuade the 27-year-old that his future lay in the north-east. With a heavy heart he decided to take his talents elsewhere. Chelsea offered the security of an attractive four-year contract and backed their belief in the player by stumping up a £250,000 transfer fee to ensure he made the switch to Stamford Bridge. The player said at the time: "After 12 years at Pittodrie it was obviously a difficult decision to leave. I have built up a good relationship with the fans and will miss them, but I've got my own life to lead and I am positive I have made the correct decision."

As well as being the master of out-muscling opponents, Rougvie was also the master of understatement. His rapport with the supporters was far superior to "good", it was fantastic. Even today he is the first name on the lips of the bulk of Dons fans when the cult-hero debate crops up periodically.

The "Ballingry Bat" and Aberdeen fitted like a hand in a glove and it was difficult to replicate that elsewhere. He made 74 appearances for Chelsea before, in 1987, he was off on a whirlwind tour of the English divisions, turning out 35 times for Brighton, 21 times for Shrewsbury and 18 times for Fulham.

In 1989 he was back on the road north to join Dunfermline and a year later he linked up with old Dons mate Chic McLelland as the duo took charge of Montrose, leading the Angus side to promotion to the First Division in 1991. He went on to savour Highland League title success as manager of Huntly and took charge of northern rivals Cove before retiring from the game.

Rougvie had the type of personality that supporters just could not ignore and his wholehearted approach to the game won him friends on both sides of the border. He made his first appearance in the blue of Chelsea against the stars of Arsenal in 1984 – and introduced himself by dumping England international Viv Anderson to the turf with a clatter that brought adoring cheers from the intrigued new audience. His fierce tackling convinced the notoriously tough Chelsea crowd that he was one of them, although referees did not always embrace the Rougvie way with the same warmth. Against Wimbledon he was once red-carded within 15 minutes of kick-off after twice crunching into John Fashanu.

It was not all a bed of roses in London and the burly Scot, hindered by a facial injury following a clash with fellow tartan crusader Joe Jordan in a game against Southampton, drifted in and out of the team before finally being ousted by the emerging talent of Tony Dorigo. Rougvie was not every Chelsea fan's cup of tea and he often divided opinion, but for sections of Stamford Bridge he became a hero and collected a clutch of man-of-the-match awards along the way.

Even at Dunfermline, in his short spell with the Pars, he became a cult figure. It was not because of a conscious effort to ingratiate himself with the supporters, it just kept happening for the man who epitomised everything that is great about football's ability to embrace every shape, size and style of player known to man. The most precious thing for the fans was the fact that Rougvie had heart. He cared about his team, his supporters and about his own professional pride. He wasn't the type to forget what had gone before, there was never a hope of him leaving his work at the office.

Aberdeen's fierce rivalry with Rangers has become part and parcel of Scottish football in modern times. Many will indicate the clash between Neil Simpson and Ian Durrant in the 1980s as the point at which the atmosphere between the two clubs became bitter, but the seeds were sown far earlier than that, with Rougvie's involvement in the 1979 League Cup final a key moment in cranking up the strong feeling amongst players and supporters alike.

The Aberdeen defender gained the unwanted distinction of becoming the first player ever to be red-carded in the final of the competition, the sending-off coming as the result of a brush with Rangers forward Derek Johnstone in the box. The alleged perpetrator and his team-mates were adamant Johnstone had taken a dive but the referee waved away the protests.

After that the grudge remained stolid, both on the terraces and in the dressing room. Even when Rougvie teamed up with Johnstone at Chelsea the Dons man kept his distance. He said at the time: "We've got an understanding – I don't like him and he doesn't like me. We both know, and it isn't going to change. Some people I know have said I should live and let live and in many ways it is water on the bridge. But there's no love lost and he knows how I feel about it. I don't go out of my way to avoid him but we're never going to be buddies. Some things are just too serious."

Certainly Johnstone's dramatic fall to earth in the final, which Rangers went on to win 2-1, caused a storm. Rougvie, goalkeeper Bobby Clark and forward Joe Harper were all summoned to the Scottish Football Association's headquarters in Glasgow to explain their public criticism of the opposition forward. In keeping with the siege mentality approach he so loved to foster, Alex Ferguson refused his players permission to attend before eventually relenting.

Rougvie became no stranger to disciplinary action, being the subject of several bans during his lengthy playing career. It led him to deduce: "I know I'm a target for opposing fans and I appear to be a target for referees as well. As soon as I go into a tackle I'm half expecting to be pulled up for it. I have to restrain my game – but there is no way I can turn over a new leaf or completely change my ways."

He and his family laughed off the hard-man accusations, with his wife praising her husband's easy-going nature. The player himself claimed the fearsome reputation was unfounded and could be traced back to a simple trait: "I like to win."

In one 1980s confessional, Rougvie explained: "At 6ft 2ins and weighing in at 14 stone, I know I am one of the biggest blokes around in Scottish football. It is true that I am a strong player. But I don't regard myself as one of the muscle-men playing in the Premier Division. I'm not a dirty player, but I could name a player or two who know all the underhand tricks of the trade and they are not afraid to use them week after week. I always go out on to the park to give nothing less than 100 per cent effort and commitment. I try to win the ball as often as I can, but I have never at any time attempted to injure an opponent. Unfortunately, some referees take the view that I win the ball unfairly, and this is what leads to fouls going against us and bookings for me. No matter where I go I seem to have the reputation of being something of a hard man. Nonsense. When I'm in the Aberdeen team I'm there to do the job of winning the ball at the back. That's what I'm best at and that's what I'm paid to do. I'll just have to accept that some referees and Doug Rougvie will continue to take different opinions."

It was not just in games that the defender was uncompromising; he adopted the same approach in training. When the Aberdeen physiotherapist suggested cycling would help ease Achilles tendon troubles, he responded by cycling to and from training every day and even made the long trip in the saddle to a family holiday in Ballater. Presumably the more sedate pedal variety was an acceptable way of getting from A to B as far as the Gaffer was concerned.

Doug Rougvie would go to any length to play the game he loved, and in return the game loved him back. You can keep your nouvelle-cuisine type of player; fans will settle for a steak-and-chips character every day of the week.

'BIG BRIAN' 1985–1997

BRIAN IRVINE

Magic Moment: Hampden was jumping, nerves were jangling, Irvine was cool and Bonner was stranded. The Scottish Cup had witnessed its first final settled by penalties and the Dons defender ensured the silverware nestled in the Pittodrie cabinet.

Dons Career: Games 384. Goals 40. Caps 9.

SCOTTISH FOOTBALL grounds have never been renowned as hotbeds of social diversity and free thinking. Anyone daring to be different runs the risk of being ostracised, or at the very least marginalised, and it takes courage to make a conscious decision to stand out from the crowd.

Brian Irvine did that when he spoke freely about his faith in an arena in which religion, on the back of more than a century of Old Firm conflict, had become a dirty word. Irvine cut through that and made it acceptable to mix faith with sport without prejudice, without preconceptions and crucially without ridicule. There may have been the occasional raised eyebrow or furrowed brow from within the decidedly industrial world of football, yet the big Dons defender won nothing but respect for his principled approach to life and his love of the game.

> "Courage is contagious. When a brave man takes a stand, the spines of others are often stiffened."
>
> **Billy Graham, evangelist**

He is the only player to have performed to a packed Pittodrie both as a player and as a preacher, having addressed the 14,000 crowd for the Aberdeen leg of American evangelist Billy Graham's crusade in Britain in 1991 with a reading in which he spoke of the moment he found God, describing it as the "best and most important decision" he ever made.

That devotion to his faith became an accepted part of Pittodrie life as Irvine worked his way into the fabric of the club and its support. He did not have the killer instinct of Doug Rougvie, nor the tricks and flicks of Charlie Cooke; he did not boast the scoring touch of Joe Harper or the exhibitionist streak of Hicham Zerouali. No, what Irvine had above all else was soul.

The sight of the towering figure of a man being held aloft by Theo Snelders at the end of the 1990 Scottish Cup final, fists clenched and held tight to his face as if to hold back the tears, only served to reinforce his status as a cult hero. Here was a player so passionate about the Dons cause that he was willing to bear his rawest emotions in front of tens of thousands at Hampden and countless other armchair fans. The celebrations were not those of a hollow badge-kisser, they were the outpourings of an individual who had just fulfilled his childhood dream. For every one of the Red Army who had ever lain awake at night fantasising about scoring the winner for their team in a cup final, there was an electrifying moment of synergy. There and then, with one fell swoop of his right boot, Irvine played out that dream for his and their entertainment.

Of course, it was no ordinary winning goal; it was the most dramatic there had ever been in the competition up to that point. When Irvine became the first man ever to score the winning penalty in a Scottish Cup final shoot-out, he earned a piece of football trivia that will forever be his own, but it was the reaction as much as the act which meant so much more to the assembled admirers.

The spectacle had not been devoid of drama prior to Irvine's decisive intervention. Charlie Nicholas, playing his last game in Aberdeen colours before moving back to Cup opponents Celtic, had put his Hoops loyalties to one side to convert his penalty with admirable professionalism and coolness. Kick after kick flew into the back of the net but something had to give and it did. Snelders, another cult-hero contender with his booming shouts which echoed around Pittodrie almost as noisily as the chants of "Theo, Theo", had set Irvine up for the biggest moment of his football life by saving Celtic defender Anton Rogan's effort to tie the shoot-out at 8-8.

It presented Irvine with his moment – score and his side won the match, miss and the Hoops were right back in it. He made the long walk forward to the penalty spot in silence, not a single team-mate dared to break the tension which had enveloped both sets of players amidst the bedlam of the national stadium on Cup final day. Pat Bonner was the goalkeeper facing Irvine, a man who would become a penalty shoot-out hero in his own right at the Italia '90 World Cup just weeks later. It was the ultimate test of wills and it was the Irishman who cracked first, shaping to dive to his right-hand post and giving Irvine a split-second opportunity to side-step his shot into the opposite corner of the goal. With the aplomb of a seasoned striker, Irvine stroked home the winner and sparked unbridled celebrations amongst the Dons squad and the supporters who had held their breath from behind the goal as he had prepared for his moment of destiny.

Almost two decades on from the toughest of character assessments, Irvine still beams with pride as he recalls the moment he became a fully fledged Dons hero. He said: "It was a unique moment for me, and having been an Aberdeen supporter since I was a boy, it was extra-special. Although I was brought up in Glasgow, among Rangers and Celtic fans, I always followed the Dons because my family's roots were in the north-east. To have the chance to score the penalty which would win the Scottish Cup was special.

"I was far from first choice for taking penalties – only the goalkeepers were left after me. The shoot-out went on and on until Anton Rogan stepped up to take his. At that point Theo Snelders roused the Aberdeen supporters behind the goal and made it difficult for Anton, who still struck a good penalty but saw Theo pull off a magnificent save. The walk from the halfway line to the penalty spot went quickly for me – I was in a no-lose situation really. If I scored then we won the Cup, if I missed then it was still level at 8-8. There was less pressure on me than those who had gone before me. I never had a good record with penalties when I was at school and in senior football I only ever took one – to decide the final. I never took one before or after that game. The feeling I experienced when the ball hit the back of the net, and the noise from the fans behind the goal, will live with me forever."

He was calmness personified as he strode up to place the ball on the spot and he later revealed that his church links had a big part to play in his approach to the most highly charged moment in his career. At times the media obsession with his faith irked Irvine, particularly when some headlines screamed that God had helped him convert the penalty. He soon set the record straight, insisting: "I never said that. On the Friday night before the game I received a message from one of my friends from the church I attend in Aberdeen. It read: 'Remember, you will never walk alone.' When I walked up to take my penalty I couldn't get those words out of my head. I told that to a reporter – and ended up with all those embarrassing God headlines. I was genuine when I said those words took all the pressure off me in the shoot-out."

Despite his occasional annoyance at the way his faith was handled in the football world, Irvine had the game to thank for his spiritual awakening. As unlikely as it may sound, it was a discussion about the meaning of life with Falkirk team-mates in 1985 that led him back to the Bible, having drifted away from religion after being brought up as a Church of Scotland member. He even turned to his family's minister for advice when it was time to move on from the Bairns. After moving to the north-east, Irvine and his wife Donna became members of the independent evangelical church of the Deeside Christian Fellowship, and his involvement grew and grew.

He told me: "I found that the Aberdeen fans supported me and my faith. It was great to have that because it is not very common in football for players to be open about their beliefs. To be honest, I don't know why it happened the way it did for me at Aberdeen. All I know is that I appreciated it and still do."

Irvine was one of the lucky ones in football. His faith was accepted at Pittodrie, unlike other professionals in Britain.

The highest-profile example was Alan Comfort at Cambridge United, who was ordered to leave the club after admitting he put God before his manager, Chris Turner. Comfort went on to be ordained as an Anglican minister. Chelsea star Gavin Peacock was another who encountered problems, with constant challenges to his faith from team-mates and managers.

Irvine was careful not to ram his faith down the throats of his team-mates, particularly conscious of keeping a low profile in the immediate aftermath of his arrival in the 1980s as he set about turning dreams into reality. Although he grew up in the central belt, his parents hailed from Inverurie and he was brought up as a staunch Dons supporter. His father's work as a policeman had taken the family south in the 1960s but they never forgot their Aberdeenshire roots.

It was in the summer of 1985 that Irvine got the chance to join his boyhood heroes. Sir Alex Ferguson agreed an £80,000 fee with Falkirk to spike Charlton's guns as the English club prepared their own bid. Irvine, who had starred for Scotland in a four-nation semi-professional tournament just a month earlier, had also been targeted by Nottingham Forest, but his heart was with the Dons. He jumped at the opportunity to sign for Ferguson, serving his notice to end his career as a bank clerk and move into full-time football. Prophetically the 20-year-old new recruit said: "I know I have been signed as a long-term prospect but I believe I am joining the best team in Scotland and I am willing to wait. I know I'll have to be patient, especially as Aberdeen have the likes of Willie Miller, Alex McLeish and Neale Cooper in central defence. I'm sure my time will come."

He lodged with his aunt and uncle in Kintore, and would make the cycle ride to Kemnay each day to catch a bus into Aberdeen for training. It was all part of an adventure which would lead him in directions nobody could have predicted. He first appeared for the first team in a 6-0 win at Clydebank late in the 1985/86 season, offering the travelling supporters the first chance to catch a glimpse of the powerfully built central defender who had caught Ferguson's eye.

Irvine went on to deputise at the heart of the back four almost 100 times over the next four seasons before finally establishing himself as a first choice in 1990/91. By then he had his first medal in the bag after appearing as a substitute in the 2-1 League Cup final win against Rangers in 1989.

Cup finals were not all a bed of roses for the stopper. He was dropped from the team for the 1992 League Cup final, then in the 1993 Scottish Cup showdown with Rangers one slip proved costly and led to the Ibrox side taking the lead in the Celtic Park match against the Dons before going on to collect the trophy with a 2-1 win. Irvine was inconsolable, left in a daze. He said at the time: "I have never been so down after a game. I can't even remember going up to collect my runners-up medal. I felt so down for the manager, the rest of the team – but especially for our supporters – that I didn't want to lift my head. I wasn't feeling sorry for myself. I just felt so bad because I thought I had let everyone down."

He was picked back up by Scotland manager Andy Roxburgh, who immediately announced Irvine would get a quick chance to bounce back by winning his third cap in the World Cup qualifier against Estonia at Pittodrie days later. Roxburgh hinted that he saw Irvine as the natural successor to Richard Gough, who had controversially announced his decision to quit the international scene.

By the mid-1990s Irvine was coming into his own, established as a Scotland player and a regular winner at Aberdeen supporters' club player-of-the-year functions as his reputation and popularity soared. Then in July 1995 he rocked the Scottish game when he read a short statement to the media who had gathered at Pittodrie for the most unexpected of news. The defender announced the problem which had kept him out of pre-season training, which up to that point had been described by the club as a back injury, was in fact multiple sclerosis. It sparked a media frenzy, with prophets of doom openly predicting the end of Irvine's career and preparing for the degenerative condition to take hold of his life. It didn't, though. Irvine stayed strong, buoyed by his strong faith, and focused on getting better. Doctors had assured the Scotland international that he had a mild form of the disease and that a full recovery was possible but many feared the worst.

Not for the first or last time, Irvine defied the odds and did indeed battle back to full fitness. In the low moments he consoled himself with the fact he had a loving wife and two healthy daughters behind him, figuring that nobody had any guarantee that they would breeze through life without illness. Being a footballer did not make him immune from life's pitfalls and he was more interested in looking to the future than dwelling on the diagnosis which had been broken to him at Aberdeen Royal Infirmary seven weeks prior to the public confirmation. For the conscientious Christian, one of the hardest parts of the whole episode was not dealing with the potential impact of the disease, but in concealing the truth behind his absence from frontline duty.

Once it was out in the open there was a sense of relief and a push to return to first-team action, with the full support of a club who had been rocked by the troubles of one of their most committed and well-liked members of staff. Chairman Ian Donald said: "Brian recently signed a two-year contract with the club as a player. We are looking for him to honour that and hopefully beyond. The main thing on everyone at the club's minds at the moment is seeing Brian back in the fold with the first team. He has already been assured the club will back him all the way. Brian and the club have been told he will be able to resume playing for us in the same fine manner he has for the last ten years."

His fellow worshippers at his Deeside church also provided a vital support network during the most testing of times. Irvine was quick to pay tribute and said at the time: "I doubt if I would have been able to cope without my faith. It was make-or-break time in my career and knowing all the Aberdeen fans were 100 per cent behind me was a tremendous comfort. But the practical support I received from my Christian friends was the single most important thing in the most difficult days. I also received hundreds of letters from fellow Christians saying they were praying for me. I was overwhelmed by it all. It didn't take me long to get physically fit again, training with Aberdeen, but the mental and spiritual fitness – which is just as important – was knocked back on the right road by my Christian friends. After that, the Dons fans took over and swept me along the road until I was fit enough to return to playing at the top level."

The process had been another galvanising moment in Irvine's far from standard career. His already devoted followers in the Pittodrie crowd became even more protective, willing him on in his fight back to full fitness. And he made it, even walking the gruelling 95-mile West Highland Way the following summer to raise funds for the Multiple Sclerosis Society.

Irvine had made his playing comeback in October 1995, playing in front of a 1,000 crowd in a friendly against Ross County to mark the opening of the East Stand at the Dingwall club's ground, and scoring to cap the occasion. He dedicated the event to the scores of supporters from across Britain who had written letters of support during his recovery period. His competitive return came in December and his introduction as a substitute in the 56th minute led to an emotional standing ovation from the 8,500 crowd. The comeback was short-lived, with floodlight failure just a minute later leading to the game against Kilmarnock being abandoned with the scores locked at 1-1.

Irvine saw off the challenge of John Inglis, the man who had been bought by Willie Miller to replace him, and signed a new two-year contract at the end of the 1994/95 season. He candidly revealed his negotiating strategy as the new deal was announced, admitting: "As long as Aberdeen offer me contracts I will sign them. I have never haggled over how much money I should receive. Roy Aitken told me how much the club could afford and I accepted it."

Part of his reward was a testimonial against Wimbledon in 1997, a mark of his loyal service to the club over 12 years and an event which brought 9,000 fans through the turnstiles to pay their own tribute. The match was a time for reflection, with the great and good of the game coming out to share their thoughts on the merits of Big Brian.

Alex Ferguson simply said: "Brian is a worthy successor to the all-time greats, like Willie Miller and Alex McLeish, and he has served the club magnificently" while manager Roy Aitken described him as "one of the club's true heroes". Former boss Alex Smith added: "He was one player I could always depend on to give me everything he had. Brian really does take pride from pulling on an Aberdeen shirt and would do almost anything to help the club win a match."

There was more than a grain of truth in what Smith had to say. In one game under his charge, Irvine volunteered to take over from Theo Snelders in goal following the keeper's red card against Hibs at Easter Road in November 1991. Irvine saved a penalty, but could not prevent the Hibees from emerging with maximum points.

Alex McLeish echoed the sentiments of the men who had coached the big defender, harking back to the dark days when the club flirted with relegation in the 1994/95 season. McLeish said: "What he did during that relegation fight should be treated as highly as all the successes Willie Miller and I had in our day. It was a time when the club needed men who were willing to fight in the trenches to get out of trouble. Brian was the biggest battler of them all and played a big part in pulling Aberdeen back from the brink of disaster."

One-time Aberdeen team-mate Robert Connor joined in the testimonial tributes, recalling: "I once heard a football manager say that being a winner has nothing to do with winning and losing. A winner is a guy who gives his all every time he steps out on to the pitch. Speaking as a fellow professional, I have to say Brian Irvine is the embodiment of that sentiment. But speaking on a more personal level, I would just say he is a big dumpling." That tongue-in-cheek comment from Connor actually mirrored the serious views of many Dons fans when the 6ft 2in defender from Falkirk first appeared on the scene. Over time he won them over with his honesty and devotion to the cause, with several episodes bridging the gap which once existed between Irvine and the club's fans.

In a frank and revealing interview in 1996, when his recovery from MS had been completed with a string of outstanding displays, he admitted: "The Aberdeen supporters have played a massive part. They have helped me build up the strongest bond any player will ever have with the followers of a club. That bond is now far more valuable to me than any of the medals I have won as a player – or may win in the future. Their support and encouragement has not only helped get my career back on line, it has helped me get my whole life back on line. The fans have even made the warm-up before our matches a memorable experience. In the past it would be fair to say I was pretty much left to get on with that. Now the fans are shouting almost non-stop encouragement and wishing me all the best.

"That wasn't always the case. When I first started to play for the club it was hard to be accepted by the Dons fans because they had such an excellent relationship with Willie Miller and Alex McLeish. Those two great servants to the club were far better players than I will ever be. I think the fans found it hard to accept anyone stepping into their boots. Things began to change when I scored the winning penalty in the 1990 Scottish Cup final. I think the fans took to me a wee bit more last season because it was obvious I was feeling just as bad as they were about Aberdeen having to fight against relegation. My illness problems since then have helped cement something between us that is unlikely to be seen again. The fans and I have been through a lot together. No matter what may lie ahead for me, I will always cherish the fact they were willing to give me help when I needed it most."

Irvine was quite right to highlight the difficulty he faced in succeeding the formidable McLeish and Miller. McLeish himself had alluded to the same thing and for any player it would have been a daunting task, whether he had cost £80,000 or £800,000. It was a thankless job but fortunately one which fell to possibly the most modest and level-headed player ever to call Pittodrie home.

It was Miller's knee injury late in 1989 which finally opened the door for Irvine and led to him becoming established in his own right after a patient wait in the wings. He had become accustomed to playing the third-man role, deputising for either McLeish or Miller when the need arose, but stepped forward from the shadows effortlessly when it became clear the legendary skipper's days were numbered.

In September 1990 he won his first international cap, playing alongside McLeish in the opening qualifying match for Euro '92 against Romania at Hampden. His call-up for the 2-1 win cost Aberdeen £30,000 due to a clause in the deal which took Irvine from Falkirk five years earlier, but the Dons were happy to pay the Bairns the money as one of the club's favourite sons continued his rise to the top. A total of nine caps went his way between that first appearance and his last international game, under Craig Brown in a 3-1 defeat at the hands of Holland in 1994.

For the next seven years he became a key man for the Dons, his time with the club ending in the summer of 1997 when he was handed a free transfer by Roy Aitken. There were plenty of takers but he opted to make the short hop to Dundee to play a part in the Dens Park side's bid for the First Division title. He made 79 appearances for Dundee before joining Ross County in 1999. With the Dingwall side he turned out 143 times, finally retiring in 2003 – a full eight years after some had written him off following the MS diagnosis. He was almost 38 when he moved on to the County coaching staff and went on to manage Elgin City in his own right, steering the Borough Briggs side to the brink of the Third Division play-offs in 2006 with a fifth-place place finish, which remains their highest ever in the Scottish Football League.

Since then he has concentrated on his role as a match summariser with BBC Radio Scotland, covering Caley Thistle and Aberdeen games, as well as his work outside the game, which includes a role with Inverness organisation Youth Inclusive, a church-led community group reaching out to Highland teenagers. In between juggling those commitments the big man still finds time for his dose of frontline action, jetting off to the US each summer in recent years to assist with the coaching of the fledgling United Soccer Leagues side Cleveland City Stars. The role in part stems from the affection which every Dons fan has for Irvine, as he revealed: "Martin Rennie, the head coach at Cleveland, is from Falkirk originally, like myself, but he is also a Dons fan and I met him many years ago through that link. We also have a mutual contact in Richie Huxford, who assisted me at Elgin City. Richie put Martin and me back in touch and it has all gone from there. I've enjoyed the opportunity to experience football in the States. It is difficult to match the adrenaline rush of being directly involved with a team and working with the City Stars players has been a breath of fresh air."

In 2008 the Stars won the Second Division championship in a title play-off match, emerging victorious in a three-goal thriller. The continent may be different, but the man from Bellshill is proving that the winning habit is difficult to shake.

'THE ARK' 1989–1992

WILLEM VAN DER ARK

Magic Moment: Van der Ark to Nicholas to Mason – goal. Willem played a lead role in the 1989 League Cup triumph and sent himself into the Aberdeen history books as a Dons winner.

Dons Career: Games 77. Goals 17.

BIG NAME, big man, big hero. Willem van der Ark was as far removed from the traditional Dons shooting stars as you could possibly imagine, but somehow he just fitted, arriving in the right place at the right time and weaving a permanent place in the rich and colourful tapestry of *Pittodrie Idols*.

"You can stand tall without standing on someone. You can be a victor without having victims."

Harriet Woods, American politician

From Paddy Buckley to Joe Harper, Pittodrie has been graced by more than its fair share of busy little forwards who thrived on balls into the box. What the old ground has rarely seen is a traditional target man, the big one to sit alongside the succession of little ones.

In van der Ark there was every reason to suspect that was about to change. At 6ft 5in tall he had the frame to play that role, but the towering Dutchman was far more difficult to pigeon-hole than his distinctive frame would suggest. Anyone who had the good fortune to see "The Ark" play will testify that aerial ability was not what his game was about. In fact, at times it looked as though he got smaller when he jumped.

In keeping with his country of origin, he was a player who preferred passes in to feet rather than back-to-front high balls. Which was just as well, because he came into a Dons team which liked to play the game the right way and was blessed with creative talents in midfield, such as Jim Bett and Paul Mason.

With the benefit of glorious hindsight, it was a golden era for the club under the wily management of Alex Smith. Van der Ark arrived in the early weeks of 1989 at a time when the Dons were pushing dominant Rangers in every competition season after season.

Not only that, but the side was packed with character and much of it was imported. Aside from the beanpole focal point of van der Ark there was the rest of the Dutch contingent in and around the same period, led by star striker Hans Gillhaus and also featuring the cultured skills of Theo Ten Caat and the more pragmatic Peter van de Ven.

Gillhaus should have been the cult hero among that batch. He was the big name, a Dutch international who had been compared to his former PSV Eindhoven team-mate Romario. It was Gillhaus who was by far the most dramatic, scoring 31 often spectacular goals in 94 appearances, yet there was something alluring about the ungainly figure of van der Ark. Gillhaus was clinical on the pitch, perhaps too clinical. He did not have the chink in the armour that the best cult heroes display, while his compatriot did, mainly his failure to take full advantage of his height and refusal to bully defenders in the way his physical presence would have allowed him too.

Van der Ark was far too nice for that, an all-round good guy. The Dons fans did not hold that against him, how could they? Instead they took to him and lavished him with the type of praise and sentiments that so many of the overseas players who landed in Aberdeen received. Manchester United supporters made the "Ooh Ah Cantona" chant famous. Less well-known was the "Ooh Ah van der Ark" ditty favoured by their Dons counterparts years previously, or "Oops Up van der Ark" depending on which section of the ground you sat in.

Just like Jock Hutton more than seven decades earlier, appearance was a major factor in van der Ark's instant appeal. While Hutton was a stout and stocky figure, the Groningen-born forward was the polar opposite and tipped the scales at just 13st 2lb, despite his great height.

His brother Albert was an international basketball player, befitting the family stature, but for Willem it was football all the way. In between shooting hoops with his brother, he spent hours honing his soccer ability, particularly practising his heading skills. For that, Dons fans can be thankful, having had their lives lit up, albeit in unconventional style, for a brief period by the quirky attacker. Not that van der Ark was devoid of talent. He propelled himself to the fringes of Dutch recognition, earning a B cap in a team which included household names such as Ed de Goey, Aaron Winter and Robert Witschge.

If van der Ark had been Mr Average and waltzed into Pittodrie at 5ft 10in, there's every chance he would be a distant memory by now, just as the likes of Peter van de Ven have become. We all remember him because of his stature, just as we remember football's army of other sky-scraping stars. Take Jermain Defoe as a perfect example. Defoe has matched Peter Crouch virtually cap for cap with England but he's unlikely ever to have the same recognition and all because he surrenders a whole foot in height to him.

Crouch is the most famous of football's lanky legion and more analysed than any other of the lofty lot. Graham Taylor made a wonderful observation about Crouch that will ring true with any Aberdeen supporter who watched van der Ark in his prime. Taylor pointed out that Crouch and his fellow tall players were not naturally good in the air because as youngsters they did not have to work at it, they stood head and shoulders above every other teenager on the field and didn't have to even lift a foot off the ground to dominate. The former England manager argued that when players of that ilk stepped up to the man's game they struggled to adapt because their spine and upper body was not tuned to jump or able to compete with the more physical defenders they faced. And he might just have a point, certainly in the case of Aberdeen's towering talisman.

Taylor, of course, had his own experience of that particular breed of player, having leaned heavily on the midfield presence of Carlton Palmer during his England reign. Palmer, at 6ft 3in, looked more suited to a basketball court than the football field, with his rangy stride, but he did collect 18 caps and held his own among more conventional company. It was in the same era as Stockport County's player of the century Kevin Francis, who wreaked havoc in the English game thanks to his 6ft 7in rig.

In comparison to some of the giants patrolling the world's football fields, van der Ark was just an ankle-biter. Nikola Zigic leads the way at at 6ft 10in, depending which report you read. Officially he is marked down at 6ft 7.5in – and that half an inch sets him apart from Czech dangerman Jan Koller, perhaps world football's best-known great oak. Funnily enough, Koller began his career as a goalkeeper before a quick-witted coach spotted the potential of sticking him at the other end of the park to terrorise defences across the globe. Koller did return between the sticks in one Bundesliga match for Borussia Dortmund when Jens Lehmann was red-carded against Bayern Munich – he shut out the red machine and was voted the League's best keeper that week.

But it is as a striker that Koller excelled, amid an eclectic bunch. What so many share is as much, if not greater, ability on the deck as they display in the air. Yes, the physical attributes make them awkward customers, but none are entirely prolific with their heads. Portsmouth's FA Cup hero Kanu, with his tricks and flicks, is 6ft 5in tall but he has the close control you might associate with a winger a foot closer to the ground. Emmanuel Adebayor is just two inches smaller than Kanu but it's his deadly ability with the ball at his feet that makes him one of the most feared forwards of his generation, not dominance in the air.

Scotland, let alone Aberdeen, has not had a wealth of extraordinarily tall players to keep supporters intrigued and entertained in equal measure. Pierre van Hooijdonk at Celtic, and more importantly at 6ft 4in, was one, and there's no doubting the impact he made on the top flight.

Kevin James, most recently galloping around the park at St Johnstone, registers 6ft 7in on the height chart, but has endured a career plagued by injuries which must surely be traced back to beanpole physique, a parallel which can be drawn with van der Ark. Derek Townsley, of Motherwell fame, matched James inch for inch but the home-grown variety never quite managed the overseas version when it came to mass appeal.

Just as Aberdeen fans of a certain vintage recall van der Ark's antics with fondess, Dundee United's followers from the late 1990s will remember vividly Joaquim Ferraz. He came from Portugal, mustered all of 15 League starts but became a cult hero for a short but memorable period thanks to his 6ft 7in frame and knack of scoring against bitter city rivals and neighbours Dundee. Twice in consecutive Tayside derbies against the Dark Blues, he popped up with a last-minute winner as the Dens Park defence struggled to get to grips with him. Then his form faded and within a year he was off, back home to Maritimo.

There is undoubtedly something instantly appealing about football's big men, not least a sense of vulnerability. For one thing, there's no place to hide when you are literally head and shoulders above the rest.

For managers too there's a pull towards the ultimate target man. Jimmy Calderwood is the most recent Aberdeen coach to try and nurture one of the high-and-mighty brigade, shipping Dyron Daal across from the Netherlands in 2006. Daal had the makings of a van der Ark Mark II but never quite lived up to the promise. He was signed on an amateur contract, and his ability did not quite measure up in the way his body did. At 6ft 4in he should have been a handy option for Calderwood, but after just one SPL start and six cameos from the bench he was sent out on loan to Dundee and later went on to St Johnstone before winding his way back to Holland and then on to Ross County. Five goals in seven league appearances for the Dark Blues did propel him to the verge of cult status in the city of jute, jam and journalism, but his place was taken by Jan Zemlik – all 6ft 7in and 15 stone of him. Alex Rae is another of the managerial mafia to have been wooed by the promise and potential of a cloud-bursting striker.

Much earlier, Alex Smith fell under the same spell. It cost him a fee of £280,000 to secure his extra attacking dimension, van der Ark, from

Willem II. His best period was as part of a three-pronged attack, sandwiched between the more subtle talents of Eoin Jess and Charlie Nicholas in a clever piece of managerial design orchestrated by a coach who resisted the obvious temptation of using his most imposing player as a one-man frontline. Just as Peter Crouch works best hunting as part of a pack, so did Aberdeen's earlier equivalent.

Between his arrival at the start of 1989 and his last game in 1991, van der Ark mustered 77 games and 17 goals. His contribution was hindered by injury, which sidelined him for a ten-month spell, but the modest statistics mask the impact the Dutchman made during his brief stop on Scottish soil.

Now working as an estate agent in his homeland, he maintains his link to the Dons through an honorary presidency of the Rob Roy Reds, a London-based supporters club which turned to a true cult hero when it was looking for a figurehead. He still looks out for his Scottish club's results, able to reflect on his tartan time with pride.

The softly spoken van der Ark, breaking into laughter as he recalled his time as a Dons star, told me: "It was a surprise when the Rob Roy Reds got in a touch a few years back, but a pleasant one. It was funny when I got the call to ask me to be president but it is nice to think the supporters remember me and I've been to their club meetings a few times in London." So why is the big man still in demand among the Red Army? Van der Ark is bashful when it comes to tackling that subject but beneath that modest exterior is a man who knows just what it takes to get the fans onside.

He said: "It's always difficult to speak about yourself – I don't know why I was popular with fans, that's not something I can really answer. I did always have a good relationship with them and that was partly because I liked to stop and talk to them on my way on and off the pitch for warm-ups and that type of thing. As a player I always liked to connect with the crowd, not just at Aberdeen but at all of the clubs I played for. I enjoyed the conversations with the people in the stands. I think they appreciated players having the time to stop and speak to them but they also noticed me because I was a different type of player. I stood out in any game."

Van der Ark savoured the cut and thrust of the Premier Division. His heart still skips a beat when he chews over his memories of bruising encounters against the Old Firm and some of his most formidable opponents. The amiable Dutchman said: "I enjoyed the type of play in Scotland. The football is at a fast pace and that suited me – it is also aggressive, in a positive way. I loved playing Rangers and Terry Butcher. Terry was a tough man and a difficult opponent. It was fun to try and get the better of him. I will always remember my first game against Rangers. It was at Ibrox at the end of the 1988/89 season when they were celebrating winning the League. We beat them 3-0, played really well and I scored one of the goals. They were the champions but we were the better team that day and we ran them close in every competition."

It was a good time to be an Aberdeen player and the club's relative success ensured an easier life in and around the city than the players who have followed in van der Ark's footsteps have enjoyed. The Scottish adventure will always have a special place in his memory bank, with the north-east public helping to ensure it was a special experience for a young striker many miles from home.

He said: "We lived in Boyd Orr Avenue in the south of the city, among lots of Dutch exiles who worked for Shell at the time. It was a home from home in that respect but the Aberdonians also had a big part to play in helping us settle. We had the city on one side and the hills towards Deeside on the other, so it was a lovely spot to stay.

"We were made very welcome in Aberdeen. Of course, I got recognised when I was out in the city, that goes with the territory, but the supporters were always enthusiastic and encouraging. Sometimes, of course, I would get recognised out and about in Glasgow too – but even as an Aberdeen player I never had any problems. Of course, it was different in a game situation, when the opposition would call me all of the names under the sun. You accept that as a player, although maybe people in the stands don't realise quite how much you hear of what is shouted from the stands.

"I always liked having contact with the Aberdeen supporters. What I really enjoyed were the supporters club functions at the end of the season, when I would be invited along with my wife. We had some fantastic evenings at those events. It was great to be able to eat, drink and let our hair down with the fans at the end of a long, hard season. Maybe some players don't enjoy that type of thing but for me it was always a great pleasure and an honour to be invited."

The lure of the Netherlands eventually proved too strong to resist for van der Ark and he has since gone on to carve out a successful second career, which has played to his familiar strengths. He added: "I've been back to Aberdeen a couple of times with my wife and I hope to return again soon. I've also kept in touch with former team-mates, including Alex McLeish, and I'll always treasure my time at Pittodrie. Now I'm back home and doing a job I love as an estate agent. It means I have plenty of contact with all sorts of people and I enjoy that – just as I did in football."

Van der Ark had caught Smith's eye banging in the goals for relegation threatened Willem II. He had netted eight in 16 games for the Dutch strugglers before being tempted over the North Sea by the lure of foreign football. Prior to his season with Willem II, he had turned out for provincial side Cambur, bagging 27 goals in his most prolific season during four years with the club. He cost £70,000 when he moved to the top flight with Willem II.

Smith said at the time: "I think the fans will find Willem an exciting penalty-box player and his size will make him an awkward customer in the air for defences." The rangy forward made his debut at Motherwell's Fir Park and marked it by scoring one goal, galloping through to slot the ball past Ally Maxwell, and winning a free-kick from which Robert Connor netted.

Smith was entitled to breathe a sigh of relief, having blooded the far from standard issue striker. The manager said: "All that I saw confirmed my earlier impressions of him. He gets around the park quickly, is good in the air and fairly good on the ground. He is also a brave player – but the most important factor is the additional options he gives us up front in permutations with Charlie Nicholas, Paul Wright and Davie Dodds."

Van der Ark was another client of Dutch agent Tom van Dalen, chief fixer in all of the club's raids on the Netherlands, but Smith was the coach with the guts to invest in the unorthodox import. He was the type of player never seen before at Pittodrie and his recruitment represented a risk, but it worked in the manager's favour as he soon ingratiated himself among the north-east public.

Scottish defenders did not know what to make of him – and neither did the referees. Described in one match report in the aftermath of his debut as "all legs, arms and elbows", he was booked on his first appearance in the Premier Division. Injury stalled his early promise and, by his own admission, he had to come to terms with a change in style, having previously thrived on a bombardment of crosses aimed at him in the box with Willem II. At Pittodrie the onus was on more patient and subtle build-up.

Just as he became a popular figure with supporters, van der Ark was a well-liked member of the Dons staff, even if he did have to stoop to clear the main doorway on his way into work each day. He became a figure of intrigue for the media, too, one of the newspaper pack's favourite sons. Every move was covered, down to his reunion with his Old English sheepdog Dusty. Van der Ark was big news, partly because of his novelty value but also because he proved very amenable for the chasing reporters. Nothing was too much trouble for the affable Ark and his chirpy demeanour won him many friends.

That was true among the players as much as it was among the media and supporters, with several bridging the gaps created by geography and time to keep in touch with him following his return to the Netherlands. Alex McLeish was among those to retain a link, treating his old teammate to a VIP day out at an Old Firm game during his stint in charge of Rangers.

With his wiry frame, Willem was no powerhouse. Terry Butcher was the nearest to him in height in the Premier Division but despite giving up an inch in height the Rangers captain, himself an athletic rather than beefy figure, was still one and a half stone heavier.

Van der Ark's game was not about power, though, and when, in his first full season, he was given freedom to roam across the frontline the Dons fans saw him at his best. With his long strides and deceptive control, he enjoyed nothing better than running at terrified defences. Sports journalist Jim Dolan, writing in the *Press and Journal*, noted: "One of the most noticeable signs of the big man's improvement is his control on the ground, which, if it will never be at George Best level, is certainly very respectable."

A groin injury which required surgery disrupted van der Ark's second season and it was a frustrating period on the sidelines for the player, who admitted he felt isolated during his enforced absence from training and games. The niggling injury led him to miss the 1990 Scottish Cup final triumph, but the prescribed rest did nothing to ease the problem and all in all he sat out ten months of action, not getting back to training until February 1991.

Despite his return to fitness, the break had given the loping goal-scorer time to assess his future and the verdict was that it lay closer to home. Like countryman Hans Gillhaus, he decided he would not be seeking a new Dons contract and made it clear he would be looking for a club in the Netherlands.

Manager Smith said: "Willem has a very good attitude and has been unlucky during his time at Pittodrie. He is only unhappy because of the unfortunate injury situation which has plagued him for the past year. Willem is entitled to move at the end of the season under freedom of contract and there is nothing we can do about it. I am a realist. It would be naïve to believe every player signed from the continent would want to extend his contract when it has been completed. Some players may be happy to experience Scottish football for a couple of seasons, then move on to another country and a different challenge. There are others, such as Theo Snelders, who settle quickly and decide they are suited to the set-up and want to stay longer."

Even after he had expressed his desire to leave, the player was still part of Smith's first-team plans and when he eventually returned to match action he did in style – scoring with a spectacular diving header in a 5-2 friendly win over IFK Gothenburg. But despite efforts by the Dons to keep the striker in Scotland, his mind was made up. The only snag was that Dutch clubs could not afford to meet the £300,000 valuation in those pre-Bosman days. Eventually he backed down and signed a new two-year contract in time for the 1991/92 season, after intense negotiation over terms, but he did not see out the deal.

In January 1992 it was announced that a £200,000 agreement had been struck with Utrecht in the Netherlands to pave the way for his return home. Smith said: "Willem needs first-team football and has done a good job for Aberdeen. With so many young players beginning to emerge at Pittodrie, and Hans Gillhaus coming back to form, we felt there was a need to make room in our first-team squad."

He later returned to Cambur and his career ended at the club at which it had begun. A groin injury in 1995 led to a warning from specialists that playing on could leave him crippled in later life and the forward took the sensible decision, calling time on his playing career just days before Christmas that year. The Ark had taken its final football voyage but the memories were always guaranteed to outlast his career.

So what did the distinctive Dutchman do to earn his place in Pittodrie folklore? In black-and-white terms, not too much – but that's the beauty of football, the grey areas in between the hard statistics.

After his goal-scoring debut against Motherwell in January 1989, there was not another goal until the final game of the season. The fact that it came in that 3-0 victory against Rangers at Ibrox helped erase the memories of his mini-drought and further endear him to the travelling Red Army. That victory was too little, too late though, with the Light Blues already demob-happy having clinched the Premier Divison title, emerging with a six-point margin over runners-up Aberdeen.

The second term was more profitable for van der Ark, in every sense. From a personal perspective he was in and around the team for the bulk of the season, with 16 starts and 11 substitute appearances in the 36 top-flight games, as well as eight outings in the domestic cup competitions and UEFA Cup. From a total of 18 starts and 17 shorter bursts from the bench he bagged 11 goals, all but two of them coming when he was in the first XI, to give him a strike rate of a goal for every two games. Not bad in anyone's book. That 1989/90 haul included The Ark's one and only Dons hat-trick, part of a 6-2 demolition of Partick Thistle at Firhill in the first game on the road to Hampden in the Scottish Cup. Despite being in at the start of the run, he missed the dramatic penalty shoot-out win against Celtic in the final.

By then van der Ark had already bagged what turned out to be his solitary Aberdeen winner's medal. Earlier in the season he appeared as a substitute in the League Cup final victory against Rangers, playing a part in the build-up to Paul Mason's winner in the 2-1 win with a deft headed flick into the path of Charlie Nicholas, who in turn provided the assist for the goal-scorer.

The strong-willed foreigner was disappointed not to have played from the start, having scored after his late introduction in the previous League game against Hearts, but manager Smith opted to recall promising young forward Eoin Jess instead to partner veteran Charlie Nicholas in attack.

Despite missing a large chunk of the notorious 1990/91 season through injury, van der Ark returned in time to play a key role in the nail-biting end to the adventure. Aberdeen fans need no reminding of the last-day defeat at Ibrox which handed Rangers the title by the two points they claimed that day, but the part the towering forward had to play may be less clear in the collective memory.

In fact, he started six of the last eight games of that campaign as the Dons tried to edge clear in the thrilling championship race and chipped in with four goals. One came in a 2-1 victory at Dundee United, another in a 2-1 victory at home to St Johnstone in the penultimate League match, and there was an earlier double in a 3-0 success at Pittodrie against Motherwell. The long and short of it is that without van der Ark's crucial counters, the final-game showdown would not have happened, as Rangers would have had the title wrapped up weeks earlier.

That purple patch was the best the Dons faithful would see of their man, who never experienced the rush of netting for the club again despite appearing, mainly as a sub, in a further 20 games in 1991/92. He signed off on a low note, playing his last game in front of just 3,071 paying punters at Broomfield as Airdrie pulled off a 2-0 win to pile pressure on the misfiring Reds.

Van der Ark was long gone by the time Alex Smith became the first manager in the history of the club to be sacked, and his successor, Willie Miller, could not prevent the team from finishing in sixth spot, the lowest League placing since 1975. The slump proved to be less than temporary, as a succession of managers tried and failed to restore the Dons to the trophy-winning knockout glory of Smith's team while facing similar frustrations in the League.

It was not until 1995 that the League Cup returned to Pittodrie and the subsequent lean spell has only served to highlight just how good the Dons fans had it during the late 1980s and first year of the '90s. Van der Ark eased himself into the role of oddball hero during that period. Who knows whether he would have done the same had he played when the club was toiling? Fortunately for the likeable Dutchman, he appeared on the scene at a time when the Dons were in the ascendancy, when Pittodrie players were there to be loved. He may have been all legs, arms and elbows, but he most certainly was a cult hero into the bargain.

'DEADLY DUNC' 1992–1997

DUNCAN SHEARER

Magic Moment: With another Shearer goal the Red Army are in wonderland as Dundee are undone and the League Cup returns to Pittodrie in 1995.

Dons Career: Games 193. Goals 78. Caps 7.

ON 10 AUGUST 1993 the Red Army ushered in a brave new era with a sparkling addition to Pittodrie life which promised to haul the Dons into the modern era and help the club compete with the game's pacesetters. The grand unveiling was not a new player but a more permanent fixture, the Richard Donald Stand.

Towering above the rest of the ageing ground, the RDS was a conspicuous statement to football followers near and far that Aberdeen were not ready to fade into the background. Just as the likes of Rangers and Celtic pressed ahead with modernisation and stadium redevelopment, Aberdeen were determined to hang on to their coat-tails and maintain their place among the elite.

In fact, the £4.5 million revamp never stretched beyond the eastern tip of Pittodrie. More than a decade and a half on, the RDS still sits incongruously on Golf Road, a fitting and impressive tribute to the late and legendary Dick Donald who lent his name to the structure, but its surroundings offer a stark reminder that in the post-Donald era the club has had to cut its cloth far finer than the supporters would have liked. Back in 1993 the Red Army could not have predicted the financial woes the next decade would bring. As they settled into their shiny new seats within the two tiers of the Dick Donald monument, beneath the gleaming glass of the new executive boxes, it felt like the start of something special.

That spirit of optimism and exuberance was not based solely on the bricks and mortar that had sprung up to form Scottish football's latest multi-million-pound enclosure. Some pure-bred Highland flesh and blood also had a massive part to play. Duncan Shearer ran out in front of the RDS on that August afternoon and produced a virtuoso performance for the assembled audience watching their first competitive game from their new vantage point. Shearer banged home a hat-trick against Clydebank as the Dons followed the opening ceremony with a 5-0 trouncing of the Bankies in the League Cup. Not surprisingly the response was a rapturous one, with Shearer leaving the field to a standing ovation from the fans in what had become the best seats in the house.

Joe Harper had been the undisputed King of the Beach End, but the beloved, sprawling and rambling old stand was gone. In its place was the sharp-edged RDS and a new generation of Dons fanatics were in the market for a new hero to match. For Shearer the endless comparisons with Harper and the other Pittodrie goal-scoring legends became familiar, but were never encouraged. After his central role in the baptism of the Richard Donald Stand, Shearer laughed off suggestions he could become the second King of the Beach End.

He said: "Our fans are all around the stadium and I want to have them all cheering. The atmosphere generated by the supporters in the new stand was amazing. It was a terrific feeling looking up and seeing the packed top tier celebrating when all the goals were scored. I hope the fans can keep that type of atmosphere going for the rest of the season. My first game at Ibrox was a bit of a shock because of the noise their fans made. I'm convinced our fans can do the same now Pittodrie has been rebuilt and make it intimidating for visiting sides. As for trying to become the new King of the Beach End – I have to admit that isn't my major aim. I have read enough about Joe Harper's relationship with the fans from that area to know it was special. All I want to do is beat his scoring records. If I can be remembered as the goal king of all Pittodrie I will be delighted."

By the time the new stand opened its cavernous concourse to the paying public for the first time, Shearer was into his second season as Aberdeen's main goal threat.

He signed in 1992 and his debut season went a long way towards ensuring he would become a cult figure. Within four months he had tucked away three hat-tricks and scored 21 goals to catapult himself into the bracket of past shooting stars, including the enigmatic Frank McDougall – the last player before Shearer to have passed the 20-goal milestone, eight seasons earlier. He went on to bag 28 by the end of his debut campaign in red.

Tagged the 'Modest Marauder' by the press gang he wowed with his consistently devastating displays for the Dons, Shearer justified manager Willie Miller's decision to invest heavily in the talented forward with his sparkling early form. At £500,000 he was the second most expensive signing in the history of the club, but he was an unqualified success. Miller said: "When fans watch highlights of Dons matches on TV and see shots at goal or opposing keepers making saves I'm sure they would notice Duncan is always in the picture. He is the first player waiting for any slip-ups, hoping to get even a half-chance of scoring. It is an instinctive thing for Duncan and he is doing what he was brought here for."

"The superior man is modest in his speech, but exceeds in his actions."

Confucius, Chinese philosopher

The fact that Shearer hit the ground running should have been no surprise to Miller or the Dons fans. Even in his first pre-season outings for the club he was on red-hot form, firing a familiar hat-trick against Nairn County in one of those early appearances on his way to seven goals in four warm-up games.

The Red Army had waited a long time for a true scoring star to fill the boots of McDougall, so cruelly cut down in his prime by injury in 1986. Billy Stark bravely picked up the mantle in the absence of McDougall, becoming leading scorer with his 14 goals in 1986/87, and Davie Dodds was next to top the Pittodrie charts when he went one strike better the following term. The high-profile arrival of Charlie Nicholas promised a more permanent striking option for the Aberdeen followers to hang their hopes on, but the expensive recruit was as much a creator and link-man as he was a scorer. Although Nicholas, with 18 goals in the 1988/89 season, did finish as leading scorer, it was left to Paul Mason, who netted 14 times, and Hans Gillhaus, on the same tally, to shoulder the burden over the next two seasons. In the season prior to Shearer's arrival it was the young head of Eoin Jess who was left to mastermind the attacking missions. While his 12-goal haul was enough to earn him the leading scorer's crown, it also highlighted just where the squad needed strengthening if a realistic challenge to Rangers' dominance was to be mounted.

Miller first tried to buy Shearer from Swindon at the tail-end of the 1991/92 season but Kenny Dalglish and Blackburn blew the Dons out of the water with a £750,000 bid. By the summer of 1992 the English side were ready to release Shearer for a Scottish homecoming and the deal was struck to make him a Don – at the fourth time of asking. The first occasion was far back in 1981 when a young flame-haired Highlander, who had been shining for Clach in the Highland League, bagged five goals in an Aberdeen practice game under the watchful eye of Dons manager Alex Ferguson. Despite the 19-year-old's purple patch in front of goal, illness led the player to miss a second trial stint and the deal was off.

He had overcome adversity to get to the Granite City in the first place. A stray sheep had almost cost Shearer his chance to pitch for a contract, when a car carrying the forward and three fellow Clach players collided with the unlucky beast near Spean Bridge and careered into a ditch. Surprisingly all four escaped unscathed and fit to play for the Inverness side later the same day.

At the same time as Aberdeen were circling there was interest from Celtic as the powerful attacker continued to make a name for himself across the country. At the age of just 17 he had been courted by Partick Thistle, but the Jags also rejected the northern starlet. Little did the Firhill side realise he would come back to haunt them in the year that followed. It was obvious to everyone who watched him that Shearer, who for a period played centre-half and midfield as well as up front for Clach, had ability mated with braveheart passion. Yet none of those early suitors took a gamble.

It got to the stage that his Highland club barred him from going out on trial, with an approach from Middlesbrough proving the straw that broke the camel's back. Shearer's brother, Dave, was already on the Ayresome Park playing staff but 'Boro were told if they wanted the younger sibling they would have to pay before sampling the goods.

Clach chairman Alex Chisholm said: "I'm getting sick and tired of clubs trying to get something for nothing. They come along expecting us to release the player for a trial period and undermine the strength of our own squad. It's just not on. There is no doubt that Duncan will eventually get his chance – but we must protect the interests of the club as well as the player. We get no compensation for losing their services: they expose themselves to the risk of injury and when they return home they might be out of action. If Scottish or English League clubs are sufficiently interested, it should not be beyond their means to make an on-the-spot check by watching the player in the Highland League. The days of bargain-hunting up here are long past. With most clubs facing cash problems, they cannot expect to get something for nothing. I would say this is a realistic, more than a tough approach. I'm hopeful Duncan will get his chance soon."

The hardline approach did not waver when Chelsea came calling early in 1983, exactly a year after 'Boro had been rebuffed. By October that year the Clach hierachy relented and allowed Shearer one last shot at glory, allowing the unemployed Lochaber lad a chance to go on trial with the Blues in London. He did not let the big opportunity pass and made a lasting impression on Chelsea manager John Neal, who returned to Clach with a name-your-price request to the Clach board. The price was £22,000 and in November the paperwork was complete and Shearer, at the age of 20, became a full-time professional for the first time.

He had joined a club pushing for promotion back to the English top flight but faced a fight to establish himself during his two and a half years in London. In March 1986, aged 23, he signed for Huddersfield Town for a nominal fee and it proved to be a bargain. Savouring a return to regular first-team football, he hit the goal trail for the Yorkshire side despite their struggles against relegation. Although he wasn't long at the club, he became a hero to the Terriers supporters and is still fondly remembered more than twenty years after his stint at Leeds Road. A four-goal performance against Barnsley is still the talk of the Town.

Duly bigger clubs began to take notice, and Shearer was linked with a £300,000 move to Derby County in the summer of 1987. The big-money move never happened but his struggling club needed the revenue and offered Shearer on a plate to Scottish clubs, including Aberdeen. Manager Ian Porterfield insisted the west-coast lad was not an option and claimed: "Shearer couldn't get into Aberdeen's team at the moment, so you can dismiss his name."

At the start of 1988 Swindon Town felt differently, making a £250,000 club record offer to take him to Wiltshire. He went on to become a legend at the County Ground. He is still talked about as the best striker the club ever had and as one of the finest players to pull on the red jersey. Fort William's finest left his mark on that corner of little England, too. A trend was developing and it would not halt upon his return to Scotland years later. With the Robins he hit a mean streak of scoring form, with 97 goals in just 199 appearances for Glenn Hoddle's side. That stirred Aberdeen's interest for a third time, and this time Willie Miller was the man at the helm. Unfortunately for the Dons the Jack Walker-funded Blackburn revolution was in full flow and it was Dalglish who won the race, so Ewood Park was the next stop for Shearer in March 1992.

Fortunately for the Red Army it was not the final stop and he bounded into Pittodrie just four months later to found a mutual appreciation society. Aberdeen became *the* club for the man of many clubs and the supporters responded by elevating him to the status of *the* man.

Shearer only recently left Aberdeen behind to return to his roots, taking his family back to the Highlands and settling in Inverness, having finally severed his physical ties with the Granite City. The emotional ties remain, however, and Shearer holds his relationship with the Dons fans dear.

He told me: "In England I had a great rapport with the Huddersfield supporters and it was the same at Swindon after my first season, but at Aberdeen it was different. The crowd at Pittodrie saw me as one of their own, a Highlander playing in the north of Scotland. I had come home. Of all the clubs I have been with, the relationship I had with the Aberdeen supporters was the best. Scoring goals is the quickest way to win over any group of fans and I was fortunate that I scored in six of my seven debuts. If you can score regularly it certainly helps and I got a lot of goals early in my career with the club."

But Shearer is the first to acknowledge that his pedigree in front of goal was only part of the story. He quickly gained a reputation as a man of the people, free from the airs and graces which had crept into football in the 1990s.

He said: "If the team went out for a few drinks on a Saturday night, I'd stay for one or two, then go my own way. I didn't like to drink in the typical footballers' pubs or go to the nightclubs, I preferred the more traditional type of place. Because of that I spent a bit of time with the fans I met in the city and became good friends with a group of about half a dozen. They could tell I was a down-to-earth sort of guy and no big-time Charlie. I've always considered myself working class, if I can put it that way. I think word soon got around that I had my feet on the ground, never saw myself as being any different from the fans, and they knew how desperate I was to win every game – just as they were. There also hadn't been a main goal-scorer at the club for some time, so I was welcome in that respect, too."

As unassuming as Shearer was as he mingled with Aberdonians in the city centre, his single-minded approach when he crossed the white line at work set him apart from the average striker. It is often said that you cannot make a goal-scorer, that the talent lies deep within. In conversation with one of Pittodrie's all-time greats, it is difficult not to concur.

He explained: "I often hear players, strikers particularly, saying they don't care who gets the goals as long as the team wins. I hate that. For me it was totally the opposite – I wanted the team to win and I wanted to score the goals. It got me into trouble sometimes. I remember one game against Kilmarnock that we had won, but I wasn't happy because I hadn't scored and felt I should have done because of the positions I'd got myself into. I was having a real go at anyone who would listen and refused to go out for the warm-down because I was boiling with rage. Roy Aitken was furious with me and ready to dock my wages. I had one foot in the bath but decided to get my shoes back on and go out and join the fitness coach Stuart Hogg and the rest of the players back out on the park for the exercises. When I look back now I realise I was throwing my toys out of the pram, but that was the way I was. I wanted to score in every game. Don't get me wrong, I would still play other people in if they were in a better position, but I saw my main job as scoring goals. I realised there were other people who could do other things better than me outside the box, or who were more mobile, but I always felt as a finisher I did okay."

Okay is, naturally enough, an understatement. Shearer's potency made him a huge hit with the supporters and none more so than those who were nestling in their new surroundings within the Richard Donald Stand. It may only have been bricks and mortar, but for the passionate Highlander it proved to be an inspiration.

Shearer said: "When I first arrived the stand was being built, so there was nothing behind the goal apart from the wooden boards. It was strange playing towards that end and amazing to see the stand growing behind it. My big thing was that I wanted to be the first player to score in front of the Richard Donald Stand – but Alex McLeish beat me to it in the first game. He was hardly in the habit of scoring goals but I couldn't grudge him it after everything he had done for the club over the years and all the times he had played in front of the old Beach End. I remember after his goal, grabbing him and turning him round to face the stand, and just saying to him 'look at that'. If I remember right, he replied with a few choice words – it was a phenomenal sight, a sea of red and white with fans towering above us. That got the ball rolling and the new stand really did create a tremendous atmosphere. It was always a little bit more special for me when I scored in front of the Richard Donald Stand."

The fact that Shearer was able to create such a buzz around Pittodrie sets him apart from so many of his forerunners and successors in the red shirt. The Aberdeen support has been intensely loyal throughout the club's history and particularly in the quarter of a century since the finest hour in Gothenburg. As that famous team broke up, success began to dwindle to the stage of all but evaporating. At the time of writing, the League Cup in 1995 remains the last trophy to rest on the Pittodrie mantelpiece and prior to that there had been a five-year wait for silverware.

Shearer said: "We had a really good year in my first season with the club, pushing Rangers in the League and coming close in both cup finals, while qualifying for Europe. Then, for whatever reason, it went off the boil, which was frustrating for everyone. The League Cup win in 1995 was enjoyable – but I didn't for a moment imagine it would be the last trophy the club would win for more than a decade, especially when you look at some of the teams that have won cups since then. A club like Aberdeen should be winning things an awful lot more regularly than it has been."

The devotion of the Red Army in the face of such on-field paucity is unquestionable, even if the Pittodrie crowd has never gained a reputation as the most fervent on the football map. Billy Connolly once remarked that northern audiences were different to those elsewhere in the country, that the further up the country he travelled he found the reaction to his routine was different. In the south the applause came throughout the performance, in the north the paying public reserved their reaction until the whole production had unfolded. Then they let their appreciation be known.

Football crowds can be similar. Even if the sweet-wrapper-rustling jibes are an exaggeration that has built over time, it is fair to say the Aberdeen crowd can hold back. Hold back, that is, until there's really something to shout about. Shearer was that something for five years between 1992 and 1997, when the Dons fans rose to their feet to chant his name and sing his song in full voice. The Red Army had been united by one man and it took a special player to do that over such a prolonged period of time.

It's a goal, Duncan Shearer
It's a goal, Duncan Shearer
Walking along
Singing a song
Walking in a Shearer wonderland

The verse rang out loud and proud throughout the 1990s following Shearer's almost instant installation as a cult figure for the Dons fans. When that wasn't being belted out, the simpler chant of "Shearer, Shearer" left the opposition support in no doubt about on whom the Dandies pinned their hopes.

With Aberdeen he averaged exactly a goal for every other League start, with 54 strikes in 108 starting appearances in the Premier Division. In the Scottish Cup the ratio was better, with eight goals in 13 starts and five sub appearances, while in the League Cup it was better again – an impressive 14 goals in just 11 starts and four entries from the bench. In Europe it was a respectable two strikes in four starts and four ties as a substitute. The reward was perhaps not fitting to the contribution, with a single winner's medal to show for Shearer's eventful and entertaining period at Pittodrie. That came courtesy of that 1995 League Cup success, when he was on target along with Billy Dodds in the 2-0 victory over Dundee in the final at Hampden.

It was not only on club duty that Shearer would grace the national stadium. He won all seven of his Scotland caps while on the Aberdeen staff, the first coming at the age of 31 in 1994 against Austria in Vienna. Shearer had served his time as a foot soldier with the Tartan Army, first sampling the Hampden roar as a Scotland fan in the 1970s as a Highland schoolboy. To run out in the dark blue of his country was the realisation of a teenage dream and he savoured every second of his surprisingly brief international career.

It began in April 1994 and ended in August 1995 in a 1-0 victory over Greece at headquarters in Glasgow. In between he featured in a 0-0 draw against Russia in Moscow and matching 2-0 wins away to San Marino and the Faroes. His two Scotland goals came in a 3-1 defeat against the Netherlands in Utrecht and a 2-0 win against Finland in Helsinki.

The same period in his club career was full of frustration. It was no coincidence that a knee injury which sidelined Shearer for four months of the 1994/95 season led to a slump in the team's form, a lull which ultimately led to manager Willie Miller's sacking. One of Miller's final acts was to secure his fit-again star striker on a new two-and-a-half-year contract designed to make him a Don for life, but for Miller at least it proved too late to save his job.

Shearer spoke out at the time about his guilt at the manager's departure and his debt to Miller. Ironically, it was Miller nine years later, in his new role as director of football, who fired assistant manager Shearer and manager Steve Paterson in 2004. Proof positive that there is no sentiment in the dog-eat-dog world of football. There is, however, licence to forgive and forget – as Shearer found during his time at Pittodrie. He played in the Dons side humiliated by part-timers Stenhousemuir in the Scottish Cup and admitted he was ashamed to leave his Aberdeen home in the aftermath, but it did not blemish his Aberdeen record in the long term.

The Pittodrie fans never let their appreciation of the powerful striker waver, even when his days at the club became numbered. With his contract due to expire in the summer of 1997, manager Roy Aitken made it clear there would be no new deal on the table. No, Aitken was ready to throw his weight behind the next generation: Dennis Wyness, Malcolm Kpedekpo and Michael Craig. Hindsight is a glorious thing, but it is safe to say that even at 34 years of age the veteran forward would have outscored that trio, put together, in the seasons that followed.

Dundee United, Bolton Wanderers, Motherwell and Turkish outfit Bursaspor were all linked with the player but eventually Aitken saw sense. Shearer was staying, having been offered a new one-year contract to tie him to the Dons until the summer of 1998 after the marksman made it impossible for him to be ignored with wholehearted appearances from the bench.

Despite the briefness of his contributions, the loyal Red Army ensured his place out of sight in the dugout did not let him drift out of mind. The chants of "Shearer, Shearer" continued to ring around Pittodrie and the man in demand admitted at the time: "It is a little embarrassing at times, but also a big thrill to know the fans haven't forgotten me. Hearing the fans so much behind me has helped keep my head up and I can only hope I get the chance to repay them."

The chance never materialised. Within weeks of the 1997/98 season beginning it became clear he would be primarily a reserve player and for a proud international with such a phenomenal scoring record it was an uncomfortable position.

Thus in September 1997 the love affair with the Dons came to an end when Inverness Caley Thistle stepped in to end his second-string stint and bring him back home to the Highlands. As he prepared for his Caley Jags debut, Shearer allowed his thoughts to drift back to the north-east. He said: "I'm obviously disappointed that I didn't get to say my farewells to the Aberdeen fans in a game at Pittodrie, but the Dons supporters knew deep down as well as I did that it was time to go."

He was hailed as the biggest signing in the Inverness club's history by the chairman and as an "inspiration" by manager Steve Paterson, who had brought him in as a coach as well as a striker. In time that role expanded to make him assistant manager and the pair turned the men from the Moray Firth into one of Scotland's most attractive football sides, a force in the First Division without quite making the giant step to the top flight.

In 2002, following the failed experiment with Ebbe Skovdahl, that promise was tapped into by a Dons board desperate to bring the good times back. Paterson and Shearer were unveiled as the new Aberdeen management team on 11 December that year, with Shearer rejecting the opportunity to become Paterson's successor as Caley Thistle manager in order to follow his boss to Pittodrie.

Shearer ignored a concerted campaign to keep him in Inverness, with the Highland club throwing money in his direction.

Speaking as he settled back in at Pittodrie, he said: "I was surprised by what Inverness went through to try to keep me. If it had been any other club trying to take me away I would probably have stayed at the Caledonian Stadium – but the Aberdeen job is different and everyone knows it. I made my decision in about 20 minutes after speaking to my family. It was a great emotional pull coming back here."

It would all end in frustration for Shearer, elbowed out of his beloved club alongside Paterson in 2004. The decision cut deep. To this day the pain is still never far from the surface for a man who felt more at home within the red-brick confines of Pittodrie than at any other club he served during an impressive playing career. Celtic had been Shearer's boyhood heroes but his affection for the Hoops was swamped by the passion he developed for the Dons and his feelings for the club made him a massive hit with the fans.

There was never a sense that Shearer was just passing through, that he was looking for the next big pay cheque or that he was on an ego trip. The overwhelming impression he gave on and off the field was that he felt privileged to play in the famous red shirt and that he was desperate to repay the club for the opportunity it had given him. He was humble until he stepped over the white line, then he became a supremely confident marksman with a goal celebration to match.

The classic Shearer pose, prone on the ground imitating a sniper, has gone down as one of the most iconic Aberdeen images of modern times.

At one point or another he gunned down every top-flight club in the country, so the distinctive celebration was a fitting one for deadly Dunc.

His coaching career with the club never hit the same heights as his time as a player, but then he never had long enough to try. His absence from the game after leaving Aberdeen for a second time was only temporary and in 2005 he was appointed as a manager in his own right for the first time, taking charge of Buckie Thistle in the Highland League. That reign ended in 2008 after disappointment in the championship, with several challenges at the top end of the table failing to deliver the club's first title since the 1950s. Shearer did savour cup success, winning the Aberdeenshire Cup and Aberdeenshire Shield with the Jags in his final season.

He was quickly snapped up by opportunistic Caley Thistle, who installed him alongside former Inverness manager Charlie Christie as a youth-coaching dream team in 2008. He was back in the game with his desire firmly intact, and it would be unwise to bet against Shearer the manager resurfacing in the near future, with familiar hunger to succeed and the scent of success driving him on.

'RICCO' 1992–1994

LEE RICHARDSON

Magic Moment: A sensational strike from Rico and the Serie A stars of Torino teetered on the brink of suffering an upset. The Dons' joy was short-lived, but the memory lingers on.

Dons Career: Games 80. Goals 10.

"DEAR SIR, I write in the hope you will allow me to play for your team. I have my own boots, am willing to travel and know my way to Pittodrie. I can think of 15,000 people who would be delighted to see me back and quite a few opposition players who would dread my reappearance. Please do not hesitate to get in touch if you feel I can be of assistance. Yours sincerely, Lee Richardson."

Sounds far fetched, doesn't it? But as his beloved Reds toiled in Ebbe Skovdahl's first season in charge it was exactly what "Rico" was prepared to do to win a ticket back to Pittodrie and try to help the Dons out of the relegation mire. By 1999, when Skovdahl's side stumbled from one League disaster to another, the old warhorse was on the books at Huddersfield but had been bombed out of the first team squad by manager Steve Bruce and was on loan at Bury. Regrets, he had a few – and one of those was choosing to turn his back on Aberdeen, the club which had truly taken Richardson to its heart.

Realising the error of his ways, the Halifax-born schemer was prepared to pen a letter to Skovdahl pleading for the opportunity for a second chance at Pittodrie. He reasoned that the Dane may not be aware of him and that a gentle nudge in the right direction might alert him to the possibilities. Mind you, if the manager had bent the ear of any Pittodrie regular he would have been assured of a glowing reference for a man who took the ground and the city by storm. Indeed, when news of his desire for another chance with the club broke in the newspapers the official supporters' club rushed forward to urge the coaching team to give the idea serious consideration and that was no surprise.

The plea to Skovdahl, as unlikely as it sounds in an age when players hold the balance of power and pursuing clubs are left to do the leg work, was not an isolated incident. During Roy Aitken's reign Richardson also volunteered his services, ready and willing to return to the frontline if required. It was a refreshingly honest approach for a player to admit he had made the wrong call in leaving a club. Rarely is any top-level pro willing to swallow his pride and make the first move in the traditional game of transfer chess. But that was typical of Richardson and his straightforward approach to life and the game he loved.

In the decade and a half since Richardson walked away from Pittodrie, the act of persuading players to make the switch to the Dons has become more and more difficult. The traditional excitement surrounding summer arrivals has been replaced by a sense of trepidation as the annual game of patience painfully draws to a conclusion as another deadline looms and a string of players from home and abroad hold out in the hope of feathering their nest as desperation among clubs creeps in. Imagine how refreshing it would be to have a player, and one of the calibre of Richardson, banging down the door asking to sign.

As it happened, the second coming never materialised. Perhaps that is not a bad thing. Why run the risk of undoing the good work that created the adulation in the first place? Instead the Dons faithful could content themselves with the blissful memories of Richardon's terrier-like displays, tenacious tackling, crisp passing and wicked shooting.

Like so many of *Pittodrie Idols* he did not hang around for the long haul but packed a lot into his short time in the north-east. In Richardson's defence, there were mitigating factors for the brevity of his service – with perceived persecution from Scotland's referees cited as one of the reasons for his decision to quit the country in 1994, after just two seasons with the club, and return to his home patch.

There were parallels with Richardson and engine-room predecessor Neale Cooper, who had left Aberdeen behind in the 1980s for exactly the same reason. The Pittodrie supporters could not get enough of Cooper's heart-on-sleeve performances but the whistlers north of the border, according to the player and Sir Alex Ferguson, failed to handle that commitment in the right way. The bookings piled up and Cooper flitted south to Aston Villa in the hope of finding a more accommodating arena for his talents.

"There are all sorts of cute puppy dogs, but it doesn't stop people from going out and buying Dobermans."

Angus Young, AC/DC guitarist

Rico was not as high-profile as the Gothenburg great but, in a very different and less successful era, he had the same ability to raise the temperature in a game by rolling up his sleeves and wading into the thick of the action. His all-action style dragged his team-mates with him into the heat of battle and Rico sparked some adrenaline-fuelled contests during his time with Aberdeen. That heart-pounding approach spread to the stands, too, with the Red Army responding by giving back the 100-per-cent commitment they got from their man in the middle. As a huge rock fan, Richardson once claimed he would rather play drums for AC/DC than turn out for Inter Milan. His taste in music echoed his style of play, full of passion and aggression. But Richardson was no hammer-thrower. He could be subtle with his promptings from the centre of the park when he wanted to be and was a potent attacking weapon thanks to his ability to fire off dangerous shots at will from distance.

With those attributes it sounds as though he had the makings of an England international, but that is where the contradiction crops up. Ask supporters of the bulk of his eight English sides about what Richardson brought to the party and the response will be complimentary, but still nowhere near as vociferous as if you popped the question in a bar in

Aberdeen. The 23 months he spent in the Granite City represented his peak.

He had arrived in 1992 from Blackburn Rovers, where he had made a half-century of League starts. Manager Willie Miller saw something that caught his attention while watching Duncan Shearer in action for the Lancashire side and, after a lengthy but committed pursuit, eventually got his man. In his quest to turn the Dons from perennial challengers to hard and fast winners, Miller operated something of a revolving-door policy while in the manager's chair. His first act was to sign Mixu Paatelainen for £400,000 and the spending did not stop there, with Roy Aitken following along with the likes of Duncan Shearer, Ray McKinnon, Peter Hetherston, John Inglis and Billy Dodds.

Paatelainen, with his bulky frame and goal-scoring knack, became something of a hero in his own right while Dodds also proved to be a shrewd investment and Aitken, for what he brought off the field as much as on it, was viewed as a solid recruit.

Yet when asked to single out his best buys, Miller does not hesitate. Shearer and Richardson, neck and neck. The pair cannot be separated by the man who signed them, just as they cannot be by the supporters who chanted their names. The duo had the X-factor, that little something extra every manager looks for but so few find as they tot up the miles on cross-country scouting missions. A twist of fate brought Richardson to Miller's attention as he tracked Shearer. It wasn't quite two for the price of one but it was the next best thing.

Before landing in Aberdeen's lap he had turned out for Halifax and Watford, commanding transfer fees of £175,000 and £250,000 when he moved on to the Hornets and then Rovers, in a steady climb up the ladder. The unexpected switch to Scotland was the making of the player. His home-town team were struggling at the wrong end of the old English Fourth Division when Richardson made his breakthrough back in 1987. Indeed, they were flirting with the indignity of relegation to the Conference when their young home-grown midfield talent was invited to leap up two divisions with Watford and join their challenge for promotion from the Second Divison in the second half of the 1988/89 campaign. The Vicarage Road side were edged out, with Chelsea joined by Manchester City and Crystal Palace in making the step up to the top flight, but Richardson was making his mark.

After just one full season with Watford he was back on the road north to join Blackburn just in time for the Kenny Dalglish-led revolution. It was another Scottish manager, Don Mackay, who signed the gritty Yorkshireman for Rovers but at the end of the midfielder's first season, in which they languished in the lower reaches of the Second Division, he found himself under the command of Dalglish and a part of the squad being built to challenge for promotion. Richardson played his part in regaining respectability, with Blackburn climbing to sixth in 1991/92, but as the big money began to wash around the Lancashire club the players from more modest backgrounds began to be edged out. Scotland provided the exit clause, Falkirk vying with Aberdeen for Richardson's services when it became clear he was open to offers in 1992. The Dons won the day and the team's supporters won a new hero.

Describing the midfielder's debut against Partick Thistle, *Press and Journal* reporter Jim Dolan wrote: "Lee not only provided the pass for the goal that lifted the Dons to victory, but impressed with his ball control and willingness to take on opponents and get to the line." From that promising 33-minute introduction, the Englishman blossomed into a star man – loved by his own team's followers, often loathed by those of the opposition and seemingly not embraced by the refereeing fraternity either.

In 80 appearances he was booked 22 times and sent off twice, enduring suspension after suspension at a time when his team were desperately attempting to break the dominance of Rangers, finishing runners-up in the League in each of his two seasons in Scotland's top flight and featuring in two Cup final disappointments.

He arrived in the infancy of Miller's first full season in charge, a campaign which followed on the heels of the disappointment of a sixth-place finish in the Premier Division. Rangers had won four consecutive championships and the Dons had been runners-up three times. That trend continued following Richardson's transfer to Scotland, with his side nine points off the title pace in 1992/93 in second place and moving to within three points the next term.

The knockout showdowns also pitted Richardson against Rangers, the Dons falling to matching 2-1 defeats in both the Scottish Cup and League Cup in the 1992/93 season. Richardson's goal in the Scottish Cup showpiece was scant consolation as the final piece of what had been a treble challenge disappeared into the Glasgow air.

He had developed a fierce rivalry with Rangers, something not lost on Dons followers with the same passion for what had developed into a fixture to run the Old Firm clashes close in terms of tension and intensity. The player was not slow in coming forward with his views on the Ibrox side, most vocally following his dismissal for a challenge on Light Blues youngster Lee Robertson in the final weeks of the 1992/93 campaign.

The Dons midfielder was stung by the negative publicity the incident generated and it cajoled him into defending his honour and integrity in public, while at the same time taking the opportunity to stoke the flames by insisting Aberdeen had nothing to fear from Rangers and that the Pittodrie youth policy put the Glasgow side to shame. Rico was at pains to point out that he felt his reputation as the "Dirty Don" was not merited, but he was by no means apologetic. Misunderstood rather than misdirected was his take on the aggressive approach he took to the game.

For manager Willie Miller the stream of suspensions which befell his midfield star man were a repetitive source of frustration. It prompted the boss to call on referees to lay off his player and to urge opposition players not to try and take advantage of the apparent willingness among officials to seize on the smallest of misdemeanours by over-reacting to challenges from the imposing man in red. Miller, speaking after a Richardson red card for a double-booking against Falkirk, said: "I do hope referees are not singling Lee out and treating him differently from any other player. I am saying this because in Saturday's game against Falkirk there was a kick by Kevin McAllister on Stephen Wright that could have brought a booking, yet the referee did nothing about it. I looked at the Lee Richardson incident again on television and thought it was hardly worth mentioning. Yet he gets ordered off. I hope the player is given a chance from now on. There have been comments passed about honesty in the game these days and I would hope that there could always be a certain amount of honesty shown by fellow pros."

Before moving north, Richardson had never been booked more than four times in a season yet in front of the Scottish officials the Englishman developed a reputation which tarnished him before a ball had been kicked. The evidence backs up the midfielder's assertion that he was not reckless by nature and while tackling was a large part of his game, it was far from the only aspect.

Jim Dolan observed: "Off the field, Richardson is an affable and courteous young man with a sense of humour – but some referees undoubtedly react to a combination of a Sherwood Forest aspect and at times over-exuberant play."

The Robin Hood reference may have been tongue-in-cheek, but there is little question that Richardson's appearance added to the rough-and-ready aura which surrounded him. The sight of the long-haired and unshaven midfield general patrolling his beat gave his team's supporters a sense of invincibility but there is every chance it also alerted referees. Inconspicuous he was not.

At one stage during his Aberdeen career Richardson opted for a change of approach, having his hair shorn and beard shaved off as part of an image change which he hoped would help him blend in with the Premier Division crowd. Apparently it came too late, with Scotland's referees' club already well aware of the snarling anchor man who was never far from the action wherever it occurred on the park. Richardson's belief that his appearance had an impact on his disciplinary record has never wavered and there have been examples since which illustrate his point. Zander Diamond's shaven-headed phase coincided with a rash of cards for the defender, something Richardson seized upon as an example of why individuality can be a curse rather than a blessing in football.

Appearance was not everything, though, with allegations of bias against the entire club rather than Richardson as an individual readily being aired during the 1990s. In November 1996 the *Evening Express* ran what the paper billed as an exposé of refereeing in Scotland, claiming an unnamed referee had lifted the lid on the widespread membership of the freemasons within the country's officials. The newspaper contrasted the disciplinary record of both halves of the Old Firm, pinpointing amazing statistics relating to the lack of action taken against Rangers when compared to Celtic.

The conspiracy theory was clear and Richardson was called upon to act as the expert judge and jury. He did not disappoint, claiming his bookings against Rangers were largely down to frustration over the inequality of refereeing decisions he witnessed in games against the Ibrox men. He also claimed he would never have had to leave Scotland had he played for Rangers rather than Aberdeen because he would not have been punished in the same way. It was controversial stuff, but then Ricco was never a man to shy away from the type of territory that would have had others running for cover.

That forthright approach, so typical of *Pittodrie Idols* through the ages, was endearing to the Red Army. Richardson was one of the boys as far as they were concerned and, in increasingly media-savvy times, his honest appraisals were a welcome relief from the mundane straight-bat replies so often fired in response to the occasional curve balls from the press inquisitors.

Now in his late 30s, time has mellowed him but the passion has not diminished. Richardson, taking a break from pre-season training with the Chesterfield side he now manages, told me: "I didn't understand that players at Aberdeen were on a pedestal, didn't understand that anything

I said would be headline news. Roy Aitken used to tell me to be careful with what I said, but I felt I was only being honest. That didn't always go down too well outside of Aberdeen. To me it isn't controversial to say we were up against 12 men – that was the way it was, with the attitude of the officials.

"Referees would warn me after five minutes. It was as though they were school teachers who saw me as some sort of disruptive pupil. I remember being sent off against Hibs and against Rangers, absolutely farcical decisions. I probably did go in a bit quick or a bit hard sometimes, but I was never a dirty player and never hurt anyone. That just wasn't what I was about. At every other club I had a reputation as a playmaker, but I was labelled as something different in Scotland. I don't understand why. I certainly would look after myself physically but there was much more to my game than winning the ball. The English game, certainly back then, was more physical and I had grown up learning that I had to protect myself in order to make the passes and play the way I wanted to play."

The way Richardson wanted to play was wholeheartedly but, by the same token, with flair and drive. That was exactly how he went about his business with the Dons and the reward was instant approval in the north-east. How he misses the buzz of kick-off and the roar of the crowd.

He said: "It seems like a long time ago. It's almost 15 years since I left Aberdeen and six since I stopped playing – I only wish I could turn back the clock and play again because I really miss it. I have always looked back at each of my moves with a hint of regret, but by far the biggest feeling I have is about the decision to leave Aberdeen. I never even spoke to Willie Miller about another contract, my mind was made up. In hindsight I should have given it another year or two. I didn't do myself any favours by moving on, but by March of the year I left I had already set my heart on going to Oldham. There was part of me that wanted to play for as many clubs, sample as many new experiences, as possible. But I was too hasty in leaving Aberdeen. When I made up my mind, Oldham were in the semi-final of the FA Cup and mid-table in the Premier League. By the end of the season they had missed out on the final and hadn't won another game, being relegated in the process. Instead of joining a club flying high I moved to a team on the crest of a slump. It was a downward spiral and that had an impact on my career.

"One of my great unfulfilled ambitions was to play abroad. Had I stayed at Aberdeen, where my profile was high, that would have been possible. Scott Booth did it, Gary Smith did it – I am sure I could have, too. Instead I ended up moving on from Oldham to Huddersfield and then Livingston. By the time I got to Livingston my ankles were shot, just through wear and tear. I really felt I let Ray Stewart down at Livi. He is the only manager I feel I have failed, simply because my body wasn't up to it. Had I been fit I think we could have won promotion and he would not have been sacked, so there's a deep sense of guilt. I had great respect for Ray."

While the mere mention of Richardson's name is enough to bring a smile to the face of the Aberdeen supporters who sang his name, the man himself cannot view his time in Scotland as a total success. Like all players with his level of determination, second place is one short of where he expected to be.

He said: "I should have, and could have, done better by winning the League or at least a cup. The team went on to win the League Cup a couple of years later and I was envious of Paul Bernard, who I had been with at Oldham, for having the chance to be part of that. To do well with Aberdeen you have to break the stranglehold the Old Firm have, or Rangers had at that time. It was so frustrating because we nearly managed it but fell at the last hurdle each time. It didn't quite happen and perhaps we didn't have the belief, or the venom, to do it. Stuart McCall and I still have a friendly rivalry – we love to hate each other. He lives not too far from me and we're from similar stock, but every time I see him I have an urge to kick him. Nothing has changed, even after all this time. Ian Ferguson was another one who I had a few battles with during that period. Nobody shirked any challenges in those games. One of the greatest qualities any team can have is the ability to see a game through or grind out a 1-0 win. All of the top sides have that and Rangers at that time were masters at it.

As a manager in his own right, most recently with Chesterfield prior to his 2009 departure, Richardson is now discovering at first hand the conundrum Willie Miller faced as he tried to unlock the undoubted potential of the Pittodrie squad in that period. Richardson believes it was a losing battle for Miller and the rest of the managers in the Scottish top flight.

He said: "Because I came up from England I had no preconceptions about the Scottish game. To me, Rangers were simply adversaries and the team we had to beat to win the League. There was no sense of awe. It is difficult for me to say because I'm from a different background, but I think the Scottish lads have had a different attitude drummed into them. A lot of players north of the border are closet Rangers or Celtic supporters and to me that isn't healthy because it can lead to too much respect being given to those clubs. I shared Willie's frustration at the way things were and I felt I always got on well with him. Willie was very intense and very focused on overtaking Rangers, which is the way it should be. We did get close, second in virtually everything during my time, but not getting beyond that was difficult to take.

"In the final analysis there were stages during the 1993/94 season when we could have taken the initiative. I remember a game at Pittodrie when we threw everything at Rangers apart from the kitchen sink, but Andy Goram played like two goalkeepers and Mark Hateley, who was always a thorn in our side, scored the winner. Had we won that night we would have put ourselves in a great position and I remember coming off the park and feeling like we had just lost the title. I could feel it slipping away from us."

Richardson's time to shine was without question in the 1993/94 European Cup Winners' Cup campaign. The first round saw the Dons cruise past Icelandic outfit Valur with a 3-0 away win followed by a 4-0 triumph on home soil. That teed up the second-round clash with Torino, the type of glamour tie the Red Army craved.

Richardson had the look of a Serie A midfielder, but the question was whether he could hold his own in that type of exalted company. The answer was a resounding affirmative.

In a pulsating first leg in Turin he was at the heart of the Dons team which came so agonisingly close to causing a European upset. In front of more than 30,000 passionate Italian supporters, the Dons caused a hush in the Stadio Delle Alpi when they carved out a two-goal lead through Eoin Jess and Mixu Paatelainen. The Italians roared back to win the tie 3-2 and set up a nerve jangling affair at Pittodrie a fortnight later.

The old ground was weighed down by 21,655 fervent and expectant supporters, the bulk roaring on the hosts. Richardson, ever the man for the big occasion, grabbed the match by the throat. His ferocious long-range volley made the impossible seem possible, giving the Dons a 1-0 lead and crucially a 3-3 aggregate draw which would have been enough to put them through on the away-goals rule. The hopes and dreams were shattered when Torino bit back with two goals of their own and the European adventure was over, albeit having been indelibly marked by Ricco, in what proved to be his final season.

He recalled: "I will always remember that goal, although I haven't watched it back for a long time. It was on my left foot so I really had to concentrate on the technique – had it been on my right, I might have relaxed a bit more and slashed it wide. Although the goal is a great memory, there's a sense of disappointment because we didn't finish the job. Torino went on to play Arsenal in the quarter-final and we were left wondering what could have been. Everyone who plays for Aberdeen knows how much the European success in the 1980s did for the profile and stature of the club and every player since must have dreamt of emulating that. I should never have played in the first leg. I'd been terribly ill with a virus leading up to it. Willie asked me to play and do a man-marking job on Benito Carbone – I was absolutely exhausted, but I did a good enough job. Again, though, we didn't quite make it over the finishing line."

When he moved on in 1994 he commanded a £325,000 fee, joining Oldham Athletic as he pursued his dream of Premiership football. He never quite reached that level, spending three years with the Latics before a loan stint with Stockport and a permanent transfer to Huddersfield. After his temporary stint with Bury in 1999 it was back to Scotland with Livingston in 2000 and then back across Hadrian's Wall to link up with Chesterfield six months later.

With that club he flourished once again, first as a midfield general and then as assistant manager. Early in 2007 he was promoted to take charge of the team in his own right and he has set about the task with the type of vigour which made him such as a hit as a player.

Dons fans may struggle to recognise the clean-shaven, short-haired manager in his suit and tie. The long hair and stubble were part of the Ricco persona, true to his rock roots and his rugged style of play. The Aberdonians may also struggle to recognise the man in a distinctly respectable profession, a position of responsibility. After all, this is the same person who just 15 years ago was making contingencies for life after football by formulating plans to create his own rock band. He had the name, PFA, pencilled in and older brother Nick, who turned out for Cardiff City at the time, as well as Manchester City's Rick Holden and Bolton Wanderers' Phil Brown – now boss of Hull City – signed to complete the line-up.

Richardson struck up a friendship with Aberdeen band One God Universe during his time on the Pittodrie roll-call, jamming with the group on occasions at Café Drummond on Belmont Street and becoming a regular at their gigs across the north-east. He even got a chance to play percussion on the band's debut album Schiffer, despite describing himself as an "enthusiastic amateur" as far as drumming was concerned. The bottom line is that he was as comfortable in a back-street venue as he was playing to a crowd of 50,000 in one of Glasgow's hotbeds of football, a real man of the people.

He admited: "I didn't appreciate everything I had at Aberdeen as much as I should have. The relationship I had with the supporters was like nothing I had experienced before and it was never repeated. At Halifax the crowd were protective to me, as a young pup, and I was fortunate that at every other club I played for the supporters appreciated me – but at Aberdeen it was something else. To hear your name being chanted fills you with pride. I even got it in bars when I was on a night out. That was a bit embarrassing but I'd far rather have it that way than have people calling me all the names under the sun, something you have to get used to as a manager. When I think about it, being coined at Motherwell or having 50,000 Rangers supporters waiting to boo me when I ran out on the park was good preparation for becoming a manager because you have to have a thick skin in this business."

When he left Pittodrie in 1994 it was a shattering blow to the supporters who had quickly grown to love and appreciate the distinctive number seven. There was to be no quick fix but time can be the game's greatest healer. After a year of longing, the Dons finally had a man fit to fill Ricco's boots when Dean Windass arrived in a £750,000 deal from Hull City in 1995.

By that time it was Roy Aitken at the tiller but the management was immaterial; what was important was the character on the park. Windass and Richardson could have been cut from the same chunk of Yorkshire stone, both opinionated and both no stranger to the red mist. Or the red card. Windass famously was shown the red on three occasions in one stormy match against Dundee United, something even Richardson never managed.

Windass even inherited the chant created for the idol he had replaced, the strains of "Oh, Oh, Ricco" replaced by calls for Deano. Windass, as it happened, barely lasted much longer than Richardson but made just as big an impact. He spent three seasons in the Scottish top flight but won the type of adulation many before him and since have failed to do in an entire career playing to the Pittodrie audience.

In 2008 Windass achieved what seemed like the impossible, firing his beloved Hull to the Premiership through the Championship play-offs at the ripe old age of 39. For a man who had never been blessed with the frame of an athlete, it was testament to his stamina and desire.

Even while living the dream with the Tigers, Windass never let Aberdeen drift from his thoughts. He approached the club with a view to a testimonial against the Dons in 2009 and in August of that year an army of Dons fans made the long haul down the east coast to pay tribute to another of their favourite sons.

Richardson and Windass in quick succession proved to be an embarrassment of riches, adding much-needed steel and skill to the spine of the Dons under Miller and then Aitken. Alex Miller, the next incumbent as Aberdeen manager, tried to repeat the magic formula when he signed a cheque for £300,000 in exchange for Bradford City midfielder Nigel Pepper. He may have come from Yorkshire, but Pepper was not a chip off the same block as his illustrious predecessors. The new recruit showed an ability to get sent off, but little else during his time in the north. Then he was gone, and largely forgotten. Unlike Richardson or Windass, who hit the mark in spectacular style with the Red Army. Ebbe Skovdahl, picking up the baton from Miller, had a dig at securing his own equivalent. Again Rachid Belabed had all the makings of a cult hero, but he fell short.

Players like Pepper and Belabed, who caused a stir more for their recklessness than simply for their commitment to the cause, come and go. What the Dons fans, as much as any other set of supporters, savour more than anything are the players who bring steel to their team, but such shrewd observers demand more than just resistance. "Hard but fair" has been the mantra for generations, from those who roared on Jock Hutton in the 1920s to those who watched in awe as Don Emery charged into another challenge in the 1940s. From the days of Davie Robb, the self-appointed minder for Joe Harper in the 1970s, to those of Doug Rougvie and Neil Simpson in the 1980s, there has been a hunger for the players who would fight tooth and nail for the cause without forgetting the family foundations the club was built upon or its sporting traditions. Richardson scored so highly in the popularity stakes by falling effortlessly into the slipstream of those revered characters who went before him. The referees may have been glad to see the back of Richardson, but the Dons fans who watched him at his peak would have taken him back like a shot.

'UNCLE EBBE' 1999–2002

EBBE SKOVDAHL

Magic Moment: Paul Bernard's goal made it a cool half-dozen as the Dons defeated Motherwell 6-5 to give Skovdahl his first League win. It was victory Ebbe-style.

Dons Career: Games 159.

IN FOOTBALL there are few certainties. Once upon a time, one was that that journalistic gold dust was about to be scattered liberally around the Pittodrie press room as soon as Ebbe Skovdahl muttered the immortal line: "We have a saying in Denmark". Those six words were the precursor to some of the most enchanting trains of thought the old ground has ever played host to and for the press pack of the time, myself included, a break from the old routine and the game's familiar clichés.

"The character of a man is known from his conversations."

Menander, Greek dramatist

In 1996 I walked through the door of Aberdeen Football Club as a teenage reporter, primed and ready for my first Dons press conference. Roy Aitken was the manager and, while his approach off the field was not as fierce as he had displayed on the park, at the back of your mind you knew "The Bear" was capable of snarling his way through a session if the questioning was not to his liking.

When I left the Pittodrie beat behind for pastures new, Aitken was still in office. In 2001 I returned to the old stomping ground and into a very different era. "Grizzly" had gone and in his place was old "Uncle Ebbe". Skovdahl was like nothing that had gone before in the Dons manager's office and like nothing since. He was refreshing, yet infuriating at times, intriguing when he chose to be yet capable of clamming up when the mood took him. Every day was different with the Dane behind the desk and nobody could predict what would come next. That was part of the fun, a major part.

As Aberdeen's first and only foreign manager, Skovdahl always held a trump card – he could play on the language barrier. Only the man himself knows for sure, but my guess is that barrier was more of a tool to throw up a shield of innocence than a hindrance for the wily old managerial fox. Skovdahl got away with some outrageous comments courtesy of the benefit of the doubt. A Scottish manager using the same turn of phrase would have been viewed with scepticism, his credibility placed in the balance, but it became an accepted part of life under the continental coach. And for that we should all be thankful.

Following in the brogue prints of a succession of respectable yet dour coaches, Skovdahl was manna from heaven for those who made it their mission to see the light side of some of the darkest days Pittodrie has ever experienced. Chris Crighton, editor of Aberdeen fanzine *The Red Final*, still pines for the charismatic Dane. Crighton recalls: "If statistics really are like miniskirts, then the ones surrounding Ebbe Skovdahl's Pittodrie tenure are like those which are often to be found struggling to maintain the decency of some of Aberdeen's sturdier clubbers on a midwinter Belmont Street night. Thoroughly inappropriate for a set-up of such magnitude, yet intriguingly alluring nonetheless. Ebbe's reign is remembered largely, fairly or unfairly, for two things – the Dons being pasted more regularly than a train station billboard, and the manager's Confucius-like musings upon the travails of his team. Not for him the glazed look of a man frozen in the middle of the tracks when the lights begin to glare out of the tunnel. Skovdahl had a world-weary analogy for every footballing disaster which came his way, if not necessarily a formula to stop them happening.

"When Skovdahl arrived in the north-east in the summer of 1999 he must have thought there was a buttery strike on or something, such was the assortment of scunnered expressions printed onto the Aberdonian faces which greeted him. Having watched through their fingers the reigns of Paul Hegarty, Alex Miller and Roy Aitken, and the final few months of Willie Miller's vain struggle, regular Pittodrie punters were easy to spot on King Street – they were the ones not using the pedestrian crossings, in the knowledge that coming head-to-head with the 1A to Garthdee would give them an excellent excuse to miss the match and probably guarantee them a more entertaining afternoon into the bargain. Whether this dishevelled Dane was the saviour was debatable, but he couldn't be any worse, surely."

> *"Why should we train for marathons when it is football we want to play?" – July 1999.*

With that, the Skovdahl story began in earnest. In his own acerbic manner, the new coach set about stamping his authority on the club on his first day in office. Gone were the traditional Scottish pre-season beastings and in their place a more refined, modernistic approach to physical conditioning. Skovdahl's son had followed in his father's footsteps by becoming a coach in his own right, serving within Brondby's youth academy, and had a reputation for sophisticated and innovative methods. Aberdeen's own fitness coach at the time, Stuart Hogg, even took the opportunity to visit Denmark and tap into Skovdahl Junior's expertise.

While the words were cutting, the actions spoke even more loudly. One of the first major spending sprees during the new man's tenure was not to bring in a Scandinavian goalkeeper, a South American striker or a French midfielder. Instead he dug out the chequebook to buy 40 mattresses, which were spread around the inner sanctum at Pittodrie for players, from youth team to first team, to bed down on in between the newly introduced daily double training sessions. That was training taken care of; all there was to take care of now was the football.

For the fanzine editor and his fellow Dons fans, a new era was about to dawn, but what it would bring was anyone's guess. Crighton said: "Summer came and summer went without any additions to Paul Hegarty's squad. Finally, on the eve of the season, in came David Preece, a goalkeeper, and two days later he picked the ball out of the net five times as Celtic set a disturbing tone. Six weeks later, he had fetched it on a further 13 occasions without any of his outfield team-mates making an impression on the SPL scoring charts. Aberdeen were not so much propping up the table as drowning in the damp course somewhere under the floorboards. Things had got so bad that celebrations of title-winning proportions met the Dons' first League goal of the season, in the last game of September, despite the fact that they were already 2-0 down and still ended up losing."

> *"Like the fans, I have dreams for Aberdeen and would love to only speak about them. But dreams are one thing … the real world is a different thing altogether." – July 1999.*

If that was Skovdahl's way of suggesting the Dons fans required a reality check, once again actions spoke louder than words. The Dane's first game following his 1999 appointment was the above-mentioned farce at Pittodrie on 1 August against a Celtic team still stung by the disappointment of missing out on the previous season's League title by six points to Rangers. The Hoops came out fighting and steamrollered over the top of Skovdahl's shell-shocked side. Crash – inside four minutes Henrik Larsson made it 1-0. Bang – Mark Viduka had the net bulging in the 35th minute. Wallop – six minutes later the Australian had bagged a double. A second-half Larsson penalty and an injury-time goal from Mark Burchill made it five and the miserable start to what was supposed to be a brave new era was complete.

Between Paul Hegarty's final game in charge at the end of the 1998/99 campaign and Skovdahl's competitive debut, there were five changes to the starting 11. New goalkeeper David Preece made his debut, in place of Hegarty's loan signing Tony Warner, while Mark Perry dropped out along with Andreas Mayer, Jamie Buchan and Michael Hart. In their places came Nigel Pepper, Paul Bernard, Dennis Wyness and Derek Young as part of the reshuffle. Jamie McAllister, a substitute on the day, also made his debut and that injection of fresh blood was to become a common occurrence as the increasingly perplexed coach searched for a solution to woes which rapidly became clear. Staggeringly he went through 37 players in his first season. The new faces included Thomas Solberg, Darren Mackie, David Lilley, Cato Guntveit, Juan Cobian, Arild Stavrum, Rachid Belabed, Kevin Rutkiewicz, Hicham Zerouali, Phil McGuire and Chris Clark. With 13 debutants in a single season they may as well have fitted a revolving door on the home dressing room to go with the mattresses.

> *"I always tell people, when you point a finger at anyone three other fingers are also pointing at yourself." – August 1999.*

It went from bad to worse for the new manager, who watched helpless from the sidelines as his inherited side drew a blank in their opening six League games while shipping 18 goals in those encounters. They lost a seventh consecutive game before picking up a point against Hibs, the first of the season, on October 2. Normal service was resumed in the next SPL outing, which resulted in a humiliating 7-0 defeat at Celtic. It remains an unwanted club record in the Premier League.

In an honourable, yet perhaps over-generous display of solidarity, the manager was quite happy to take the blame for his team's failings. It was clearly a source of frustration for an experienced coach who had carved out a strong reputation throughout Europe and supporters could have been forgiven for wondering if he did, in fact, have any answer to the malaise enveloping Pittodrie.

But they didn't. Instead the supporters rounded on chairman Stewart Milne and his directors. Anybody, in fact, apart from the Danish import who had charmed them in his brief introduction to their club and city. There were demonstrations against Milne, a reaction which had become common, but the support for his bold managerial appointment remained strong when the circumstances were taken into account. There was an element of giving him the benefit of the doubt but there was also a less quantifiable element which can only be explained by Skovdahl's rapidly developing cult status.

After the fifth defeat in that horrible sequence, a 3-0 reverse against St Johnstone, a crowd of 200 gathered outside Pittodrie to vent their fury at Milne. One supporter interviewed at the time said: "I'm disgusted to see my club in the shape it's in at the moment and, like any number of fans out here tonight, my biggest concern is that Ebbe Skovdahl will walk away from the job here because he's not getting the support he deserves from the Aberdeen board." In previous years the Dons support would have been urging the board to pay the manager to walk away, but Skovdahl's distinctive brand of enthusiasm for the job had turned the tables. It was the employers, not the employee, who fell under the spotlight.

> *"It was close to the strangest game I have ever been involved in. I won't hear anyone say we are not entertaining." – October 1999.*

Life with Uncle Ebbe on the scene was never boring. The crazy, crazy 6-5 victory against Motherwell in October 1999 broke Aberdeen's League duck for the season and brought the manager his first set of full points. The 11-goal thriller has gone down as one of the most exhilarating the Dons fans have been treated to in modern times and it was as unpredictable a contest as Skovdahl appeared to be as a manager. Robbie Winters bagged a hat-trick while Eoin Jess, Andy Dow and Paul Bernard were also on target to give hope to the Red Army who had made the trip to Fir Park. In a total of 36 League games there were only eight victories that season as the rock-bottom Dons remained rooted solidly to the muddy foot of the SPL table. Only the dilapidated state of First Division champions Falkirk's ground saved Aberdeen from the ignominy of relegation. With Brockville's crumbling old stands failing to meet top-flight criteria the Dons were handed a get-out-of-jail card worth millions.

Despite those League woes – which included 5-1 and 5-0 defeats against Rangers and a 5-1 collapse against Celtic, yet featured the highs of a 5-1 victory against Kilmarnock and a 4-0 win over Hibs – it was not an unmitigated disaster. Under old Uncle Ebbe, the Dons reached both domestic cup finals, only to fall at the final hurdle each time. The League Cup was first up, with the Dane steering his side past Livingston, Falkirk, Rangers and Dundee United to set up a Hampden date with Celtic in the final. The Hoops won 2-0 to prevent the Dons from claiming their first trophy in five years.

> *"We have an old saying in Denmark that you must never sell the skin until you have killed the bear." – February 2000.*

With his musings on bear hide, Skovdahl was, in his by now familiar fashion, preparing a soft landing for the fans who were expecting a comfortable passage past seemingly inferior opponents. The opposition in this case was the Steve Paterson-inspired Caley Thistle and the competition was the Scottish Cup. The First Division Highlanders did not let Skovdahl down, putting up stiff resistance to claim a 1-1 draw in the initial tie before the Dons eased through to the fifth round. Wins against Dundee United and then Hibs in the semi-final teed up another shot at glory. This time it was Rangers who stood in the path and nobody will ever forget the outcome, with Jim Leighton's loss through injury within minutes of kick-off leaving the lost figure of Robbie Winters standing in for the bulk of the match. Not surprisingly Rangers ran out 4-0 victors and the manager found himself backed into a corner, furiously defending his decision not to include a substitute goalkeeper on the bench for what transpired to be the biggest match of his reign.

Skovdahl, who had reeled at the criticism of negative tactics earlier in the season, claimed the decision, which proved flawed, was testament to his attacking nature. The Dane could cling to the wreckage of his second final defeat, safe in the knowledge that the UEFA Cup place which came with the appearance in the showpiece game at least offered the prospect of salvation in the season which followed. That European qualification should have been an occasion to celebrate, but turned out to be a millstone around the neck of the manager.

Chris Crighton recalled: "If it felt like a corner had been turned as Andy Dow's free-kick ruffled the net for the first goal of Ebbe's first season, the Dons merely emerged into oncoming motorway traffic. Despite breaking their League duck with a suitably bizarre 6-5 win at Motherwell, Skovdahl's Aberdeen finished a distant last, losing 21 of their 36 matches and conceding an horrific 83 goals, albeit having taken their eye off the Premier League ball when it became clear early in 2000 that the scheduled relegation play-offs would not be required. Because, remarkably, they had bigger fish to fry – the worst team in the land somehow managed to see off Livingston, Falkirk, Rangers, St Mirren, Inverness, Hibs and Dundee United twice – to power through to not one but two domestic cup finals. Of course, they lost both, the second with a striker in goal because, yes, Skovdahl had decided not to include a keeper amongst his substitutes. But the Hampden days out were just reward for the supporters who had left their embarrassment and shame on the shelf and continued to follow his ramshackle team across the country."

Bohemians Football Club was the name plucked from the bowl alongside the Dons in the UEFA Cup draw for the 2000/01 season. The eclectic bunch of Dubliners, led by their eccentric manager Roddy Collins, should not have posed a problem. But once again Ebbe's words proved prophetic and supporters were left referring back to bears and their skins. A shock 2-1 reverse at Pittodrie left the Dons with a not unconquerable mountain to climb – but they found themselves stranded at base camp in Dublin, unable to score and tumbling out on the away-goals rule when a Bohs own goal proved too little, too late for their European cause. The 2-2 aggregate draw was as big a humiliation as the club had experienced in the continental game, even taking Skonta Riga into account, but it did not damage the manager's reputation among the travelling Red Army.

By that stage the cult of Skovdahl was growing by the day, with every droll comment. The media took no prisoners in the wake of the humbling in Dublin but reporters were left bemused by the support for the forlorn coach. The *Evening Express* noted in the aftermath: "Legendary United States president Abraham Lincoln was wrong ... it appears you can fool all of the people all of the time. How else do you explain 1,400 Dons fans giving their team and manager a standing ovation after their most humiliating European exit ever? Having witnessed their anger after previous shockers against FC Copenhagen, Skonto Riga, Zalgiris Vilnius and Stenhousemuir, I was prepared for the worst. As the Dons were being hailed as heroes I sat there in the shadows of the Tolka Park stand wondering if the Red Army has been the victim of some sort of mass brainwashing."

Brainwashing it may not have been, but Skovdahl certainly had a hold over the Aberdeen fans during his brief dalliance with the Scottish game. The 2000/01 season had got off to the worst possible start with the shocking events on the Emerald Isle but things, it transpired, cannot only get better. They can get an awful lot worse.

In December 2000, having already been beaten 4-2 by Rangers earlier in the season, Aberdeen travelled south to Parkhead hoping to break their Old Firm hoodoo and record a victory against one of the Glasgow giants. Having held the Hoops 1-1 at Pittodrie already that term, there was reason for optimism but Celtic had not read the script and produced a 6-0 thumping to once again raise serious question marks about the direction in which the club was heading.

> *"Only cowards walk away when they have problems." – December 2000.*

With that simple statement the manager made it clear. He was in it for the long haul, for better or worse as well as for richer and for poorer. Before the season was out he had signed a new contract and agreed to a significant pay cut, believed to run into six figures, to ensure he could stay on and see through the rebuilding vision he had when he first arrived on north-east soil. That financial sacrifice did not go unnoticed by the Dons support, so used to watching players and managers come and go without any public sign of real commitment to the cause.

The new contract coincided with a decent run of form by Skovdahl's team. Five defeats in the last 15 games of the season at least hinted that the frailties were beginning to be shored up. Instead of propping up the division, there was mid-table anonymity, which after the previous season's struggles was just fine for the Dandies. Seventh place in a 12-team league was hardly the stuff of dreams but it was progress all the same.

> *"Statistics are like mini-skirts: they give you lots of good ideas, but hide what's important." – 2000.*

The mini-skirts quip is undoubtedly the most famous pearl of wisdom rolled out by Skovdahl and was a retort to a claim that statistically Arild Stavrum was a better striker than Henrik Larsson. As crass as it may have been to compare the two, Skovdahl was doing himself a disservice. In luring Stavrum to Pittodrie, he had, in fact, pulled off a masterstroke, even if it did take the Norwegian time to find his feet in the hectic confines of the SPL.

Stavrum banged home 17 goals in 2000/01, his second campaign in a red shirt, and was the reason for much of the optimism that prevailed in and around the ground. His nearest challenger was Robbie Winters, on nine goals, so there was no doubt Stavrum had justified Skovdahl's faith and proved he could cut it at the top level. If only he had stuck around longer, Stavrum himself would surely have etched a permanent place on the Aberdeen Cult Heroes roll of honour. As it happened, on the back of his 2000/01 campaign, he opted for a midnight flit to Besiktas in Turkey and the burgeoning relationship with the Red Army was severed.

The loss of Stavrum should have been a body blow for Skovdahl but the progress continued in the 2001/02 term as the Dons clawed their way up to a fourth-place finish in the League and once again clinched UEFA Cup qualification. Life was good, the chain-smoking manager was a becoming a god. He was often seen puffing on a cigarette as he made a leisurely stroll up the touchline towards the dugout on match-day. Soon the relaxed attitude impregnated the club at every level and the tea-cup throwing days of Sir Alex felt like a lifetime ago.

> *"The operation went well but the patient died." – September 2001.*

The laid-back approach did lend itself to an occasional blip but there were encouraging signs that the message was getting through. The five- and six-goal thrashings which had become a hallmark of the previous seasons disappeared; in their place came a more assured and competent team moulded by the shrewd Scandinavian.

That in itself brought issues, with the famous "patient died" defence coming in the wake of a clammy performance in a 2-0 defeat against Celtic. As Skovdahl was learning, improved performance brought expectation levels creeping back up and simply competing admirably with the Old Firm was never going to be enough in the long term for a success-starved outfit. The half-complete building job would have to continue at rapid pace if the ambitions in the stands were to be matched on the park.

> *"Even though it is written in the newspapers, it might be true." – August 2001.*

In response, Skovdahl continued to flood the north-east with new recruits and the steady stream of arrivals was welcome fodder for the headline-writers. His cutting observation about the intense newspaper interest in his transfer dealings related to a story revealing Ben Thornley's imminent arrival, a deal which provoked a flurry of enthusiasm amongst an Aberdeen faithful deprived of out-and-out wingers up to that point.

By the time the 2001/02 campaign kicked-off, the mark of Uncle Ebbe was stamped across the Aberdeen team. When he picked 14 to tackle Rangers on the opening day, there were only four survivors from his first selection of 14 back in 1999. One of those, David Preece, was a Skovdahl signing so only a trio of inherited players made it past the manager's first two seasons at the helm: captain Derek Whyte, Derek Young and Robbie Winters. It was a remarkable turnover in personnel but deemed necessary and paid off with that fourth-placed finish and another shot at the European game.

The players brought in to fill the gaps created by Skovdahl's revolution included imports Cato Guntveit, Roberto Bisconti, Thomas Solberg and Rachid Belabed, as well as youngsters Kevin McNaughton, Darren Mackie, Chris Clark, Phil McGuire and Kevin Rutkiewicz. Darren Young had also forced his way back in as a key man in the master plan. Experienced Danish goalkeeper Peter Kjaer, arguably the biggest transfer coup of them all, arrived during the 2001/02 campaign and lodged himself in the team, while Leon Mike, a promising Manchester City reserve, arrived amid much fanfare. Mike, a former *Coronation Street* actor, did not take the Scottish stage by storm.

In the summer of 2002, with the club buoyed by the imminent UEFA Cup campaign, cultured French defender Eric Deloumeaux was tempted north after starring for Motherwell and everything was rosy in the Pittodrie garden. For a while, at least.

Nistru Otaci, and the potentially treacherous Moldovan trip that tie involved, were successfully negotiated in the qualifying round to set up a glamour tie with Hertha Berlin. Glorious failure ensued, with a 0-0 draw at Pittodrie followed up by a 1-0 defeat in the Olympic Stadium courtesy of an agonising 89th-minute goal from Michael Preetz. Nobody had given the Dons much hope of troubling their Bundesliga opponents but Skovdahl walked out of the sprawling old Berlin ground with his head held high – and straight into a barrage of body blows in the months which followed.

After the curtain fell on the European adventure, a truly horrible run of just one victory in nine League encounters followed before the end of the Skovdahl era finally arrived. That sequence included a return to the dark days against the Old Firm, with a 7-0 annihilation at Parkhead against Celtic as John Hartson ran riot with four goals. Amid tales of boardroom unrest, Skovdahl uncharacteristically threw in the towel, claiming he had taken the club as far as the financial restrictions would allow. Whether he jumped before he was pushed, we will never know. His final game was a 1-0 defeat against Kilmarnock at Pittodrie on 2 December 2002. The chants of "Ebbe must stay" rang out around the ground but the words were hollow. The man the fans hoped would turn out to be a managerial messiah already had his bags packed and his return ticket to Copenhagen booked.

> *"There is an expression often used over here, which is 'Play for the manager'. On the continent the players played for the club, so I was unaware of this." – November 2002.*

Initially, when the announcement of Skovdahl's decision to stand down was made, the timescale was left open-ended. He was willing to see the season out if required, but within days the departure had been hastened and Steve Paterson was being lined up to take his place. While Paterson was a popular choice, there was no hiding the disappointment among sections of the Dons support who were desperate to see their idiosyncratic coach succeed.

Writing in the *Press and Journal*, Aberdeen reporter Stuart Darroch observed: "When the history books record Ebbe Skovdahl's time at Aberdeen, his colourful quotes and his penchant for the occasional cigarette will figure as prominently as his achievements on the field. Skovdahl has achieved the impossible at the club by failing to improve on the club's League position, yet still remaining a favourite among the majority of the fans. The man initially dubbed a Danish dud by certain sections of the media will return home with, perhaps, his credibility not completely intact, but with a hard-earned respect in a football-mad foreign country. Skovdahl remains one of the favourite Pittodrie imports in the eyes of the fans. Not many managers can walk away from Pittodrie with his team in fourth-bottom position and still be warmly greeted on Union Street."

And there you have it – in a whirlwind of words the life and Aberdeen times of Ebbe Skovdahl in a neat nutshell. Behind his three years and four months steering the good ship AFC lay a complex character whose background shaped his unique approach to the game.

For a start, Skovdahl is not his surname. It is, in fact, his middle name. According to his passport he was Mr E S Hansen, and Mrs Hansen was the lady on his arm. The Skovdahl tag first surfaced when he played alongside Ebbe Johansen in his homeland and he switched moniker to avoid confusion. The pair were team-mates during the Dons hero's days in part-time football – he never even sampled the full-time game until he became coach of Brondby in 1986.

Up to that point he had carved out a niche for himself as a salesman and it isn't difficult to see how he managed it, the gift of the gab being a prerequisite. He gambled with his future when he gave up that lucrative career in sales to venture into the professional game but it paid off with instant success, guiding Brondby to the League title and being snapped up by Portuguese giants Benfica soon afterwards.

Despite leading the Lisbon side into the last eight of the European Cup, and sitting nicely in second spot in the League, he was dismissed after six months and returned to Brondby. There he regrouped and led the Copenhagen side to three titles and two domestic cups during his tenure. It was an impressive record, enough to catch Stewart Milne's attention and create one of the most colourful chapters in the history of the club.

The chairman has often been criticised for thriftiness and urged to dig into his own personal wealth to give his managers clout in the transfer market. In the case of Skovdahl, it would be wrong to suggest there was not backing for the grand plans. He spent £1.4million in his bid to put the Dons back on the football map, the type of funding his successors could only dream of.

He used the new players to make his vision for 4-3-3 football a reality, but the attacking connotations of that formation did not come to fruition on the park. Aside from that, a perceived lack of passion from the touchlines also raised eyebrows among supporters and the media alike.

Stuart Darroch reported: "His laid-back nature in front of the media and in the dugout led to the criticism he didn't care. Clearly not the case. Time after time he would respond to this criticism by saying he refused to waste energy and time shouting at the players when he could calmly point out the error of their ways."

In the main, the Dane's dealings with the media reflected his touchline persona, cool and collected. But there was another side to the man, one which was rarely seen in public but lurked beneath. When irked, Skovdahl could show steel and had a stubbornness which served him well in every aspect of the job. While the continental coach fostered a relaxed mood within his camp, his dealings with players he deemed to have crossed the fine line were swift and resolute.

Fans' favourite Eoin Jess was one victim, sacrificed when the manager questioned his commitment to the cause, while German midfielder Andreas Mayer was also swiftly removed from the books after querying Skovdahl's leadership qualities. Nobody reaches the heights he did without that grit and determination, but the difference between him and so many of his peers was that there was no bravado involved; he preferred to try and keep his shows of strength behind closed doors. The fans were treated to the friendly face and they enjoyed it as a break from the norm.

Crighton said: "After the early struggles there was progress. Skovdahl flooded the team with youngsters – Kevin McNaughton, Phil McGuire, Ryan Esson, David Rowson, Chris Clark and the Young brothers all became first-team fixtures, with 225 starts between them in Ebbe's second season compared to 15 in his first – and as they grew in stature so, too, did the team. From tenth in 2000, they rose to seventh in 2001, and a fourth-place finish in 2002 that seemed almost as unbelievable as the comedy of two years previous.

"In just three years, Ebbe Skovdahl had turned a team which struggled to even run on to the park without bumping into one another into a side which had qualified for Europe with a run of home wins not seen since the glory days of Alex Ferguson. German giants Hertha Berlin were inches away from being eliminated by the Dons in that UEFA Cup, and if the boss had stumbled into the Irish Bar that night there would have been no shortage of Reds queuing up to buy him a Carlsberg. One month later Ebbe's nemesis, Celtic, smashed yet another seven past poor Preece – the sixth time the Hoops had scored five or more against

Skovdahl's Aberdeen – and a further month down the line he was gone, like a hurricane blowing itself out over Pittodrie, leaving us all wondering what on earth just happened.

"Ebbe was often pilloried for his lack of ambition – even the famous mini-skirts quote was his response to the revelation that some criteria suggested his own player Arild Stavrum was better than Henrik Larsson, a sentiment which you might have hoped he would have tried to brazenly defend in some way – but as with any manager he can only be judged by whether he left the club in a better state than he received it, and in Skovdahl's case the answer to that question is a definite yes.

"One of Skovdahl's most famous truisms was, fittingly after yet another Parkhead defeat, that 'the operation went well, but the patient died'. It was to prove his own Pittodrie obituary. If the operation was to restore some pride to a beaten-down club, then one has to say, even though it was a time-consuming procedure, it worked. But if the patient was Ebbe himself, more specifically his reputation in Aberdeen and in Scottish football, then, sadly, he didn't make it. One suspects history will judge Ebbe Skovdahl considerably less harshly than the jackals who couldn't see past his stand-up routines, his chain-smoking and his wonky specs."

'ZERO' 1999–2002

HICHAM ZEROUALI

Magic Moment: With Aberdeen teetering on the brink of Scottish Cup first-round humiliation against First Division side St Mirren, the Moroccan magician stepped up to the plate and batted the Dons back into the tournament with a stupendous free-kick equaliser which proved to be the first step on the road to Hampden.

Dons Career: Games 48. Goals 13. Caps 17.

IN DARK, dark days one star shone bright as a glimmering, sparkling beacon of hope and light for the Dons supporters. Amidst the six-goal drubbings and other morale-sapping defeats there was relief from the despair when one man was on the ball: step forward Hicham Zerouali.

The Moroccan, probably more than any other overseas player to grace the Pittodrie turf, warmed the hearts of the football public in the frosty north-east. Zoltan Varga brought intrigue and mystery, Willem van der Ark was a true gem of a curio, but Zerouali was a purveyor of heart-stopping drama and a merchant of unbridled joy during a troubled time for the club.

Despite two cup-final appearances during the Zerouali era, typically the high spots were few and far between for a team which produced performances as erratic and eccentric as its coach, Ebbe Skovdahl. Inside his first four games for his new Scottish outfit, the Moroccan had experienced a 6-0 reverse at the hands of Celtic and a 5-0 loss against Rangers. Yes, there were good times, but the rough most certainly had to be taken with the smooth and individual performances offered fans escapism. None more so than those from Zerouali, the tricks and flicks as well as the spectacular goals that came with the territory.

His SPL career was all too brief, just 14 League starts and 31 eventful months, but his impact was instant and lasting. Zerouali's untimely death in 2004 in a car crash in his homeland at the tender age of 27 and with his best years still in front of him only served to reinforce, in the most tragic of circumstances, just how much he meant to the adoring Aberdonians and just how much he would be missed.

The tiny crumb of comfort was the fact the Red Army had savoured the midfield marvel during his foreign assignment and never failed to show their appreciation. The affection was mutual, with the player genuinely touched by the strength of feeling his talents generated, and so another cult hero was born.

He signed amid fanfare and trumpet late in 1999, making his debut in a 3-1 win over Hearts on December 8. The first goal came 17 days later, a stunner from distance in a 3-1 victory against Dundee United. His ability to carve out memorable moments materialised quickly, with his net-busting equaliser against St Mirren in a Scottish Cup tie in January 2000 typifying his contribution to the team effort in that period. In all he scored 11 League goals, many of them during his frequent cameo appearances from the bench.

"Nothing great in the world has been accomplished without passion."

Georg Wilhelm, German philosopher

Every supporter has his/her own 'Zero' moment, and every journalist, too. My own most vivid recollection is of the Moroccan marauding down the Pittodrie pitch with the Hibs team, including goalkeeper Nick Colgan, in hot pursuit after the Edinburgh team had thrown everyone forward in a bid to grab a late goal in an SPL game in November 2001. Zerouali won the race, slotting the ball into an empty net to cap a scene which could have come straight from a Benny Hill sketch.

The media fell under Zerouali's spell, just as the fans did, although admittedly his work ethic came under the microscope in the hurly-burly of the Scottish game. Critical objectivity was not always applied where Zerouali was concerned but behind the scenes the Dons did have the foresight to remain level-headed about their new prized asset.

Zerouali's status as a cult hero was not lost on Aberdeen's marketing department. Set against a backdrop of spiralling debts and annual losses which could not be stemmed, the need to increase revenue and maximise earning potential was at the top of the boardroom agenda. In Zero, there was a perfect opportunity to speculate to accumulate.

The fez became a must-have accessory around Pittodrie as fans paid homage to their African idol, but the Dons had more innovative plans in mind. They were about to rip up football tradition and start from scratch, or start from zero as it happened. Squad numbers were introduced in the SPL in the late 1990s and in 2000 the quick-thinking Reds took full advantage when they became the first, and admittedly the last, club in the country to register a player as number nought.

Zero had zero on his back and everyone was happy. The new kit had its first outing in the Scottish Cup final of 2000 and the predicted rush for replica kits materialised. The club even investigated the possibility of shipping the latest strip to Morocco to capitalise on the foreign interest in their star's progress on Scottish soil, aiming to make it the must-have fashion accessory on the streets of Casablanca and Rabat. That shipment never landed in Africa, but it's the thought that counts.

The zero lasted all of one year. By the summer of 2001 the club had agreed to a desperate plea from Zerouali to ditch the digit which he felt was the root of much of the bad luck which plagued him during the period he was, quite literally, the first name on the Dons squad list. The request was granted, the vacant number 11 was handed over and Dons general manager David Johnston was left to apologise to the supporters who had shelled out for their one-season piece of apparel.

Johnston said: "Hicham feels the number zero has been very unlucky and asked for a change. There is no point in asking a player to wear a number that makes him unhappy. I'm sure the fans will agree we had no choice on this occasion. We are also about to launch a new kit and announcing Hicham's new number now at least makes sure fans who buy it don't put the wrong one on those jerseys."

While Zerouali's cache off the park was valuable to the Dons, his recruitment was based on football merits rather than any ambitious revenue projections. The marketing melee which followed his arrival was very much an afterthought, a world away from the cold and calculated approach taken by English Premier League and even Celtic in the drive to introduce players from Japan and the Far East to the British game. Shunsuke Nakamura's introduction to the Hoops team brought dead ball ability and cultured passing, but it also injected hard cash into the Parkhead coffers. Sales of Celtic shirts bearing the Japan international's name in his homeland, and other Bhoys merchandise, have helped propel the club into the top ten of world football's money league.

Celtic ranked seventh in the 2006/07 financial table published by accountants Deloitte and were the only club from outwith England, Germany, France, Italy and Spain to feature in the top 20. They boasted record turnover in excess of £75 million and the influence of Nakamura did nothing but good things for the balance sheet. The television viewing figures reflected the enormous potential for revenue generating growth, with Japanese subscription levels to SPL coverage shooting up from 100,000 to 1.2 million following Nakamura's introduction.

The potential to earn on the back of Zerouali was explored by the Dons, but the Moroccan market offered far less potential than the Far East equivalent and the idea of exporting the Zero shirts to his native country were quietly dropped. The whole Zero phenomenon came from a chant from the stands, with the new star quickly christened with the abbreviated tag by the Red Army who could not wedge his full name into a suitable song. The club took note of the nickname, and the shirt idea was adopted after the player was persuaded of its merits by those in power at Pittodrie. Initially he was not keen on becoming a Zero, but after listening to the commercially sound arguments he warmed to the idea. Soon after, the replica kits began to fly from the shelves in a way the club had never experienced before.

Because of the freestyle nature of the retail explosion, there was no cynicism surrounding Zerouali's arrival in Scotland. The move was not born from a twinkle in a marketing man's eye, instead catching the attention of a key member of the backroom staff. Keith Burkinshaw is a much maligned figure in the history of Aberdeen Football Club, occupying the director of football's chair long before Willie Miller returned in that capacity. The former Spurs manager was enticed to Pittodrie during Roy Aitken's tenure, charged with adding experience to the coaching set-up and a guiding hand to the board. His work was done behind the scenes, largely unnoticed and unloved by an Aberdeen support who saw his considerable wage as a drain on resources at a time when their team was struggling.

If Burkinshaw can lay claim to one legacy it is the hope he provided by stumbling upon a young rising star by the name of Zerouali while trawling through the endless mountain of video tapes provided by agents peddling players of varying quality during that era. Zerouali's talents shone like a beacon amid the procession of mundane players and Burkinshaw alerted manager Ebbe Skovdahl to the possibilities of signing the man the director of football had already labelled a "Moroccan Magician". Those involved with the club at that time can still recall vividly the buzz that swept through the back rooms of Pittodrie after the first sighting of the player who quickly shot to the top of Aberdeen's wanted list. He was not an overnight box-office hit in the way established superstar Charlie Nicholas had been, but the club knew he had the potential to add something very special to the mix.

They had to work hard to conclude the deal, contending with the red tape which accompanies any move for a non-European player, but persistence paid off. For the playing squad and the rest of the staff at Pittodrie, life was about to get far more interesting. His presence gave the whole club a lift, from the team manning the club's administrative offices to the team-mates who knew one flash of brilliance could win them a game. It also brought frustration in equal measure, through the lows which followed the highs.

There was always a feeling from within Pittodrie that Zerouali would have been better suited to playing in a winning team, rather than the embattled side he found himself in amid the torrid Skovdahl reign. He was a luxury player at a time when bread and butter was the order of the day and undoubtedly the Dons never saw the very best of him, at least not consistently, because of the culture of fear and trepidation which surrounded almost every game during his stay with the club.

There was little scope for creative freedom, although Zerouali did display the ability to shoehorn his talents into games whenever possible. Away from the game he was pleasant, polite and humble. He endeared himself to his colleagues at the club, who in turn did their best to help him settle in unfamiliar surroundings. The language barrier did not prevent the African from expressing himself, always willing to share a laugh and joke with the Dons staff just as he did with the Dons supporters who wore his name on their backs. That attitude helped cement his place at the head of the popularity stakes, confirming his worth in so many ways.

He was every marketing man's dream, but Zerouali's short time in Aberdeen was not all about calm waters and plain sailing. There were tears, tantrums and fall-outs along the way, but ultimately the bond between player and the paying public was never broken.

The conflict was, more often than not, born out of frustration as the talented attacker found himself in a team which was so near to success, yet so far. In the space of one week in May 2000 the player reacted furiously to his first-half substitution in a League game against Dundee and then hammered a ball against the dugout in anger as he watched helpless from the sidelines as his team fell to a 4-0 Scottish Cup final defeat against Rangers. That led to a heated exchange with manager Ebbe Skovdahl and assistant manager Gardner Speirs.

Zerouali defended his position, admitting: "I kicked the ball against the dugout out of sheer frustration because the fourth goal meant the game was finished and there was nothing I could do about it. I'm a passionate player and in my culture you're not expected to keep your emotions under strict control. I desperately wanted to see Aberdeen win the final for the fans and I kicked the ball the way I did to get the disappointment out of my system. We all had to shout to make ourselves heard above the noise from the crowd and I tend to wave my hands about to try to make myself understood because my English still isn't very good.

"The manager had said to me that I would be playing in the Scottish Cup final but when I got to the dressing room I was told I was not in the team. I was up and down like a yo-yo doing warm-ups during the game, but when I was not getting on I lost my temper. After that I said to the manager that I would be leaving for Morocco. I said I was leaving early next day for home and that I would not be coming back, but staying in Morocco. I said if he didn't fix things up I would be gone from Aberdeen."

For a man who posed the club's greatest attacking threat and possessed a large dollop of the team's flair, it was a serious threat. The flashpoints brought the player's relationship with his coach into the foreground and it was an intriguing pairing. On one hand was the mild-mannered, reserved and softly spoken Skovdahl with a personality befitting his Norse roots, while on the other was the fiery-tempered, animated bundle of pent-up frustration who never attempted to hide an on-field persona developed amid the arid heat of the sprawling coastal city of Rabat.

With a population in excess of 1.7 million it was a world away from his temporary home in Scotland's silver city. Off the field, hampered by his efforts to learn English and get to grips with the Doric dialect of the north-east, he was less brazen, more humble and happy to fade into the background. That background often included that provided by the sanctuary of a city-centre takeaway owned by his Aberdeen-based friend Mustapha Wahbi. Often Zerouali and fellow Moroccan Rachid Belabed were found behind the counter of the busy restaurant – to the delight of the late-night revellers who could get the inside track on the latest Dons news along with their nibbles.

The restaurant offered a small slice of Morocco on the streets of Aberdeen, a small sliver of a link to home. Rabat, Morocco's capital city and a hub of industry and politics, nestles on the Atlantic coast on the tip of Africa and it was the city which launched Zerouali on the path to international stardom. Fus Rabat, the club with which he made his name, incorporates everything from basketball sides to chess teams but it is its football stars who are held in highest regard by the passionate fans desperate to add to the four championships the club has won since it burst into life in 1946. Zerouali became a firm favourite as a young Fus Rabat player making his way in the world and was a full international by the time he signed for the Dons, going on to win 17 caps and scoring three goals for the Atlas Lions.

Moroccan football has been described by one commentator as "intuitive, unpredictable, and explosive". Zerouali came from that mould and how to handle his mercurial talents represented a major challenge for a manager more used to the tamer temperaments of Scandinavian and north European charges. It proved a tough nut to crack for Skovdahl, who more often than not attempted to fight fire with fire.

In the aftermath of the Scottish Cup final showdown, Skovdahl said: "I'll be having words with Zerouali again. I know his actions came from his frustration at not being able to do anything about the situation in the match. He does have a bit of a temper. It's something we've seen on the training ground when things don't go his way. That can be a good thing if he uses it the right way, as motivation to use his skills and ability against opponents. That's what I want from him next season. He will be told that, like me, he has to forget the way he does things at home and make sure he behaves on and off the pitch in a way which does not attract the wrong sort of attention. What is acceptable in Morocco may not be here."

The crux of the matter is that the Dons fans would have loved to have seen the same level of passion from every single player who pulled on a red shirt. They put themselves through the mill week in and week out in the stands, and here in front of them was a man who showed the same emotions on the park or on the touchline, depending on where he was billeted. The expression of feeling, whether positive or negative, never harmed Zerouali's standing in the eyes of the support and his inability to keep his thoughts and sentiments hidden from view only served to strengthen the bond.

As it turned out, the challenge for greater discipline in the 2000/01 season by Skovdahl proved to be an empty one. At the beginning of the campaign Zerouali suffered a sickening ankle-break in a game against Motherwell. It shattered his hopes of representing his country at the Olympics and plunged him into a depressing period of rehabilitation. In customary style, he lightened the mood in a way that was rare to Scottish football – by taking to playing the piano. It offered some relief from the boredom of his extended period on the sidelines Despite resuming light training within months, the injury kept Zerouali sidelined for the entire season when a second operation to repair the damage was required.

It rarely mattered whether Zero was in the Dons team or not; his status as an idol to thousands outweighed the trivial matters of on-field events. He even spurned his own range of tribute food products. In 2001 Turriff butcher John Brown won a gold medal at the Scottish Meat Trades Fair in Perth with his Moroccan-style spicy Zerouali sausage. Brown created it after launching a competition for sausage recipes and the Dons tribute submitted by local GP Dr Steven Henderson caught his eye.

Outside of the lighter moments, the darker times were never far away. When he returned to action in the build-up to the 2001/02 season, the Moroccan again hit the headlines in controversial circumstances. He was ordered off in a 3-1 victory against Farum during a tour of Denmark for an extraordinary outburst at the home referee, making a two-fingered gesture at the official before aiming another verbal volley at the Dons bench as he trooped off following his dismissal for dissent. The player later claimed the referee swore at him, although that was denied by the Dane in question.

Skovdahl said: "I am devastated with what he did to the referee. I asked the referee what Hicham had said and it is not something I would like to repeat. It is not acceptable and is not something I can allow when we play League games. Our team is not strong enough to play with ten players. There is no excuse for what he did. You can always say he has a temper but you have to think of your team-mates who have to play with ten men. That is why he will be fined."

Zerouali was absent from the team when it began the campaign, although the manager claimed that was due to fitness concerns rather than the pre-season outburst. He made his comeback weeks into the new term, and capped his return by scoring against Motherwell, then earning a call up to the Morocco squad for a friendly against Italy.

He said: "It has been the longest year of my life and, at times, it was difficult to see when I would be back, but that is all now in the past. Now I have the chance to put everything behind me and get on with playing for Aberdeen and also Morocco."

Nothing in life runs without a hitch and, in Zerouali's case particularly, drama was never far away. After his triumphant return to action he was back in the headlines after an incredible miss against St Johnstone which was followed by his failure to convert from the penalty spot in the same game. Those glitches came after Dons fans had spent 68 minutes chanting for their hero to be brought on from the bench. He said: "The fans were still on my side. I went out that night and one of the fans even said to me: 'Hicham, don't worry. Even Roberto Baggio has missed a penalty' and that made me feel a lot better about myself."

Misses and all, Zerouali was still the Aberdeen player most likely to be a match-winner. By the time the calendar flicked to 2002, time was running out in the Dons' bid to keep him in Scotland. With his contract due to expire in the summer, the African was well aware of his worth to the club and was holding out for an offer he could not refuse.

He claimed: "I'm looking for a new contract from Aberdeen because I want to stay at the club. And the only way to get that is to score goals that will help the team. But everything has to be right and that includes the financial side of things. I have to do as well as I can to make sure that everyone wants me to stay at the club. So the more goals I score the more difficult it will make it for the club not to offer me the right deal. I love the club because the fans like me so much. They are really good and are always there to cheer the team on. I have got my place in the team here, and now I want to win a contract that will be good for myself and the club. The people in Aberdeen are very friendly and I like that a lot. They are always asking me how I'm doing and want to shake my hand and I enjoy that. I have been here for two and a half years and feel that I have settled well in the city. I will never enjoy as strong a relationship with supporters as I do with the Aberdeen ones. From the day I arrived in Scotland they have treated me in a very special way."

By March 2002 it had been confirmed that the Aberdeen contract offer had been rejected and the player was transfer-listed as the club tried to avoid losing what had been a prize asset for nothing at the end of his contract. When Zerouali eventually moved it was under freedom of contract, joining United Arab Emirates club Al Nasr on a two-year agreement in the summer of 2002.

The lucrative deal and warmer climate did not erase the frozen north from Zerouali's memory completely. For one thing, he had family ties to Aberdeen as the proud father of a young daughter by his Scottish partner, and for another his football experience in the SPL had left a mark on him. He was the first to admit his Pittodrie career had petered out, but Zerouali's affection for the Dons never wavered.

"I was with Aberdeen for two and a half years and the first year was great," explained Zerouali. "I was playing regularly and really enjoyed it but after that I suffered a lot of injuries and then dropped out of the team. I'm glad I came to Aberdeen because it has been a great experience for me and I've made a lot of good friends at the club and in the city. But it's time to leave because I spent the last few weeks of my Aberdeen career playing in the reserves, and that's no use to me. I want to take part in every game and it was hard to play one week but not the next. I'm going to miss the fans. They are really special because they always get behind the team, no matter what the score is. Whatever club

I go to in the future, I'll always talk about how good the Aberdeen supporters are."

In fact, within months the African was pining for a return. In the first few weeks of 2003 he claimed: "I really miss Scotland – and the cold weather. It's a lot easier for training than here in Dubai, where it is unbelievably hot at times. At first it was almost unbearable to even train in the heat, never mind play any games. From that point of view I preferred training and playing for Aberdeen. You had to train hard just to keep warm."

He saw out his contract in Dubai and came close to a return to Europe with Darlington in 2004. That collapsed due to work-permit problems and British football was robbed of its chance to see a unique talent make a return to these shores. Then in December 2004, the Dons supporters were rocked by the news their idol had been killed in a car accident. He died when his car left the road and hit a tree in his native Morocco.

The tributes flowed thick and fast, but there were no empty sentiments or tired clichés. The despair was genuine for a much-loved former player and the pavements outside Pittodrie quickly developed into a shrine to Zerouali. On the anniversary of his death the floral tributes can still be found, more subtle than the huge banners proclaiming Zero's undoubted talents, which have been unfurled across the Richard Donald Stand. Not that the unsubtle would be unsuitable – he was brash, bold and proud on the park. Just the way the Red Army like their heroes.

'THE SPECIAL ONE' 2003–present

ZANDER DIAMOND

Magic Moment: The multi-million pound stars of Lokomotiv Moscow were rooted to the floor as Aberdeen's home-grown lionheart humbled them with a towering header and kept the European dream alive. The Pittodrie crowd rose as one to celebrate with their favourite son.

Dons Career: Games 157. Goals11 (to the end of 2007/08).

IN THE days of Jock Hutton and Gentleman George Hamilton, the Aberdeen supporters had to make do with crackling weekly radio round-ups for their fix of football news. In the era of Harper, Miller and Rougvie the weekend television highlights programmes took a grip. For Zander Diamond and his team-mates, the media frenzy has kicked into overdrive and the glare of the spotlight is more intense than ever for the *YouTube* generation.

The internet video-sharing site has become a global phenomenon since it was launched in 2005. Bleary-eyed *YouTube* viewers across the world viewed 2.5 billion videos within the first six months of the site's existence and more than 150,000 clips are added every day. The marriage between football and the age of the online image was just as quick as the site's astonishing growth and the Red Army have not been slow in coming forward with their collection of favourite moments. Zander Diamond, more often than not, takes centre stage.

From the Parkhead chorus of "One Zander Diamond" to footage of the towering defender's UEFA Cup goal against Lokomotiv Moscow in 2008, Diamond has taken his place in the digital age. But it is not his tackling or rare goals that have won the Dons ace the most fame – it is his particular passion for beating one SPL team. Two clips featuring

Diamond's celebrations following Lee Miller's goal to clinch the 2-0 victory against Rangers on the final day of the 2007/08 season, ensuring that the title was destined for Celtic, were between them viewed more than 23,000 times inside the first two weeks of their existence. Put another way, that's more hits than Pittodrie has seats. The goal against Moscow was far more important in the grand scheme than any celebration, yet footage of that attracted less than 3,000 hits in eight months.

Only a Dons fan landing from a distant planet could have failed to have taken note of Diamond's leanings towards Celtic. For those who had missed it, the Sunday tabloid newspaper photographs printed in 2008 of the defender celebrating his 22nd birthday with a Celtic cake while decked out in Hoops regalia would have been enough to ensure that the penny dropped. Manager Jimmy Calderwood described Diamond posing for the snap, which was pinched from the social networking website of his girlfriend – to further demonstrate the perils of new media – as a "stupid" act. Aberdeen, after all, pay him a not-inconsequential wage for wearing red rather than green and white. Yet there was no backlash from the fans, no howls of derision from the Richard Donald Stand.

The debate, in keeping with the new media phenomenon, was conducted in internet forums rather than the barroom talking shops of old. The outcome was clear: Diamond's folly could be forgiven because the incident was typical of his character. What you see is what you get.

Diamond, in one fell swoop, proved himself to be untouchable in the eyes of the fans. Any other player caught off guard in a similar manner could expect to be pilloried, but for one member of the staff, at least, there is no shame in having an unabashed Old Firm indulgence.

His Celtic roots, the cause of so much consternation for a Pittodrie coaching team steeped in all things Rangers and the source of so much banter behind the scenes, might explain his love of putting one over on the Light Blues. The furious rivalry between his adopted club, Aberdeen, and the Ibrox men has only added fuel to that fiery passion and the results have been spectacular.

Since being sent off in 2003 during his first game at Ibrox, when Willie Young brandished a red card for a trip on Shota Arveladze, the number-five has had some memorable battles with the team from the south side of Glasgow. That victory against a Rangers team still shooting for the SPL title in 2008 was the highlight and he did nothing to disguise the fact. The 23,000 internet aficionados who have logged on to watch the Diamond celebrations in full flow have been met by images of the shaven-headed Aberdeen man leaping up the pitch past the travelling Rangers support, fist clenched and face wide with glee. Not one of those viewers will have been left in any doubt about how much that victory meant to Diamond and, regardless of the motivation, conscious or sub-conscious, the Red Army shared every emotion. For that moment in time, Diamond was the embodiment of the collective spirit within the home fans.

"The spirit, the will to win, and the will to excel are the things that endure. These qualities are so much more important than the events that occur."

Vince Lombardi, American football coach

To suggest the passion exists only when it comes to putting Rangers to the sword would be wrong. Diamond knows only two speeds: stopped and full tilt. His bounding athleticism and exaggerated body language make him stand out in a Dons team which, by the manager's own admission, lacks the vocal drive he desperately craves. Calderwood has often lamented the lack of talkers in the modern game, not just at Pittodrie, but in Diamond he has an exception to that particular trend. Off the pitch as well as on it, Diamond is more than capable of making himself heard even above the noise of a packed stadium. His animated heart-on-sleeve displays have established the type of connection with those seated around Pittodrie that is difficult to replicate, bridging the generation gaps and reaching out to all-corners from the family stand at the Merkland End to the old-timers in the Main Stand and hard-core sections of the Richard Donald Stand and South Stand.

The relationship did not take long to establish. In May 2003 Diamond burst on to the scene. Not for him a quiet introduction to first-team life. Instead he set about his debut in typical brash and raucous fashion. *Press and Journal* writer Stuart Darroch observed: "The days of million-pound transfers long gone, Aberdeen's future success will be based on unearthing a few diamonds in the youth team. In Saturday's debutant centre-back, AFC has discovered a real gem. Zander Diamond has spent the season terrorising teenage centre-forwards for the Dons' youth team. His extra-time performance in the Youth Cup final last weekend, when cramp rendered him immobile and with Neil Cooper having committed his three substitutes, was quite heroic. At Tannadice, he was more commanding in the air than Captain Biggles. Even the ever-voluble captain Peter Kjaer, at the opposite end of the career spectrum, only had cause to shout at Zander once."

That "heroic" performance was in a 3-1 defeat against Celtic, a game which attracted a crowd of close to 2,000 people. Before long the gangly defender would be playing to a new audience, having been rapidly promoted to the top team by Steve Paterson as he fought against raging budget cuts. Diamond was a Scotland under-19 international by the time he began life as a first-team player and he went on to captain the country's under-21 side on his way to 12 caps at that level.

Under Walter Smith there followed a call-up to Scotland Future, the short-lived equivalent of a 'B' international team, and it must be only a matter of time before promotion to the full squad completes the set.

After being introduced as a half-time replacement for Phil McGuire in a League game at Dundee United at the end of the 2002/03 season, Diamond made his first domestic start against Dumbarton, his home-town club, in a League Cup tie the following term. It attracted the lowest Pittodrie crowd for 28 years but Diamond helped lift the gloom for the 3,944 who did turn up. After his glowing endorsement months earlier, Darroch greeted the full debut by noting: "Zander may hop around the pitch wielding his hands like a concert pianist, but he will become a key player of a different kind."

Within weeks of his breakthrough, Diamond was being compared to Alex McLeish by the media and even his manager. The similarities in stature between Diamond and McLeish in his youth aided the link, but it was quickly dispelled by the player: "I just don't listen to all the talk about McLeish. I'm my own guy, I'm Zander. I don't like to be compared to McLeish, Willie Miller or anyone else. I'm my own person and want to make a name for myself."

Naturally, that did not stop the comparisons. *Evening Express* sports editor Charlie Allan was among those beating the drum, writing at the time of Diamond's debut: "The one Aberdeen player to finish the night with any real credit was 18-year-old defender Zander Diamond. He is as raw as the pound of mince I was once served in a restuarant in Paris because I couldn't understand the menu. I would be wary of risking Zander up against someone like Michael Mols or Henrik Larsson at this stage of his career. But the lad is strong in the tackle, rarely missed a header and I also noted his use of the ball. Zander made 25 successful passes and put just five off target, not bad for a teenager getting his first top-team run-out at Pittodrie. And he at least didn't have to worry about the atmosphere adding to his nerves.

"Zander told me he hates being compared to Alex McLeish. He is a big lad but, hey, I don't care. I was at Pittodrie on 2 January 1978 to witness 'Big Eck's' surprise first start against Dundee United, after whispers that Willie Garner had chosen to celebrate the New Year a bit more than manager Billy McNeill liked. Like Zander, Eck was rough around the edges but showed enough to leave most Dons fans sure he would be back as a first-team regular sooner rather than later. You can never be certain, of course, but I just sense Zander has something special as well."

Coincidentally, McNeill has had a big part to play in Diamond's career, just as he did in sending McLeish on the road to stardom. The Celtic legend and former Aberdeen manager is the father of Diamond's agent and the one-time Scotland international has acted as mentor-in-chief, just as he was for Big Eck three decades ago.

The McLeish comparisons were not fleeting or isolated. Three years later, in 2006, it was the turn of Archie Knox, then part of the Scotland set-up and with Diamond under his wing in the under-21 squad, to highlight the similarities between the new kid on the block and the flame-haired Glaswegian defender who was under his command during Knox's time as assistant to Alex Ferguson during Aberdeen's glory days.

Knox insisted: "It shouldn't be seen as a hindrance to Zander, it should act as inspiration. I worked with Alex when he was the same age Zander is now and they have a lot of similar qualities. It will be tough, because Alex had the advantage of being part of a very good Aberdeen team full of top-level internationals. But that doesn't take anything away from the fact Alex made his career off his own back. If he can do it by showing the right attitude, then so can Zander. Alex, like Zander, was far from being a polished footballer. But I have worked with countless players over the years and there is nobody who grafted harder than Alex to make himself the best he could be. He had unrivalled determination to succeed – nothing was going to stand in his way. That is the marker for any young player who wants to break away from the pack."

Diamond has gone on to prove his dedication to the cause and his determination to succeed, outlasting the manager who showed the faith which led to his fast-track to the Dons team. Steve Paterson, most recently in charge of Peterhead in the Second Division, has watched from outside the confines of Pittodrie as the youngster he tipped for the top has gone on to fulfil his potential in a way so many other young players have failed to do.

Paterson, now back in the social work sector following his departure from Peterhead and enjoying his first sustained break from management for two decades, told me: "Whoever had been in charge at that moment in time would have put Zander Diamond into the first team, I have no doubt about that. I was fortunate to be at the club when he reached that stage and I was confident he could handle it. He was quite clearly an outstanding prospect. He had the right attitude, a good physique for a player of his age, a really good turn of pace, was good on the ground and had tremendous heading ability. With those qualities he couldn't fail to make an impact."

Paterson left Pittodrie in 2004 but has keenly followed Diamond's career in the years since then. He can still see glimpses of the rookie teenager he worked with day in and day out on the training field, but knows the best is yet to come from the fans' favourite.

He said: "Zander was raw, and probably still is to a certain extent, but he had a willingness to learn and be coached. That does not sound like a huge thing, but any young player who wants to succeed has to have that desire to improve rather than being happy just to stand still once they make it into the first team. He is a manager's dream. Defenders are a bit like goalkeepers in that as they mature they learn to read the game better and anticipate things quicker. It is easy to forget that he is still a young player because he has been in the team for so long, but I firmly believe Zander's best years are ahead of him. He is the type of character who will carry on progressing and pushing himself on."

When Diamond made his first senior start under Paterson the teamsheet read: David Preece, Michael Hart, Jamie McQuilken, Kevin McNaughton, Russell Anderson, Zander Diamond, Leigh Hinds, Steve Tosh, Paul Sheerin, Markus Heikkinen, David Zdrilic. By the start of the 2008/09 season he was the last man standing, the sole survivor from that slice of the past following Michael Hart's move to Preston North End earlier in the year. He has seen team-mates come and go, some slipping down the divisions and others, such as Russell Anderson, going on to better themselves financially and test their talents outside of the often stifling confines of the 12-team Scottish top flight. With five years' service under his belt by the time he signed his latest Dons deal in 2008, Diamond is one of the longest-serving members of the Pittodrie playing staff, but Paterson does feel the burning ambition which has shaped the player's career could mean he does not finish as a one-club man.

The former Dons boss said: "Zander was certainly the stand-out young player during my short time at Pittodrie and the one I felt had a real chance of going all the way in the game. I still feel that is the case.

When I say 'go all the way', I mean playing for the full Scotland team and making a very good living at a high level in England. We have seen in recent times that players have been tempted south. Unfortunately for Aberdeen, I can see that happening further down the line with Zander because he is sure to attract interest, and every player dreams of testing himself at the highest level."

Having described Diamond as every manager's dream, Paterson never struggled to comprehend the warmth of feeling extended from the stands towards his former pupil. The right attitude is nine-tenths of the formula for players who succeed in making the jump to cult status, and from day one that asset was in the defender's make-up.

Paterson continued: "Supporters always like a tryer. Fans can forgive most things as long as they get total commitment from a player and that is what Zander Diamond gives every time he steps on to a football pitch. He has a determination and a will to win which the people who pay their money at the gate love to see. Yes, he has had spells of inconsistency, as every young player has, and can rush into things – but supporters know the game and they can see past that. Zander was taken to the hearts of the Aberdeen fans pretty much straight away, which is unusual for a defender. Usually it's a tricky winger or a goal-scorer who gets that type of backing but he has proved to be the exception. He has an honesty to his game which people can appreciate and relate to. A young player can have all the skill in the world but without a strong character it is wasted. There has never been a doubt about Zander in that respect and his bubbly personality can lift those around him. That type of player is priceless in any dressing room."

The supporters did not question Paterson's decision to make use of Diamond. Inside his first season he had already won over the Dons fans, who voted him the player most likely to make it big in the game. Scott Morrison, Scott Muirhead and Stephen Payne were the other players in the running and the outcome suggests the Red Army know their football. While Muirhead turns out for Dunfermline, Morrison attempts to rebuild his career with Ross County and Payne dropped down the divisions with

Queen of the South and then Stranraer, their former youth-team skipper has gone from strength to strength with the Aberdeen.

When he was very young, the Dons were well aware of Diamond's pulling power with the club's long-suffering supporters. The annual meetings around the millennium were akin to ritual verbal slayings as the fans clashed angrily with the board. Positive spin became crucial in the run-up to those gatherings and it was no coincidence that the AGM of 2003, with the team toiling and directors ready to face another barrage, was used to announce that the most glittering asset had been tied to a new two-year contract.

The displays from the defensive rookie led to a flurry of links with potential suitors. One week it was Liverpool or Celtic, the next Atletico Madrid. While it sounds fanciful, the speculation rang true with the Pittodrie punters, who had watched the tireless Trojan make an instant mark on the SPL and its strikers.

Paterson's plan was to build his defence around Diamond, a raw talent he rated as a future skipper. The captaincy issue has circled around the Dumbarton destroyer ever since he burst on to the scene, but he has had to be patient in his pursuit of the armband. Russell Anderson, and more recently Scott Severin, have filled that role. While Anderson, the home-town boy with the Dons' very essence coursing through his veins, was the obvious choice, there was a determined lobbying for Diamond to succeed him when his tenure ended. Severin's laid back demeanour split opinion, while Diamond's unbridled passion for the cause had fans flocking to back him for the job. While Severin got the nod from Jimmy Calderwood, the manager has already hinted that he views Diamond as the heir to the captain's throne.

His value to the club is not just anecdotal – the Dons manager has put his money where his mouth is. At the turn of 2008, it looked certain Diamond was heading for the exit, having failed to reach agreement over a replacement for his soon-to-expire contract. Former defensive partner Russell Anderson had made the lucrative switch south, while fellow free agents Chris Clark, Michael Hart and Barry Nicholson were preparing to do the same thing. Clark, Hart and Nicholson had been key to Aberdeen's success in reaching the UEFA Cup group stages, but the club refused to be held to ransom and reluctantly accepted their inevitable departures. The negotiating stance was hard-line, and the message was clear from director of football Willie Miller: there will be no second offer, the terms you see on the table are what you get. Except, it transpired, in one case.

Faced with the prospect of losing Diamond, the man who had risen to the challenge and made the most credible attempt at filling the boots of Anderson following his switch to the English Premier League with Sunderland, the club backtracked. With one last throw of the dice, Miller and Calderwood got together to massage the wage budget and, with the backing of the rest of the board, came up with a package which persuaded the stopper his future lay at Pittodrie.

As the ink dried on his new agreement and the player came to terms with his new role as Aberdeen's very own "Special One", as he was dubbed by one reporter during the press call to announce the deal, Diamond said: "I have always maintained I would speak to Aberdeen first and, give them their due, they have come up with a deal which both parties are happy about. I can't talk about anyone else and what they were offered. The club came up with a solution and, if I am the Special One, then so be it, but it was not a hard decision for me to make. The club changed its position for me and I felt I should show loyalty and stand by them in the same way they stood by me in my 18-month spell when I struggled with injury and poor form. I am still learning, I'm only 22 and the club is going places. We are in all the cup competitions and in a good position in the League."

By that stage, Jimmy Calderwood had already revealed that he had rejected big-money offers for the prize asset during the early days of his Dons tenure. In 2007 the coach confided: "I could have sold Zander for a lot of money but there was no way that we were going to sell him. The offer was thrown straight out the window. That is not a decision I regret."

The potential for regret that Calderwood spoke about back then stemmed from a sticky patch in Diamond's otherwise smooth career at the top level. For a period in the 2006/07 season, and even the term before that, it appeared everything he touched turned to disaster, with loose back-passes and concentration lapses leading to the loss of several high-profile goals. The youngster's confidence should have taken a battering but his resilience came to the fore and, to his manager's delight, he was prepared to stand up and be counted even when the going got tough.

Any up-and-coming player can expect peaks and troughs when it comes to form and Diamond has been no different. Where he has stood out has been in his willingness to face the juggernaut of criticism head on and learn from his mistakes, engrossing himself in post-match video analysis of his own performances when most team-mates are making the most of what remains of their weekend. Diamond's commitment to improving has won him Brownie points at Pittodrie, with that quiet dedication belying his more brash and happy-go-lucky public persona. With the media, too, Diamond has become a firm favourite. He is always willing to talk, always ready to put a brave face on things, and a respect for the forthright and honest professional has developed, his occasional blips always being followed by lavish praise.

After Diamond roared back to form in a 0-0 draw against Rangers at Ibrox in 2005, Charlie Allan wrote: "Big John Wayne played the Davy Crockett role in the movie of *The Alamo*, but it was a Diamond as opposed to a 'Duke' who grabbed star billing for the Dons. Zander Diamond, who has had a torrid time this season, bounced back with one of his best performances in a red shirt. He stood as tall in his football boots as Wayne ever did in the saddle to out-draw Rangers' main marksman Dado Prso, help shoot down Rangers' title hopes yet again and restore some confidence in the Aberdeen ranks. Diamond dived into tackles, put his head in where it hurts and refused to surrender when Rangers threw everything at the visitors. After the final whistle I saw the sheer delight on Diamond's face as he hugged team-mates and took the applause from the Aberdeen fans, who seemed unconcerned by their team's lack of a goal threat. Diamond needed a performance like that as a reminder that he had only temporarily strayed off the path that will eventually take him to the top."

Once again the story returns to the familiar theme of Diamond's passion and the revelry which he has displayed during some of his finest hours. While trophy success has been a stranger at Pittodrie in recent years, there has been no shortage of plaudits for Diamond after he survived some of the most turbulent years in the club's history.

In his rookie season the Dons finished dead centre in the 12-team SPL under Steve Paterson, but it was a false dawn. In 2003/04 the final table showed the Reds in 11th place, just avoiding relegation, and Jimmy Calderwood was drafted in as the new manager with the task of pointing the side back in the right direction. He has succeeded, leaning heavily on Diamond en-route to fourth place, then sixth, third and another fourth. Still silverware eludes Diamond, but League and Cup glory has become a more realistic prospect as he prepares for his prime years. Courtesy of his most recent contract, which ties him to the club until the summer of 2011, what should be his best seasons will be spent in a red shirt.

The personal highlights came thick and fast during the 2007/08 campaign, marking the 25th anniversary of the Gothenburg glory and fittingly bringing Aberdeen's eagerly awaited return to the European stage. The UEFA Cup campaign turned out to be the rubber stamp on Diamond's football CV. Still in his early 20s, he came of age with defiant performances against the might of Ukrainian big-spenders Dnipro, not to mention the Bundesliga stars of Bayern Munich and his goal-scoring contribution against Lokomotiv Moscow.

For anyone whose path has crossed with that of Diamond, it was no shock that he failed to be fazed by the potentially daunting prospect of stepping up to continental competition. In the first five years of his senior career, the man from Alexandria has continually risen to the challenges presented to him. That has not gone unnoticed among the supporters, who have been able to see through the flaws of youth to take note of the bigger picture and the bright future ahead.

He set about the European ties with the trademark blood-and-thunder approach, the blood usually his own as the patched-up Diamond threw himself into challenges, taking more than his share of hits along the way. The Germans and Russians must have been bemused by the sight of the marauding centre-half scrapping for every ball and launching himself into challenge after challenge. It simply isn't the continental way. The Bayern and Lokomotiv defenders, as well as those from Copenhagen, Panathinaikos and Atletico Madrid, left the park with barely a hair out of place after their encounters with the Dons. Yet the Aberdeen fans would take their man's more Rougvie-esque approach every time. They want to see signs of their star's exertions and crave the straightforward approach to defending. You can keep your refined continental ways. No-nonsense will do just fine.

BIBLIOGRAPHY

Gothenburg Glory, Paul Smith, Aberdeen Journals, 2008

The Legends of Aberdeen, Paul Smith, Breedon, 2007

The Don, Willie Miller and Rob Robertson, Birlinn 2007

The Bonnie Prince, Charlie Cooke and Martin Knight, Mainstream, 2007

Aberdeen: Champions of Scotland, Kevin Stirling, Desert Island Books, 2004

The First 100 Years of the Dons, Jack Webster, Hodder & Stoughton, 2003

Golden Boy, Nick Varley, Aurum Press, 2002

A Scottish Soccer Internationalists Who's Who, Douglas Lamming, Hutton Press, 1987

Aberdeen: A Complete Record, Jim Rickaby, Breedon, 1987

The Aberdeen Football Companion, Clive Leatherdale, John Donald Publishers, 1986

In a Different League, Rodwill Clyne, 1981

Aberdeen: A Centenary History, Kevin Stirling, Desert Island Books, 2002.

Additional archive sources:

The Press and Journal, Aberdeen
The Evening Express, Aberdeen
The Green Final, Aberdeen
www.afc.co.uk
www.Scottishfa.co.uk
The Observer